Boston, 1960 Allyn and Bacon, Inc.

Through ART To Creativity

Art in the Elementary School Program

Manuel Barkan

Professor of Art Education
School of Fine and Applied Arts
The Ohio State University

Library of Congress Catalog Card Number: 60–9679

Printed in the United States of America

for J*oel*

Contents

Preface

A great deal has been written about the teaching of art, and much of this material has been addressed to the education of elementary school children. In varying degrees, the literature presents and reflects what we have come to understand about good teaching of art. In general, most of this material, including my own, presents and analyzes ideas about teaching which are felt to be important. These ideas are often illustrated with descriptions of classroom practices and examples of the art work done by children. The general improvement of the teaching of art in recent years has come about largely though the development and use of such materials.

There are, however, some fascinating and troublesome problems in writing about teaching in order to explain the nature of the teaching act. Writing about teaching can explain many issues involved in teaching; but the act of teaching is not really the theoretical explanation. The act of teaching comprises the composite day-to-day behavior of a teacher; it *embodies* the theory which is implicit in her actions. The teacher at work in a classroom reflects the theory she has internalized into her personal manner—actions, speech and gestures.

For example, it is sound and proper to explain that teaching art to children involves the stimulation of their imaginative abilities. This is one idea which is part of current theory about good art education. But what are some of the specific and concrete things good teachers do to achieve that goal? What do they talk about, and how do they act? How do they treat children in order to stimulate their imaginative abilities? What do their children do in turn, and how do they talk and act?

The theory of good teaching of art can explain the nature of imagination and its significance in the education of children. By itself, however, theoretical explanation does not convey how imaginative children sound, nor does it convey the life-like images of how they behave. Furthermore, it does not transmit the live and moving interchange between good teachers and their children as they strive to enhance the ability to be imaginative.

In making this distinction between theory and practice, I am in no way implying any separation between theory and practice. Nor am I suggesting that good practice is not grounded in theory. Quite the contrary, teaching practice and theory are intimately interdependent. Theory grows out of the problems and possibilities observed in the process of teaching. Teaching practice is based upon theoretical ideas which guide the behavior of teachers. Each stems from the other, but each has a form which is different from the other. The teaching process is the live interchange between a teacher and her children. Theory about teaching explains the meaning and significance of the experiences of the teacher and the children.

Learning to teach, therefore, involves achieving awareness of the behavior of teachers in the light of good theory. Writing about teaching involves the development and presentation of theory to explain the behavior of good teachers. Both the student who is learning to teach and his professors who talk and write about teaching are plagued by some of the very same questions: How can good teaching be observed as the embodiment of good theory; and how can the theory of good teaching be brought to life so that it can be better understood and developed? Taken together, such questions should be able to help all of us learn how to teach art effectively, and how to learn more about what is important in the teaching of art. These were the questions I asked of myself in order to conceive the content and format of this book.

I have addressed myself primarily to the problem of bringing together some detailed examples of good teaching of art in the elementary schools with some theory about the teaching of art. I have done this through reporting my observations of a selected group of good teachers, and through analyzing these reports.

This book is based upon a series of detailed accounts, both verbal and photographic, of much that transpired in the classrooms of eighteen fine teachers. These teachers represent the kindergarten through the sixth grade. There are several classroom teachers at each level and one art teacher; their work is reported through verbatim tape-recorded discussions in their classrooms, accompanied by photographs taken at the same time. These are then analyzed to reveal how each teacher internalized the theory of good teaching of art into her own personality and hence into her own classroom behavior.

The content of this book is organized in terms of four levels—kindergarten, early, middle, and upper elementary grades. Chapters 2, 4, 6 and 8 present the classroom records at each of the four levels and can be used in a number of ways. They can be read to study the character and quality of the interchanges between the teachers and children. They can be read with special attention to the ways each teacher vitalized the discussions of particular ideas. They can be studied to discover how each teacher conducted her work with her group of children utilizing the resources of her school and community and in terms of the limitations of the facilities in her own classroom. They can be examined to see the various art activities conducted by all of these teachers; they can be studied to discover how each teacher provided art materials to be used as instruments for the creation of ideas rather than as ends in themselves.

Chapters 3, 5, 7, and 9 provide the analysis of the classroom activities, and they are each divided into the same group of sections—developmental achievements of the children; what the teachers talked about; how they organized classroom time; how they utilized classroom space; and the art works produced by the children. These sections can be read together within the single chapters in direct relation to the classroom records from which they are derived. Any one of these sections can be read separately in each of the analysis chapters to see the implications of the particular issues discussed at each educational level. For example, the sections on utilization of time can be read in Chapters 3, 5, 7, and 9 to discover the variety of ways these teachers organized their time schedules in relation to the age of their children, the activities in process, and the facilities in their rooms. Or, the sections on the art works produced by the children can be studied to see how, and why, children create ideas through the visual arts at different age levels.

There is a bibliography at the end of the book which is selective rather than exhaustive. Each reference is briefly annotated as a guide to the reader for further study of the various considerations in the teaching of art to elementary school children.

There were a number of criteria I used to select the eighteen teachers whose work I have reported and analyzed. First and foremost, I was looking for people who in my judgment were doing an excellent job of teaching art to elementary school children. In addition, I was looking for people who would provide a balanced representation of all the grade levels, and who taught in different school systems with varying classroom facilities and in different socio-economic communities. I wanted these teachers to be reasonably well separated geographically, although I needed to select them in groups according to location. This was essential because I recorded the activities in each classroom during six to ten visits spread over two to four weeks. By selecting a group of about six teachers in one general location, I was able to visit their classes every other day, or daily when necessary, for at least an hour and often for as long as two and a half hours for each visit.

For assistance in selecting the eighteen teachers, I am indebted to people I know—superintendents, principals and art supervisors—in fifteen different school systems. These people, in whose judgment I was confident, recommended to me the very best teachers in their schools in respect to the teaching of art. In this way, I gathered the names of about one hundred and fifty teachers whose classes I visited. I then selected the eighteen teachers from nine of these school systems according to my own judgment, and in terms of the other criteria I indicated. There were many other teachers whom I wished I could have included. Distribution among grades, communities, and locations, together with the limitations of the size of a book dictated the final choices. With the agreement of the school officers, I sought and received the generous permission of the individual teachers to return to their classrooms for extended periods of time in order to record their work.

The teachers who are thus presented in this book were not selected through any comprehensive survey. That was not my purpose. These teachers do, however, represent the kinds of excellent teaching of art which are current in a good many schools throughout the country. During my visits to their classes I was solely concerned with observing what they were doing with their children. I did not review the teaching of art in their school systems in general. My purpose, as indicated earlier, was to record and analyze the work of selected individual fine teachers.

My presence in the classrooms undoubtedly had some effect on the teachers and the children, in spite of my efforts to be as unobtrusive as possible. I explained my purpose in being there, and showed the children the equipment I was using. Within one or two visits, my presence seemed to be accepted without undue notice. My small battery-powered tape recorder and my high-speed camera enabled me to catch the conversations and process photographs.

It might be fair to assume that some of these teachers put a bit of extra energy into their work during the period of my visits. In terms of my purpose in this book, such extras are of little significance. If anything, they made their work that much better, which was to the good. After all, I wasn't rating or comparing them. They knew I was there because I thought they were good, and it was good teaching that I wanted to record. I visited all the classes to record my observations from January through May in 1958.

I appreciate the generosity of the administrators of the following school systems for their permission to work with the teachers I selected: Bexley, Columbus, Upper Arlington and Worthington in Ohio; Ann Arbor and Dearborn in Michigan; and Ritenour Consolidated District, St. Louis and University City in Missouri.

To the following teachers I owe the deepest debt of gratitude for their courage and professional dedication in allowing me to record what transpired in their classrooms: Elma Abele, Clara Brooks, Louise Carr, Edith Cupelli, Virginia Ellis, Margaret Harrington, Jean Hoyer, Mildred Joslin, Elsie G. Keller, Mary F. Kersting, Virginia Kessler, Peggy Lee, Eugenia McParlane, Carolyn Retzlaff, Margaret Rood, Mary Rychener, Mary Alice Shrosbree, and Berta Williams.

I am indebted to the children for accepting me in their classes to hear them talk and to watch them work. To their parents I owe my appreciation for their kind permission to use the photographs of their children in this book. I owe special thanks to John Moore, a third-grade boy who painted the wonderful bug which is reproduced on the frontispiece of this book.

Finally, my appreciation to three colleagues at the Ohio State University—Professors Jerome J. Hausman, Coretta W. Mitchell and Jeanne Orr—who read the manuscript and made valuable suggestions. The manner of presentation and the analysis of the classroom records are of course my own.

Manuel Barkan
Columbus, Ohio

February 1960

Through ART To Creativity

LEARNING

This book is about the teaching of art in the elementary schools. It is written for elementary school classroom teachers and for art teachers.

If you are learning to become a teacher, or if you are a teacher seeking to improve your teaching of art, there are surely many questions you are wondering about: What should children learn through their art activities? What are good art activities? What should you talk about to your children? How can you help them find ideas for their work? What should you expect their art works to look like? How should you plan your classroom time? And how can you use your classroom furniture, space and equipment to best advantage? Such questions are real and important. Wise answers can enable you to teach art well so that your children can expand their creative abilities.

When art is taught well, children learn to create and express ideas ingeniously, imaginatively and beautifully. Good teachers are guided by the deep conviction that the potentiality for creative experience belongs to

TO TEACH ART

all children. They know that, although the abilities among individual children vary widely, understanding, encouragement, and help lead children to develop the abilities they have.

When children create ideas, they make them up. They invent them. Their capacity to invent rests heavily on the scope of experiences they can draw upon to create their ideas. At the same time, children are attentive to the reactions of other people towards their ideas. When children's inventions are viewed with interest, they are encouraged to create more ideas. When their efforts go unnoticed or are rejected, children lose confidence in their capacity to invent. They become dependent on the ideas of others. The experiences a teacher provides as sources of ideas and the way she reacts to the efforts of children are, therefore, critical to their creative development. As a result, there is one paramount question among the many important ones which we might ask about the teaching of art: How does a good teacher talk to her children to encourage their creative activity? For example, "listen" to how one excellent teacher talked to her children. Notice the things she talked about, the way she talked, the mood she created through the discussion, and the manner in which she responded to the reactions of her children. You can see how she involved the children in the discussion by integrating their comments and reactions with the ideas she wanted to bring to them. This discussion was the experience from which they went on to create their own ideas.

Mrs. Kersting was talking with her second-grade children about a poem she was planning to read.

MRS. KERSTING: Later in the day I want to read you a little poem about a troll. What is a troll?

MARY: A leprechaun.

MRS. KERSTING: Did you ever see one?

CHILDREN: No!

MRS. KERSTING: Never saw a troll or a leprechaun?

CHILDREN: No!

MRS. KERSTING: Did you say no? Is a troll anything like a fairy?

CHILDREN: Yes!

CHILDREN: No!

MRS. KERSTING: Well now, wait a minute. Is a troll something like a fairy?

CHILDREN: No!

CHILDREN: Yes!

MRS. KERSTING: Do you say yes, Mary? What about an elf? Is a troll anything like an elf?

CHILDREN: Yes, yes!

MRS. KERSTING: Some of us think a troll is like a fairy, and some of us think he isn't. Some think an elf's like a fairy, and some think they are not alike.

Do you know what—whichever you think, that's right. Now Brenda thinks a troll's like a fairy. In her mind that's right.

Do you know, the most wonderful thing about us is that we all have a brain—something up here (she points to her head)—and nobody knows what we're thinking about. Now, if you want to

2

see my hand, here's my hand. I can see Roy's hand. I can see Brenda's eyes. I can look back there and see Jim. But you know what? I don't know what you're thinking about, and you don't know what I'm thinking about. Not really! I don't know what John is thinking about. You can feel my head, but you can't tell what I'm thinking about.

Is there anyone who could tell me right now what he's thinking about? What are you thinking about, Brenda?

BRENDA: About being an angel.

MRS. KERSTING: Who would dream that Brenda's thinking about being an angel? Nobody. I'd never think of that. Johnny, what were you thinking about?

JOHNNY: Uh-u-uh, the numbers there (he points to the board).

MRS. KERSTING: You wouldn't know Johnny was thinking about that. Mary, what were you thinking about?

MARY: Getting married.

CHILDREN: (Laughter)

MRS. KERSTING: That's not silly; all girls think about getting married some day. Jim, what are you thinking about?

JIM: I'm thinking, someday I want to be an ape.

CHILDREN: (Laughter)

MRS. KERSTING: Well, Jim, when do you expect to be that?

CHILDREN: (Laughter)

MRS. KERSTING: Now we know one thing about what Jimmy is thinking. Never in the world would you ever imagine what he was thinking about. That's the nicest part about thoughts. Nobody ever knows what you are thinking about until you tell somebody about it.

Now what else are some of you thinking about? Roy, what are you thinking about?

ROY: I'm thinking about, if I don't go home in the summer, if I don't go home anytime in the summer, I guess I'll go home on Christmas Eve. I guess I will go home on Christmas Eve. My father is fixing a new house, and I will go home on Christmas Eve.

MRS. KERSTING: Listen to all that Roy is thinking in his head. He's even thinking till next Christmas.

Do you know, we don't all have to talk about what we're thinking. There are different ways to tell what you are thinking about. You could write stories about your thoughts, or make pictures about them. Stories and pictures help us tell what we're thinking about.

Just think what we have heard: Christmastime, angels, marriage, and so many other things. Today, I'd like to ask you to paint one of your thoughts—something you are thinking about. You can paint about a troll or a fairy if you'd like to. But you don't have to. Paint something you are thinking about in your head, and tell us about it in a picture.

Now, will you put your oilcloths on your desks. Let's get some paper and brushes, and then let's put the paints out on all the tables. You can paint anything in your mind that we don't know about.

JOHNNY: I don't know what to paint.

MRS. KERSTING: I'm sure you're thinking about something.

JOHNNY: A boat, guns.

MRS. KERSTING: If that's what you're thinking about, that's good. Paint your thoughts for us.

I'm sure you recognized from the way Mrs. Kersting talked how fine a teacher she is. The discussion provided the experience which stimulated the flow of ideas. She made her children feel that they all had ideas which were interesting and worth-while. Through the things she said and the questions she asked, she helped her children to realize that everyone creates his own ideas, and that each person's ideas are his own private property until he tells someone else about them. She chose to talk about a troll because she felt that this would encourage her children to speculate and to think. She didn't really mean for them to paint trolls, even though she suggested this as a possibility. Her main purpose was to show them how they could all think about ideas that would be good to paint.

I'm also sure you noticed another thing. Mrs. Kersting made her children aware of the fact that people express their ideas in different ways. Talking is only one form of expression. Writing stories and painting pictures are others.

4

Learning to Teach Art

From this illustration you can see how teaching art to children rests first and foremost on the experience a teacher provides to stimulate the flow of ideas, and on the sincerity with which she communicates her faith in their ability to create and express ideas. Then the teacher can help her children to expand their ideas and to develop their abilities for expression. Learning to create ideas is an integral part of learning to express them. Creating and expressing ideas with sensitivity, imagination, artistry, and control constitute one of the most significant goals of the modern elementary school program.

Art in the Elementary School

Although there are many notable differences in the teaching of art in the kindergarten and the early, middle, and upper grades of the elementary school, there are three factors of perennial importance at all levels. Regardless of the particular age and level, when a teacher tries to help any group of children to create and express ideas, it is necessary to pay continuous attention to: (1) the physical, social-emotional, intellectual, and aesthetic development of the children; (2) the variety of ways in which ideas can be created and expressed; and (3) the general background for ideas among the children as derived from other studies or events of interest.

Mrs. Kersting's attention to these factors must have been apparent to you as you "listened" to her talk to her second-grade children.

Insight into *the physical, social-emotional, intellectual and aesthetic development of the children* provided Mrs. Kersting with cues for talking, for planning and conducting activities, for arranging room facilities, for selecting materials to be used in work, and for knowing the character of the art work to expect from her children.

In choosing to talk about trolls, leprechauns, and elves, Mrs. Kersting demonstrated her awareness of the tendency toward and capacity for fantasy among children at this age level. The way she developed the concept that ideas are in people's minds until they express them to others, revealed her knowledge of the intellectual ability of her children to understand such an abstract concept. The way she asked them to spread oilcloths on their desks and to get paper, paints, and brushes, demonstrated her own attention to the use of physical facilities and her awareness of the ability of her children to share the responsibility for the care of the facilities.

The variety of ways in which ideas can be created and expressed is an integral part of the learning and development of children. Their general experience in handling ideas is strongly reflected in the specific work they do with any particular form of expression.

Mrs. Kersting knew how children stimulate their own flow of ideas as they express them through different forms. Through talking about their ideas, she helped her children to realize that ideas can also be expressed through writing and painting. The way she linked oral, written, and pictorial expression to each other revealed her teaching goal, and helped her children to become aware of this relationship.

The general background for ideas among the children as derived from other studies or events of interest is the wellspring of raw material out of which they create ideas for expression. Reading, discussions, and field trips for direct observation not only provide background experiences for other studies, but serve the study of art as well. The focal points of interest in the ongoing life in and out of a classroom are the sources children draw upon to create ideas for expression.

Mrs. Kersting introduced the discussion about the troll to encourage a variety of ideas among her children. The discussion thus became the source and formed the basis for the individual ideas to be expressed by the children in their paintings.

Continuous attention to these three factors—the development of the children, the interplay among various forms of expression, and the general background for ideas—is apparent in the work of every good teacher. As a matter of fact, in observing a fine teacher at work, you can always notice how these factors have become a part of her own "second nature." Their presence demonstrates the role of art experiences in the development and education of children, because it underscores the intimate relationship of meaningful art activities to the total curriculum of a class.

Purpose and Content of This Book

My purpose in this book is to deal with some of the information for effective teaching of art in the elementary school, whether you are a classroom teacher or an art teacher. From your point of view as a teacher of children, this book should help you to learn and to understand how art can be taught within the elementary school program. When seen in this context and taught in this spirit, art can become an integral part of the education of children.

In dealing with the teaching of art, I shall include some necessary considerations about the nature of art. While it is true that there are important and general characteristics of good teaching, you cannot learn how to develop these in your own teaching without essential insight and knowledge about the particular subject you intend to teach. To conduct specific activities in a classroom, you need to know what you are planning to teach as well as how you might teach it. In fact, you really cannot pay too much attention to the teaching of art without having some basic insight into the nature of art itself. By basic insight I mean knowing something about what goes into the making of a work of art.

I am not referring merely to knowing how to use certain art materials or knowing how to draw or construct certain things. Important as these are, they are no substitutes for *your own personal experiences* expressing your own ideas through art. Knowing about art means that you have had the experience of creating your own artistic expressions. When you teach art to children, the primary part of your job is to help them to create their ideas through the arts. Your ability to help children to create will stem in large part from your own personal experiences as a creator. The insight you thus gain into the process, problems, and achievements of creation prepares you immeasurably for helping children to create artistic expressions of their own.

Although I shall include some attention to the nature of art, because it is essential to any consideration of the teaching of art, you should not expect this book to provide you with the direct personal experiences you need with art itself. Such experiences cannot be derived from a book. They come from working with art materials—from learning to create and to express your own ideas through art. They also come from looking at works of art others have made. For such learning, there is no substitute for your own involvement in making works of art, accompanied by your own looking at the art works others have created. In this sense, art is no different from reading or arithmetic. You cannot teach reading to children unless you can read yourself; nor can you teach them arithmetic without knowing something about number concepts.

I am assuming, therefore, that you have had or are now having some personal experiences in making and looking at works of art. I am assuming that you have had experiences in expressing your ideas through the creation of paintings, pieces of sculpture, collages, or through any among the many other possible art media. With such experiences of your own, you will have put yourself in the position of knowing something about what art is in order to consider what children should be taught at their various age levels in the elementary school. Such personal experiences enable you to consider how you can help children to create and express their own ideas. The teaching of art consists of helping others to create ideas of their own with imagination, subtlety, beauty, and control.

In this book, I shall discuss the teaching of art by presenting the work of a selected group of fine teachers. There are few better ways to learn to teach well than to observe excellent teachers at work, and to view them as models from whom to learn. People who do a fine job of teaching should be both admired and studied.

The teachers whose work I shall present are to be emulated for

Learning to Teach Art

their degree of excellence, but they cannot be imitated. Fine teachers teach artistically. Their work shows their individuality.

All these teachers know that they teach well, and they are confident in the quality of their teaching. Yet each one of them realizes that truly excellent teaching is the perennial goal of every fine teacher. They consequently feel that they can teach even better, and they strive to improve the work they do.

Although you will recognize important characteristics these teachers share, you will also discover significant individual differences among them. They know their children, and they know what they strive to teach. But above all, they devote themselves to their teaching; their own personal characteristics are reflected in their teaching. By observing them with care, you can learn important things all good teachers do in relation to the unique things individual teachers do. In this way you can recognize ways to build your own capacities as a teacher so that your teaching will reflect your own personality and knowledge.

Through the work of the teachers I shall present, you will be able to get a feeling for the dynamics and process of their teaching. You can "see" and "hear" how they taught their children, what they talked about, and how they responded to the reactions of their children. You can see how they planned their work, how they prepared for their teaching, how they utilized classroom time, and how they utilized the physical space and facilities in their classrooms and schools. You also can see the art works their children created. Above all, you will be able to see teachers who know what it means to challenge the creative potentialities of growing children. You can hear these teachers talk to their children with sympathy, understanding, and imagination. Their ingenuity, courage, and skill should help you realize many important qualities that you should develop in yourself and in your own teaching.

All of these teachers, except one, are classroom teachers. Several of them teach art independently and without the benefit of consultation or supervisory assistance from an art teacher. A few enjoy frequent and helpful assistance, and a few work directly with an art teacher.

Some of these teachers are in schools with limited, restricted, and difficult facilities. Some enjoy the advantages of well-planned and well-equipped classrooms. None has facilities which are in any way unusual or out of reach of any community that wants to provide an adequate level of education for the development of its children.

I shall present the work of these teachers through classroom records of the discussions between themselves and their children. The discussions were recorded in their classrooms. The photographic portions of the records were made at the same time the discussions and activities were in process.

The records of the work of these teachers were made over periods

8

of time varying from two to four weeks in each class. These were the time periods necessary to grasp the scope of each teacher's work. In some instances, the length of time was determined by the age level of the children. In others, the nature of the activities in process, and the time required for their development and completion, were the governing factors. As a result, you will be able to see how each teacher developed a span of work with her own group of children.

Although my primary concern is to report the teaching of art, to do this in the most meaningful manner I shall present the context in which each teacher taught art to her children. As a result, you will be able to get a feeling for the experiences of the children in art in relation to the backgrounds that were current in their respective classes. Consequently, the classroom records include many other activities in which the different groups were engaged. Some of the art activities were an outgrowth of ideas originating from social studies. Other art activities were developed in direct relation to the work different groups of children were doing in other studies. Depending upon the individual cases, therefore, the classroom records include some of the work done in social studies, music, drama, dance, and writing.

I have organized the classroom records into the following grade and age-level clusters: kindergarten, early, middle, and upper elementary grades. The kindergarten level is presented through the work of three teachers; each of the other levels includes from four to six teachers. The work of at least one teacher on each level is presented in great detail; the others of the same level are presented more briefly. By reporting at length the work of at least one teacher on each level, you will be able to acquaint yourself with many essential details. By seeing a group of teachers on each level, you will notice important variations and differences among the specific things they do. You will also see some natural differences in the teaching styles, temperaments, and backgrounds among the individual teachers.

To make the classroom records as useful as possible, each level is presented through a sequence of two chapters. The first contains the classroom records; the second presents an analysis of the work of the group of teachers in terms of five points on which to focus your attention: (1) major developmental achievements of the children, (2) the content of the teachers' conversations, (3) the teachers' use of classroom time, (4) the teachers' use of classroom space and equipment, and (5) the children's art works.

There is a selected and annotated bibliography at the end of the book with references that should be useful to you for further study.

As you read the materials in the chapters that follow, I hope you will see the interdependence between good teaching and theory. I think you will see how the work of fine teachers reflects the theory about good teaching. The theory as presented in this book is derived primarily from the manner in which the classroom activities of the teachers and children who are described, were conducted.

KINDERGARTEN

This chapter presents the work of three kindergarten teachers: Miss Joslin, Miss Lee, and Mrs. Rychener, each of whom teaches two groups of children. One of their groups meets in the mornings; the other in the afternoons. Each of these three teachers is represented through the work she was doing with one of her groups.

Their classrooms are large and well arranged, so that comfortable space is provided for the various activities each of them conducts. There is good floor space for the children to use for movement, rest, discussion, and play. There is good table space for work, and the rooms are well subdivided with sections arranged for special purposes and equipment. Each room is equipped with toilet and lavatory facilities.

Miss Joslin, Miss Lee, and Mrs. Rychener work independently from a special art teacher. In Miss Joslin's school system there is an art consultant for several elementary schools. She can be called upon, but the pressure of work brings her to Miss Joslin's room only on rare occasions. There

CLASSROOM RECORDS

is an art teacher who spends all of her time in the building where Miss Lee teaches. Miss Lee consults with her from time to time, but the art teacher has no direct responsibility for work at the kindergarten level. In Mrs. Rychener's school, there is a part-time art teacher who meets once every two weeks with the older children only.

Here is some further information about each of these teachers, together with excerpts from the records of the activities in their classes:

Six Days in Miss Joslin's Kindergarten

Miss Joslin is a person with boundless enthusiasm. Recorded music fills the air in her classroom, and regardless of the activities in process, it is never a surprise to hear her burst into song with the children or to join them in a dance. Her classroom is a kindergartener's treasure house with something fascinating in virtually every corner. It indeed would be an understatement to say that Miss Joslin encourages her children to create and express ideas. She literally lives the process of expression with them.

The school in which Miss Joslin teaches is located in a modest middle class community. The homes in the neighborhood are well kept. The school building itself could be called neither very old nor very recent. It has been remodeled and modernized, but Miss Joslin's room was originally not intended for a kindergarten. It is huge and high-ceilinged, with anterooms at either end. A series of glass doors along one long wall opens onto a porch which becomes a functional part of the classroom in good weather. Miss Joslin has thirty-two children in this class. It meets in the mornings.

When all the children had arrived, Miss Joslin asked them to come together. They assembled in a circle on the floor.

MISS JOSLIN: Bobby, would you like to tell us the name of this month?

BOBBY: January.

MISS JOSLIN: Oh my goodness, let's take a look at it. What letter does it start with?

BOBBY: A.

MISS JOSLIN: Then what do you think it is? Would you like to ask a friend?

BOBBY: Don.

DON: April.

MISS JOSLIN: Let's sing our April song, so we will remember about April.

CHILDREN: April is the month of showers,
April is the month of flowers,
April is the month of spring.
I'm so happy, I must sing.

MISS JOSLIN: Would someone who has his hand up like to tell us some of the things we're going to do this month?

ROBBIE: Airport trip.

MISS JOSLIN: Mark, why are we going to the airport? Do you know?

MARK: To see about planes.

MISS JOSLIN: And what else?

MARK: Pilots?

MISS JOSLIN: All right. Dora, why do you think we are going to the airport besides planes?

12

Kindergarten Classroom Records

DORA: To learn.

MISS JOSLIN: About what? Other things than planes. What about the people who work there? Are we going to find out about them?

CHILDREN: Yes.

MISS JOSLIN: Can someone name someone we will meet when we go to the airport? Bobby?

BOBBY: We might meet a hostess.

MISS JOSLIN: Yes. What would her job be, Bobby?

BOBBY: To serve the people the food, and to see if they are comfortable.

MISS JOSLIN: That's right. Let's sing about our trip.

CHILDREN: (Singing in chorus)

We're going to the airport, the airport, the airport.
We're going to the airport to have some fun.

MISS JOSLIN: Bobby would you ask if there are any science finders this morning?

BOBBY: Are there any science finders?

MISS JOSLIN: I thought I saw someone with something sticking out of his pocket. Come up Douglas. I think you're a science finder, aren't you? Tell us what you brought.

DOUGLAS: I brought some lettuce seeds.

MISS JOSLIN: And why do we want those?

DOUGLAS: To see lettuce growing.

MISS JOSLIN: Why haven't we been able to plant our lettuce, Douglas?

DOUGLAS: 'Cause the ground didn't dry up.

MISS JOSLIN: You know what the weather man said? He said it's going to rain again tomorrow.

MARCIA: It's supposed to frost.

MISS JOSLIN: It is? Isn't this a funny April month? Douglas, would you now ask someone to go into our science room and bring out something that tells us that spring has come.

DOUGLAS: George. (He goes to the science room.)

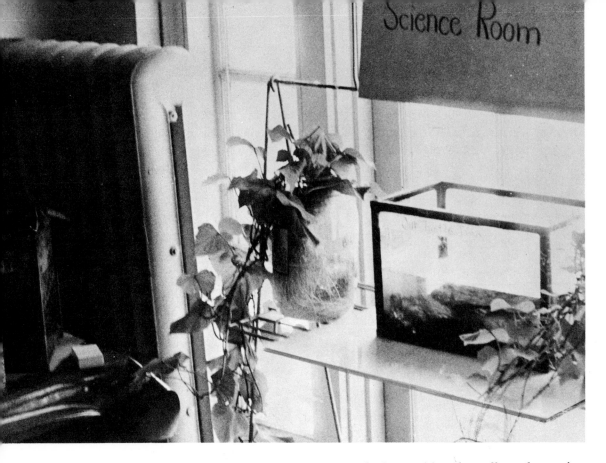

MISS JOSLIN: All right, George. Can you find something that tells us that spring is coming?

GEORGE: Some pussy willows.

MISS JOSLIN: Yes, what happened to the pussy willows? I wonder what happened to the pussy willows?

GEORGE: They're starting to blooming.

MISS JOSLIN: They're blooming. Can you see any buds? Are there any buds left —real closed-up tight ones?

GEORGE: Yes. I see one.

MISS JOSLIN: That's right. But all the others are going to seed, aren't they? Would you like to sing about the pussy willows?

CHILDREN: Yes. (Singing in chorus)

Fuzzy little pussy willow,
Standing by the brook.
Tell me where's your mother kitty,
Tell me where to look.

14

Kindergarten Classroom Records

I am not a fuzzy kitty,
I'm a growing plant.
I wish I had a mother kitty,
But you see I can't.

MISS JOSLIN: Now that April is here, we shall all look for signs of spring. Everything will begin to change. The birds will come back from the south to build their nests; and April showers will help the flowers bloom.

Do you remember last fall, before winter began, we had these trees on our tables (points to large branches stuck into cans filled with sand). What did we do to the trees?

MARK: I know.

MISS JOSLIN: What?

MARK: Put leaves on them.

MISS JOSLIN: What color leaves did we put on them?

MARK: All the colors.

MISS JOSLIN: Why?

BARBARA: Make them prettier.

MARK: No, because it was fall, and they turned colors.

MISS JOSLIN: Weren't the trees outside doing that too?

CHILDREN: Yes.

MISS JOSLIN: And then, what did the trees look like in the wintertime?

MARCIA: Like old ugly trees.

MISS JOSLIN: I don't think they were ugly.

MARCIA: They didn't have any leaves on them.

MISS JOSLIN: I know. But you can't see the branches when the leaves are on. I like a tree without any leaves. You can see the branches.

MARCIA: I like trees with leaves.

MISS JOSLIN: You have a right to like them that way. When winter came and it began to snow, what did we put on our trees?

JIMMY: We stuck cotton on them.

MISS JOSLIN: Yes, and do you remember a week ago I went out and found some more branches and put them in the sand cans? What do you think we should do to these trees now?

JOAN: Put green leaves on them.

MISS JOSLIN: You know there are so many different kinds of leaves. On my way to school this morning I looked for some leaves to bring to show you. But, my goodness, most of the leaves were just little baby leaves. I have a few though.

This one comes from a magnolia tree. I brought this one from my house. What about this leaf? This is long and pointed.

GEORGE: Like an Indian's feather.

MISS JOSLIN: It does look like an Indian's feather, but this is a rhododendron leaf.

JOHN: Look, this looks like a bunny's ear.

MISS JOSLIN: You're right. It does look like the shape of a bunny's ear. Now, what kind of leaves do we want to put on our trees?

CHILDREN: Green ones.

MISS JOSLIN: Do you know, when you make your green leaves you can make them any shape you wish. We're going to have magic trees, and you can make your leaves any shape you wish. Some leaves are big, and some are little. Some have points on the ends, and some don't.

And when the afternoon children come, they'll say, "Look what's happened to our trees." And maybe they'll put birds in our trees, and maybe even birds' nests. Won't that be fun?

CHILDREN: Yes.

Through this discussion, Miss Joslin encouraged the children to observe the characteristic details of pussy willows, trees, branches, and leaves. Such observation brought ideas to mind and provided background for the art activity. It was apparent that the children were involved in the discussion, because they revealed their individual feelings about many of the things they mentioned. Miss Joslin encouraged them to respect their own feelings in preparation for the work they were to do.

MISS JOSLIN: Now let's see how many leaves we can put on our trees. Before you start, though, I want to see how many "hundred-per-cent cleaner-uppers" we have. What is a hundred-per-cent cleaner-upper?

BOBBY: You clean up everything.

MISS JOSLIN: You clean up your table. Of course today you don't have to worry about paste or newspaper or paint, because we won't need all those things. You'll just need your scissors and sticky tape. So what will you have to clean up when you're finished?

CHILDREN: Scraps.

MISS JOSLIN: Yes, the scraps. How about your chairs?

BOBBY: Put it back.

MISS JOSLIN: Because, if you leave it out, someone might fall over it, and you wouldn't want that to happen. Now you can go to the tables and begin your work.

On each table was a tin can filled with sand with a branch stuck in it. Miss Joslin had also prepared scissors and small squares of construction paper of various green shades for the children to use. The children said they wanted to make green leaves, but Miss Joslin prepared green, yellow, yellow-green and blue-green paper, so that they would be able to choose the particular colors they wanted. They went to their tables, and proceeded to cut their leaves and tape them to the branches.

Most of the children worked on their tree branches for about fifteen minutes to half an hour. As individuals finished cutting and mounting the leaves, they went on to a free choice activity. Some of their selections included block building, painting, finger painting, woodwork, and dancing with hoops and streamers on the open porch to the accompaniment of the record player.

When they had finished their paintings, they hung them on a line with clothes pins. Miss Joslin had strung a line on a pair of pulleys along one wall so the children could reach it with ease. The children knew how to hang their finished paintings on the line to get them out of the way where they could dry.

After about a half-hour in their chosen activities, Miss Joslin announced five minutes for clean-up, and the children passed the word around like a chant. They put their things away, and assembled on the floor in a circle for juice, talk, and rest.

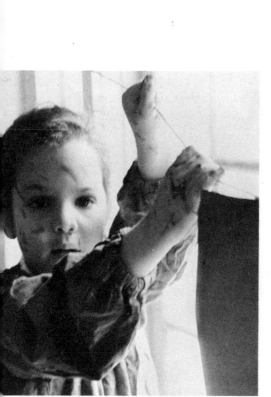

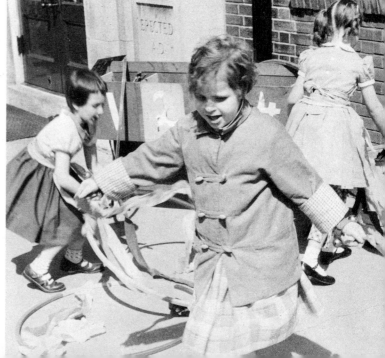

The next morning, Miss Joslin introduced four children from the afternoon kindergarten. As the year proceeds, she periodically invites some of the afternoon children to visit the morning class, and some of the morning children to visit in the afternoon. Since each group sees the work the other has done, the children enjoy visiting each other. After the introductory discussion, the visitors from the afternoon kindergarten showed the morning group some new paintings they had made and some things they had brought for the science room.

Miss Joslin then began to talk about something they could do that morning. In her hands she had a ball of clay to demonstrate to the children how to use it. She also had several clay pieces to show which were made by children in the afternoon kindergarten.

MISS JOSLIN: Today we're going to be able to work with clay. Clay is the only thing you can have fun with that you can squeeze and pull. You can't do that with paint or when you're working with wet chalk. You can pull clay up (and she demonstrates with a piece of clay), and you can push it back.

ANDREW: Oh, this here's fun.

MISS JOSLIN: You'll find that when you start with a ball—now this is really too much clay—it's better to start with a littler piece. (She breaks off a piece about the size of an egg.) If you'll roll it nice and smooth and—

BRENDA: Oh, this is gonna be fun.

MISS JOSLIN: Yes, it is going to be fun—and roll it. You know you have to be pretty strong with clay. You have to use your muscles. You can push. You can squeeze in to make all sorts of interesting things. In fact, I heard a little girl the other day while she was playing with clay in the afternoon kindergarten. She was saying to herself: "I'm making grass grow." And I heard another little boy say: "And I'm making an airplane. My airplane is going somewhere." And then I heard another little boy—(and she proceeds to roll a snake out of her piece of clay). As you can see he made a—

CHILDREN: Snake.

MISS JOSLIN: He made the snake all rolled up. Oh what a very fine round fat snake he made! Some of the children wanted to save what they made. I have them to show to you.

One little boy made a very interesting thing. He decided to call it "Three Men in A Boat."

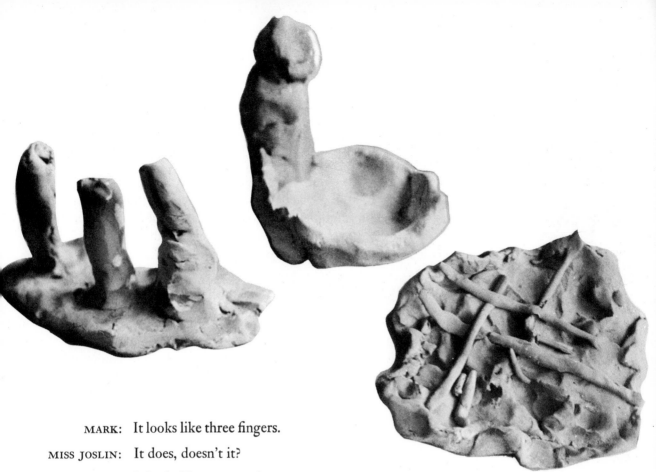

MARK: It looks like three fingers.

MISS JOSLIN: It does, doesn't it?

JEAN: It looks like a gas station pump.

MISS JOSLIN: It could be. You know this is just like when we look at pictures. A picture looks different to everyone, doesn't it? And when we make things with clay, it could look different to you.

This little boy made something his daddy could use. What did he call this?

CHILDREN: Ash tray.

MISS JOSLIN: No, he didn't. He called it his daddy's cuff-link holder. And look. He put a little man on the side. I'm glad that he remembered to smooth the clay, because what happens if you don't?

MARY: It'll break.

MISS JOSLIN: Of course, it will break.

Every child here made something different. We all like to be different, don't we? Don't we all look different?

This little boy made a cherry pie. I'll bet he likes cherry pie.

21

Kindergarten Classroom Records

MARCIA: Hey, I'm going to make me a cake like that.

MISS JOSLIN: Do you remember when we played with clay before, we had to wear our smocks?

You know, we have our two clowns—Charlie and Happy—and you have done a very good job of keeping their clothes on the hooks. Charlie and Happy aren't very happy if their clothes fall off. When you use the smocks, be careful to put them right back on the clowns when you're finished.

When you go to the other side of the room, you will see a little table with your clay boards (9″ x 12″ pieces of masonite) piled up. Take enough clay to fill your hand. You know, some children take so much clay that they can't handle it. Take a handful, and then if you need more, go back and get it. And when you're all finished, if you have pieces of clay left all over on your board like this (she demonstrates), pick them up and squeeze them together. Because when you put the clay back in the can, it should be in one ball.

Now, how many of you are going to be one-hundred-per-cent cleaner-uppers? What do you do with your clay board when you are finished?

CHILDREN: Wash it.

MISS JOSLIN: What do you wash it in?

CHILDREN: In a bucket.

MISS JOSLIN: And then you go into your bathroom and wash your hands. Remember the paper towels. Push them down in the basket so they won't pop out.

GEORGE: At first wash your hands in that soapy stuff. Then wash your board, and then go in the bathroom and wash your hands.

MISS JOSLIN: That's right. That's fine. When you are finished, be sure that your smock is hung up, and then you may do anything you want.

You know why we can do so many things in this kindergarten? Because you help each other. You help each other and that helps me.

Examination of the work done by the children in the afternoon kindergarten suggested ideas to these children. There was little risk that they would copy, because of the variety of things they saw and the emphasis Miss Joslin put on their personal interpretations. Her demonstration of the handling of clay and her preparation of the material and equipment enabled the children to go directly to work.

The children got up from the floor and went to the two clowns—Charlie and Happy—to get their smocks. At the side of the room near their work tables, Miss Joslin had prepared a bench with the masonite boards on a tray, a garbage bucket lined with pliofilm which was filled with clay, and a bucket of soapy water with a sponge in it.

The children put on their smocks and helped each other button themselves. They reached into the bucket for clay, took a board, and went to work. They squeezed and rolled the clay, built their pieces, and smoothed them with care.

When they completed their work, they gathered up the clay scraps, returned what was left to the clay bucket, and washed their boards in the soapy water. Those who finished early went on to play with blocks, build in the sand pile, and dance on the porch until the others were through.

❧   ❧   ❧

On Monday morning there was a great surprise in the kindergarten. Miss Joslin had borrowed two cages from one of the local commercial companies. One contained two rabbits; several ducklings were in the other. When the children arrived, they naturally gathered around the cages, and put their hands in to play with the rabbits and ducks.

Miss Joslin brought a plastic basin and filled it with water, and the children put two of the ducklings in the water. This was so exciting that they took turns playing with the ducks for quite a while.

The animals were the center of attraction, and the children devoted over half an hour to their unexpected surprise. Then they gathered on the floor in a circle to go on with the activities of the day. After checking the calendar and noting the day, date and month, they went on to talk about spring. The children who brought science things showed them to the group. Today's additions to their science collection consisted of some rocks, daffodils, and a slab of wood cut from the middle of a tree trunk.

MISS JOSLIN: Before we start playtime today, I want to tell you about something the afternoon children started to make—a scarecrow. It's a little early to make one, because our lettuce hasn't started to come up yet; but we'll need one soon. But because the afternoon children planted the lettuce seeds, I decided it would only be fair to have some children in the morning group build a scarecrow.

One year we had the most wonderful lettuce garden, but there were some wild bunnies in the neighborhood, and they ate all our lettuce.

PAMELA: We have a wild bunny in my back yard.

MISS JOSLIN: The birds outside leave our garden alone, but it's the rabbits we have to worry about. So I found two nice big boards. How can we put them together (shows the boards to the children)?

CHILDREN: Nail them.

MISS JOSLIN: What could this be (holds up short board)?

CHILDREN: Arms.

MISS JOSLIN: How could we make the end of our board stick in the ground?

JOHN: Cut a point.

MISS JOSLIN: Yes, cut a point to make it go into the ground. And after the board is nailed on, what would we do up on this part (points to top of vertical board)?

CAROL: Draw a man.

MISS JOSLIN: We could have someone paint a face. Maybe it would take a lot of children to make this. And, after the face is dry, we could take some of that colored yarn and make some hair.

MARK: I could.

PAMELA: And then we have to put a dress on.

MISS JOSLIN: We could dress him, because we have lots of funny clothes in the playhouse.

BOBBY: Put a hat on.

MISS JOSLIN: All right. I'd like to ask Dennis to please put this over on the work bench. Would you like to help build the scarecrow, Dennis?

DENNIS: Yes.

MISS JOSLIN: The children who would like to paint today might like to paint the animals that are in our kindergarten. You can choose to paint or dance or play records, and don't forget about the scarecrow.

The children scattered around the room. Some of them first went back to the cages to play a while longer with the ducks and rabbits. Soon they were all at work. Two boys joined together to build the scarecrow.

A few of the girls played records and danced to the music.

One girl went to the science room to examine the slab of wood from the tree trunk with a magnifying glass.

Some of the children made paintings of the animals in the room.

By the end of the morning, the two boys who began the work on the scarecrow were joined by two other helpers. They had a scarecrow to show for their efforts.

෨   ෨   ෨

The next morning, after the introductory discussion, Miss Joslin began to talk about some of the things they had made the day before.

MISS JOSLIN: Johnny made a bunny out of clay. So many of you made your bunnies in different ways. Just like yesterday, some of the boys built horses out of blocks. You taught me that. I didn't even know about it.

MARK: We make buildings with blocks, too.

MISS JOSLIN: Michael painted his bunny on yellow paper. This looks like "Funny Bunny." Do you remember him?

MICHAEL: Yeah.

MISS JOSLIN: Before he found his tail. I like your bunny, Michael. And Linda painted this beautiful butterfly. It's sitting on a bench in the rain. Soon she will spread her wings and fly away. Mrs. Butterfly must be happy that spring has come. Don't you think so?

CHILDREN: Yes.

MISS JOSLIN: I like the orange raindrops.

And here's your bunny, Cindy. Cindy's little bunny is very happy. She has such a lovely smile on her face. She must like all the boys and girls in the kindergarten. She knows that they will be kind to her.

Oh, I just love this one. You guess what it is.

CHILDREN: A scarecrow.

MISS JOSLIN: John painted that. This is the way our garden will look when the lettuce begins to grow. Our scarecrow will stand in the ground and frighten the wild bunnies away.

Look at the scarecrow that Dennis and the other boys made yesterday. You know, when I saw the scarecrow they made, I thought of the song we used to sing about the funny snowman. Do you remember the funny snowman?

CHILDREN: Yes.

MISS JOSLIN: We could almost change the song, couldn't we?

CHILDREN: (Singing in chorus)
Funny scarecrow tall and—

DENNIS: Skinny.

MISS JOSLIN: Yes, skinny.

CHILDREN: With your funny eyes and your funny hair,
With your funny shirt and your funny arms.
I have to laugh when I look at you.

MISS JOSLIN: You know, if someone has time this morning during playtime, he could do something. Do you remember what we did to our Santa Claus at Christmastime?

CHILDREN: Yes.

MISS JOSLIN: What did we do?

SANDY: We stuffed 'im.

MISS JOSLIN: We had a great big Santa Claus. What can we do with our scarecrow?

CHILDREN: Stuff 'im.

MISS JOSLIN: We could make him look real fat—fill his shirt up.

BOBBY: Yeah, we'll fill him up so the body—the paper will make him fat.

MISS JOSLIN: That's right, and we'll tie a rope around his body to keep the paper from falling out.

Sheryl, I just love your picture. It has so much color in it.

Since the two little bunnies have been visiting in our kindergarten, all of the children have been having fun painting their pictures. All the children paint them differently. This is the way Sheryl painted one of them.

In this way, the children shared, enjoyed, and appreciated the many things they had made. Miss Joslin helped them to recognize the qualities in their work—the beautiful colors and the interesting interpretations. This helped them to discover more things that were good to do. It helped them to realize that it was good to create their own ideas.

MISS JOSLIN: Boys and girls, we're going to play a little game this morning. We'll put this paper bag over someone's head so their eyes cannot see. Then I'm going to ask Carol to choose someone to go into the science room and bring something out, and the child with the bag on his head will feel it to see if he can guess what it is.

George, you put the bag on your head. And Carol, you choose someone to go into the science room and find something.

CAROL: Cindy.

CINDY: (Comes back with a turtle shell for George to feel.)

GEORGE: A turtle shell.

CHILDREN: (Cheers)

MISS JOSLIN: George, how did it feel?

GEORGE: Smooth.

MISS JOSLIN: Did it feel a little bumpy?

GEORGE: Yes.

MISS JOSLIN: And did it feel round?

GEORGE: Yes.

They played the game several more times with children bringing a piece of wood, feathers, and a stone from the science room.

MISS JOSLIN: You know that by feeling, we can tell what things are, and sometimes by smelling too. Some things feel smooth. Some things feel rough. Some things feel bumpy. Some things feel furry, just by telling with your hands.

The children enjoyed the game, but Miss Joslin's comments made the experience more than a mere game. She was teaching them to touch things sensitively in order to observe the quality of different textures. This experience formed the basis for their next art activity.

MISS JOSLIN: Do you remember the collages we made a while ago? I saved some, and I have them right here on the floor. But do you know what I'd like you to do today? I was so excited when I thought about it. We're going to make a different kind of collage.

Last time we used smooth and bumpy and rough things to make our collages, but we made them flat. I thought this time, when we make our collages, we can push them up in the air. So, I looked around and found something that's a little bit stiffer—almost like cardboard—for you to use. When we make our collages today, let's push them up into the air.

Right in the middle of your tables I have put some round trays. Do you remember when you had to say, "Please pass the paste"? Now you may turn the tray. When you see someone is finished, you may turn the tray and find the thing you wish to put on your collage—maybe a button, or maybe a feather, or a shiny bead.

Now I'm going to show you some of the things you can do. I tried to build one up into the air, but maybe you can make yours go even higher.

If there's something you want which you can't find on the tray, you may go over to the paper table. Maybe you'd like some crepe paper. Maybe you'd like a piece of colored paper. These feathers came from our—

CHILDREN: Indians.

MISS JOSLIN: Yes, from our Indian hats. And these are pieces of colored yarn which I pasted into a cup. And you know why I like this aluminum foil? You can twist it, and you can turn it. Look at this thing. It looks like a fairy tree, doesn't it?

JOHN: It's fun.

MISS JOSLIN: And I took a bead and stuck it on the end of this wire. Of course I know you can think of a lot more interesting things. I didn't have very long to play with this. Do you think that all your collages should look different?

CHILDREN: Yes.

MISS JOSLIN: Yes. All of your collages should be of your own ideas.

When you're finished I want you to slip your collage into your locker (cubby bin). And then you may do whatever you like.

When I call your name, you may come up and choose the color cardboard you would like. You may take a paste stick and a piece of newspaper, and let's see if we can have one hundred-per-cent—

CHILDREN: Cleaner-uppers.

MISS JOSLIN: All right, Laurie will you come up. Mark, Cindy, John . . .

The children selected their pieces of colored cardboard, picked up paste sticks and newspaper sheets which Miss Joslin had prepared, and proceeded to the work tables.

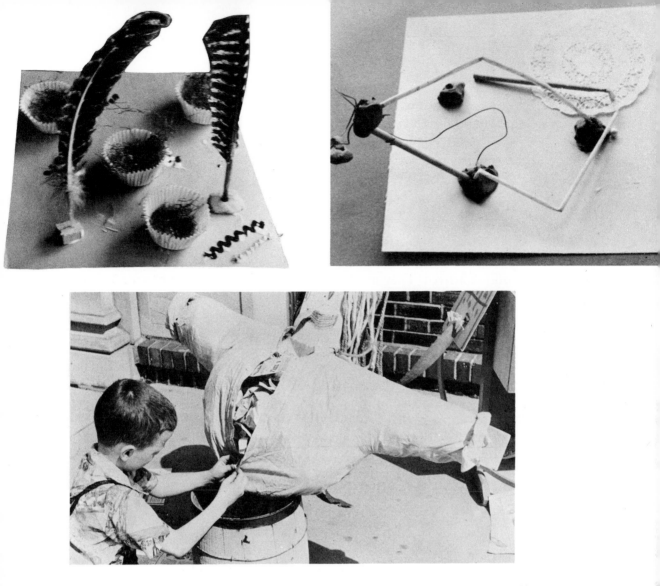

They were engrossed in this new activity. It was like the collages they had made earlier, and they knew how to handle the materials. Yet this was a new kind of construction, and they discovered many new ideas. Most of the children worked for at least twenty-five minutes before cleaning up and going on to their free choice activities. Several children worked for almost forty minutes.

Here are two of the collages they built way into the air.

After finishing their collages, three of the boys took the scarecrow out on the porch to stuff him with paper.

Here, one of the boys is buttoning the scarecrow's shirt to keep the paper in.

This was the day for the trip to the airport. The school bus was waiting, and six mothers were there to help. Each mother took five or six children for whom she was to be responsible. By making these arrangements in advance, Miss Joslin was thus free to talk to the children and to take care of details of the trip.

When they arrived at the airport, they went first to the airline ticket counter to talk to the attendant. He showed them a ticket, and they saw where the baggage was weighed. Then they went through the airport building to see the shops, post office, restaurant, and the in-coming baggage platform. A train of trucks came in with a load of luggage from a plane that had just arrived. They noticed that the sky-caps were just like the red-caps they had seen on a trip to the railroad station earlier in the year.

Then they went out on the observation deck for a perfect view of the plane loading platforms and the entire airfield. The noise of the engines was exciting, and they were fascinated by all the activity—moving of the ramps, attendants, gasoline trucks, baggage trucks, passengers, pilots, and stewardesses.

After two or three planes had loaded and departed, the children were ready to go. Miss Joslin had arranged with one of the airlines for the children to be allowed into a hangar to see how planes were repaired. They were also to get into a plane. The bus, therefore, took the group to the airline hangar. They looked around, asked questions, and proceeded to the plane they could board. They sat in the passenger seats and fastened their safety belts as passengers do when they take a trip.

Some of the children took turns going up to the pilot's cabin to sit at the controls. This was an exciting experience, since few of the children had ever been in an airplane before. Their satisfaction was written all over their faces as they got off the plane.

To make a perfect day even better, a helicopter suddenly came in out of nowhere and landed near the hangar. They stopped to watch the whirling propellers.

The trip took the entire morning, because their school was about twenty minutes' ride from the airport. On the way back, they were tired but excited. They sang songs about airplanes and talked about the things they had seen.

〜〜 〜〜 〜〜

The next day, reverberations of the airport trip filled the classroom air. The children quickly took care of the calendar and began to sing.

CHILDREN: (Singing in chorus)

What did we see on our trip to the airport?
What did we see on our trip to the airport?
What did we see?

MISS JOSLIN: What did we see? Barbara?

BARBARA: Well, we saw a jet taking off.

MISS JOSLIN: What other types of planes did you see out there? Douglas?

DOUGLAS: Copeller plane.

MISS JOSLIN: Yes, but let me hear all of you say propeller.

CHILDREN: Propeller.

MISS JOSLIN: What kind of a plane did we see over near the hangar?

BOBBY: That was—ah—a—passenger plane.

MISS JOSLIN: It was. But what about the one we saw up in the air?

MARK: Well, that was a helicopter.

MISS JOSLIN: It was. What can a helicopter do that other planes cannot do? Laurie?

LAURIE: Go straight up in the air and straight down.

CHILDREN: (Singing in chorus)

What else did we see on our trip to the airport?
What else did we see on our trip to the airport?
What else did we see?

MISS JOSLIN: George.

GEORGE: Where the co-pilot and pilot sits.

MISS JOSLIN: All right. Would you like to tell us about that? Why do they have to have a co-pilot?

GEORGE: If the one—if the pilot gets hurt or something, the co-pilot takes over.

MISS JOSLIN: That's right.

MARK: Yeah, but who takes over for the co-pilot?

MISS JOSLIN: If you build an airplane, how many steering wheels will you need for your pilot's cabin?

CHILDREN: Two.

MISS JOSLIN: What else did you see in the cabin? Linda?

LINDA: A radio.

MISS JOSLIN: Linda says she saw a radio up there in the cabin. What else was up there?

MARCIA: A microphone.

MISS JOSLIN: All right, why would a pilot need a microphone and earphones? Bobby, what do you think about the earphones the pilot puts on his head?

BOBBY: Well, if he puts the earphones on, he can hear what the man in the control tower is saying.

MISS JOSLIN: That's very important.

I'd like some children to paint at the easels this morning and make something you saw. Now it doesn't have to be an airplane. We saw so many things at the airport. The airport inside reminded me of the Union Station—just like a city. It had all of the same things. Cindy, can you tell us something you saw?

CINDY: Oh, the people buy things for the trip.

MISS JOSLIN: What do they buy for the trip?

LINDA: Tickets.

MISS JOSLIN: When you go on an airplane, you do not have your ticket punched the way you do on a train. Does anyone have an idea what happens to the ticket after you buy it?

LINDA: It's already punched.

MISS JOSLIN: No. Bobby, do you know?

BOBBY: When you get on a plane, you give it to the—you give it to the ticket man.

MISS JOSLIN: That's a pretty good guess. George, do you know what happens to the ticket?

GEORGE: When you get on the airplane, you give it to the stewardess.

MISS JOSLIN: That's right. And the stewardess has a kitchen. She gets hot meals for you. She brings them on trays. I borrowed these trays from the cafeteria today, so if you wish to serve food in the plane, you can use these. You can use the food we have in our playhouse.

If some of you should make some clay airplanes or some airplanes out of wood, where do you think you should put these when you're finished?

PAMELA: On that table.

SHEILA: I want to make a collage.

MISS JOSLIN: Sheila, that's a good idea. Could Sheila make a collage showing something she saw at the airport?

CHILDREN: Yes.

MISS JOSLIN: Good. You can begin now, and wear a smock if you need to.

In this way, they talked over a great many of the things they saw at the airport. As they talked, Miss Joslin mentioned a variety of possibilities for work they could do. She had everything prepared for the children to use, like wheels for the pilots, trays for the stewardess, and paint for those who wanted to make pictures. During the course of the discussion, the children were able to decide what each of them wanted to do, and they were ready to begin.

The children scattered over the room. Several went to work with the large blocks and laid out a huge airplane in the center of the floor. This attracted quite a few of the children, and throughout the entire morning different children took turns dramatizing the roles of passenger, stewardess, and pilot.

Two of the children worked with Miss Joslin to build a ticket office. When they were finished, one of the boys took over as ticket-seller.

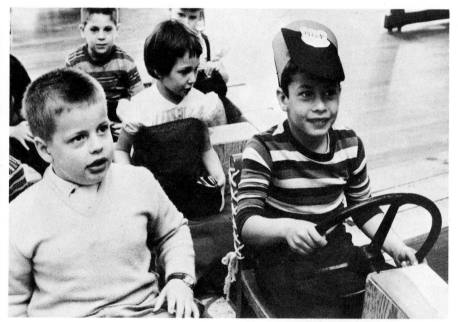

38

Kindergarten Classroom Records

When two of the boys were asked what they were doing, they replied: "We're building an airport."

One of the girls worked for quite a while at the woodwork bench sawing, hammering, and building an airplane. When she finished, she put on a smock, and went to the paint table to paint her plane.

One of the boys made a helicopter out of clay.

Among the paintings was this one of an airline stewardess.

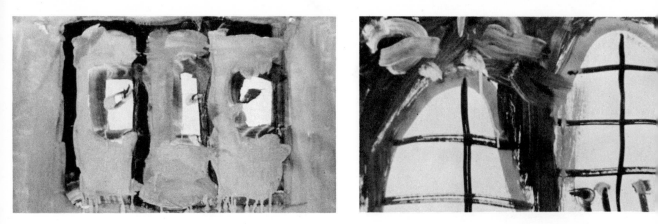

Two surprises appeared among the paintings made that morning. Through all the discussion no one had mentioned the telephone booths, and no one had said anything about the huge glass windows in the airport building. These were the surprise ideas that two of the children painted.

Seven Days in Miss Lee's Kindergarten

Miss Lee is a very orderly person. She is not too demonstrative toward her children. She arranges her work carefully and systematically, and reacts calmly and sympathetically. Miss Lee loves stories and poems, and she truly has an unlimited fund of them. Individually and in chorus her children speak and sing the poems she has taught them. They are delighted with the tingle of the language and the images evoked. Frequent opportunities for work in art is one of the keystones of Miss Lee's teaching.

The school in which Miss Lee teaches is located in a comfortable residential neighborhood of a small industrial city which adjoins a huge metropolitan center. Her building is quite new and modern; her classroom is sunny and bright. There are thirty-seven children in the group whose activities are described.

This was Miss Lee's afternoon kindergarten group. Like many kindergarten teachers, she began with the children seated on the floor and gathered around her. They looked at the large calendar chart and noted the day of the week, the date, and the month. It was Wednesday, March 5. They counted the number of boys and girls and calculated how many people were absent that afternoon. This is the daily introductory routine.

MISS LEE: I have an interesting story I think you'll like. It's called "Raggedy Ann." Raggedy Ann did a lot of things, and after you hear the story, I think you might like to make some pictures about her.

The children listened intently, and after the story was over they talked about Raggedy Ann's many adventures. Miss Lee suggested they use crayons to do their pictures. The children got up from the floor and went to

40

their tables. She brought the crayons and a bundle of 12″ x 18″ manila paper from the cupboard. The children helped themselves and went to work. Most of them finished their pictures in about twenty minutes; some took about half an hour. When some of the children began to complete their pictures, Miss Lee asked them all to stop and listen.

MISS LEE: When you have finished your pictures and are all through, you may play. Some of you might like to build with blocks, or play on the see-saw. Two of you may ride the tricycles. And a few of you might like to use the playhouse today. Two of you might like to paint at the easels, and some of you might like to play with clay.

I'm going to put the big hand of the clock (a cardboard clock dial) on number ten. You watch the clock on the wall and when the big hand gets to number ten, let's all clean up and sit on the floor again.

Most of the children thus had fifteen to twenty minutes in a free-choice activity. When they gathered together on the floor, Miss Lee had all their crayon pictures in her lap. She held up a few to comment about them.

MISS LEE: Look at the beautiful colors Jane used in her picture. And, I like how Johnny made the hair on his Raggedy Ann, don't you?

I think it would be nice if some of you people would tell us about your pictures. I'd like to have four people to come up at a time, and hold up their pictures, and tell us what part of the story or which Raggedy Ann they made a picture of.

Four volunteers came up and found their pictures. They faced the class and showed their pictures.

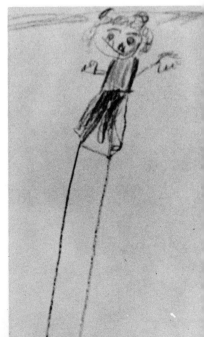

MISS LEE: Tommy, tell us about your Raggedy Ann picture.

TOMMY: She has a bird's nest in her hair.

MISS LEE: A nest?

TOMMY: That was the time she got her hand caught.

MISS LEE: I like that. Bobby, tell us about yours.

BOBBY: Raggedy Ann went to a stranger's house.

MISS LEE: Good, Bobby, thank you.

They continued showing and looking at each other's pictures for about ten minutes, when Miss Lee recognized that attention was beginning to wane. It was time to shift to another activity.

MISS LEE: I think I'll hang up the pictures we didn't have time to look at together, so we'll be able to see them all. Now it's time for us to go out to the play yard.

❧   ❧   ❧

The next day after the children had checked the calendar and attendance, Miss Lee read the words to a folk song. She called it a poem.

MISS LEE: I have a new poem to read to you today. You're going to like it. It's about an old woman.

There was an old woman who swallowed a spider,
Right down inside her, she swallowed a spider.
She swallowed a spider because of the fly,
Oh my, swallowed a fly.
Poor woman, I think she'll die.

Miss Lee continued to read the rest of the poem about the old woman swallowing a cow because of the dog, a dog because of the cat, a cat because of the bird, and a bird because of the spider. In the last stanza, the old woman swallowed a horse.

MISS LEE: There was an old woman who swallowed a horse.
She died, of course.

The children, of course, were delighted with the poem, and Miss Lee reread it to them more slowly. As she read, they joined in a chorus. By the time they had recited the second stanza, some of them began to move to the accompaniment of the words. Soon all the children joined in the movements and gestures. They enjoyed the rhythm, were amused by the humor, and swayed to the words as they spoke.

Listening to the poem, reciting it, and making up gestures to accompany it made this whole experience exciting and meaningful to the

children. When they had adopted the poem as their own, Miss Lee knew they were ready to do something about it.

MISS LEE: Did you like that?

CHILDREN: Yes.

MISS LEE: How would you like to do a real big painting of any one of the things in that poem? We can use our big roll of white paper to do this. We all won't be able to make large paintings at one time. We don't have enough space for that, but some of you can paint today, and the rest can make them tomorrow. Who would like to paint today? (About two-thirds of the group raised their hands.)

All right. I think we can manage. Those who will wait till tomorrow can play house, build with blocks, or paint at the easels.

Get your smocks and paints, and I'll cut the paper. Then spread your paper on the floor, and be careful not to spill any paint.

Miss Lee took the roll of paper and cut large pieces which varied in size from 30" x 36" to 30" x 40". Each painter took a sheet, spread it out on the floor, and went to work. The paint had been prepared in fruit juice cans, and the children selected the colors they preferred. The rest of the group divided among the other activities.

❧   ❧   ❧

The next day, they again recited the poem about the old woman who swallowed a fly. They knew it well and spoke it with spirit, movement, and gesture.

MISS LEE: That was good. I have your pictures that you made yesterday. I thought you might like to cut them out. Then we can put them on the wall. This is Carolyn's, and this was a picture of—

CAROLYN: The cat.

MISS LEE: That's right. You can cut out the cat, and the tree and the flower, and we'll put them on the wall.

Marc. Tell us about yours.

MARC: I think that was the fly.

MISS LEE: Good. Now come cut it out. Look at the nice bright sky Marc put in his picture.

In this manner Miss Lee distributed the pictures to the children who had painted them. They spread their pictures on the floor, went to the cupboard for scissors, and began to cut out the painted objects. Miss Lee continued to talk to those children who hadn't yet painted a large picture.

MISS LEE: Do you remember yesterday, some of you didn't get to paint a large picture. If you'd like to do one today, I'll give you a sheet of paper and you may paint one now.

I know something else some of you might like to do. Bobby has been sick several days now, and some of you might like to make a get-well card for him. You may choose to paint a large picture or make a get-well card for Bobby. While you're all working, I'll begin to fix our new cut-out pictures on the wall.

In this way all the children selected their work. One of them made a get-well painting for Bobby.

While they worked, Miss Lee began to hang their cut-out pictures on the wall.

As some of the children began to complete their work, the room naturally became noisy. Miss Lee stopped what she was doing, went to the piano and played a phrase.

MISS LEE: Look at the big clock and tell me what number the big hand is on.

JEAN: Three.

MISS LEE: Almost. When you finish your work, you can have playtime to-day until the big hand gets on number five. (She set the large hand of the cardboard clock to point to number five.) Then I want you to clean up and put everything away.

If you happen to get any paint on the floor, don't forget to wash it off with a sponge when you are finished.

෨ ෨ ෨

The following day, after having taken care of the calendar and attendance, the children sat on the floor and listened.

MISS LEE: What a lovely book I brought today—a book about—can you guess what it would be about? (She holds the book for them to see.)

JOHN: Fishing.

MISS LEE: It might be. What else?

JANE: Spring.

MISS LEE: Jane, what makes you think it might be about spring?

JANE: Because, um—in the spring, um—the water looks real pretty like that, and the grass is nice and green.

MISS LEE: Let's see how many other things we can find in this book that would tell us that it looks like spring. Can you see the name of the story? Do you want to tell the boys and girls the name of it?

JIMMY: Yes. *City Springtime.*

MISS LEE: How can you tell it's *City Springtime* instead of country spring-time?

JIMMY: Because the sun's out.

MISS LEE: Well, wouldn't the sun be out in the country too? Look at the picture and see if you can tell why it's called *City Springtime.*

MARC: Because it's a city.

MISS LEE: What makes you think it's a city?

MARC: Because it's buildings.

MISS LEE: What kind of buildings?

MARC: Skyscrapers.

MISS LEE: Yes. Sure. Look at them.

MARC: Because it's big buildings, and they need stuff like that to work in, and banks.

MISS LEE: Is there anything else that tells us it's spring?

MARY: The leaves on the trees.

MISS LEE: Yes. The leaves on the trees. Look out the window. What do you see on our trees now?

CAROLYN: Nothing.

MISS LEE: Well, how are we ever going to get some things on the trees to tell us it's spring? Are there leaves, or is there something coming before the leaves?

MARY: Something coming before.

MISS LEE: What has to come out on the trees before the leaves will get there?

MARC: Flowers.

MISS LEE: Even before the blossoms. Something else.

JOHN: Buds.

MISS LEE: Yes, buds. What do buds look like?

JEAN: Um—, round.

MISS LEE: Yes, a lot of little buds—little bumps. How many of you have seen any little bumps on the trees in your yard? Did you notice any?

And there are other things to tell us signs of spring too. What are they? Maybe you've seen some more things in your backyard, or around your house—some other things that tell us spring is coming?

MARY: We have little green parts of the tulips coming out up around our house.

MISS LEE: Yes, they're starting to push up through the ground.

MARY: Every day spring's coming.

MISS LEE: What happened to that little plant you saw, Tommy? Where was it all winter long?

TOMMY: Under the grass.

46

Kindergarten Classroom Records

MISS LEE: Sure. And what was the ground like in the winter? Kenny?

KENNY: Hard.

MISS LEE: Because it was cold. And what happens to the ground in the springtime?

KENNY: Warm.

MISS LEE: Yes, the ground gets warm.

TOMMY: Um—. It gets softer.

MISS LEE: Sure. When the ground gets soft and the flowers start pushing their way up, what else is going to push up in the warm weather too? Do you know what, Tommy?

TOMMY: Grass.

MISS LEE: Grass. Good for you. The little blades of grass are going to start pushing their heads up.

Every day let's see if we can find some new things that tell us spring is coming.

This story is about spring in the city. It's a story about a little boy, and his name is Lewis. And Lewis lives in the country. He can tell about spring in the country, but he wondered how you can tell about spring in the city where the buildings are tall.

She reads the story of Lewis' trip to the city with his mother to visit his aunt. They go to the park. They feed peanuts to the squirrels, and then Lewis' aunt buys him a kite. The story about spring brought many things to mind—warm weather, buds on trees, new grass pushing up from the ground, fishing, and kite flying. There were many ideas here for things to do.

MISS LEE: I wonder if you'd like to make something today—something that would be kind of "springy," something we would have fun with out on the playground, something Lewis had fun with, before it got caught up in the tree?

CHILDREN: Kites.

MISS LEE: See if you can close your eyes and think about some kites flying up there in the sky with some bright spring colors for trimming? How many of you have had a chance to fly a kite?

CHILDREN: I did. I, I—

MISS LEE: You know, it's just about right for a kite, and there is a kite we can make. We have great big sheets of colored paper, and we could fold them and cut them a certain way and make kites.

Let's go over to the tables. You choose your own color, and I'll use this sheet to show you how to fold it. Can you all see?

CHILDREN: Yes.

MISS LEE: First, you'll have to fold the paper in half. You'll have to see that the corners match, and you'll have to make sure that it fits just right. Now make a nice fold, and we have a book. You can help each other if you want to.

Now we have to fold it one more time. Make sure that it matches at the corners. Fold it real hard into a littler book.

Now we're going to cut from one corner all the way across to the other corner. That's going to take a lot of steady people. You'll have to hold onto the part where the fold is and really think. Hold the closed side real tight. Start from one side and cut clear across. When you cut it, then open it up, and you'll have a kite shape.

Now what are we going to put on here?

CHERI: All different colors.

JERRY: Decorations.

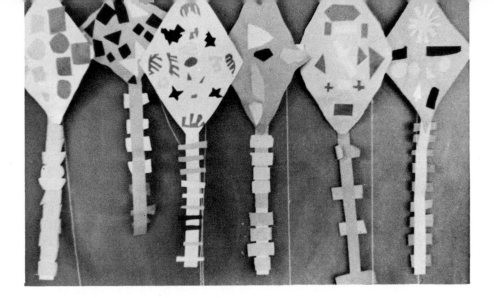

MISS LEE: What kind of decorations would you like to put on your kites?

MARY: Stars.

GARY: Boats.

MISS LEE: How about some "springy" looking things too? Marc, what would you like to put on yours?

MARC: Flowers.

MISS LEE: All right. You can put whatever you'd like on your own kite. To-day we'll try to decorate one side of our kites, and when you finish one side, I think we'll stop. That'll take quite a lot of work, so we'll stop when you get that much done. Then tomorrow, we'll do the other side and make the tail. You know, a kite needs a tail to fly. Then we'll need something else on the kite. What will we need?

CHERI: String.

MISS LEE: Yes, string. After we put the string on, we'll go outside together. Maybe we'll have a nice windy day and we'll make our kites sail in the air.

Now choose whichever colors you like and go to work.

༄ ༄ ༄

The following day required only a very brief discussion before they returned to the work on their kites. They completed the decorations on both sides and made the tails. As they finished, Miss Lee hung their kites on the wall.

༄ ༄ ༄

49

Kindergarten Classroom Records

The next day was kite-flying time. The children were anxious to take their kites out of doors to make them fly.

MISS LEE: Let's sit down and plan all the things to do this afternoon. We want to fly our kites today, so let's save enough time to do that. I think today it might be fun to start out with playtime. We've been doing a lot of work making our kites. So, let's have playtime first today.

Let's look at the clock. The big hand is almost on number one. We can have playtime until the big hand is all the way over here on number six. When it gets on six, it will be time to clean up. Put everything away and make a big circle. How many can remember that?

CHILDREN: Yes.

MISS LEE: All right. There are a lot of things you can do in playtime. Which boys and girls would like to crayon a picture today? Which people would like to play in the playhouse? How about clay? Library table? Trains? Puzzles? We have two bikes. Who would like to ride a bike today?

The children selected their individual activities and scattered around the room. At 1:30 p.m. they began to clean up. As they gathered into the circle, Miss Lee played several records of songs they knew, and they joined in the singing. She then played some dance rhythms and invited the children to dance in the circle—first the girls, then the boys, then together.

MISS LEE: I think it's time we went outside to fly our kites. The playground is pretty muddy, so I think it would be better if we went along the sidewalk in front of the school. You're going to have to give yourself lots of room, so don't get crowded. Hang onto the string, and run as fast as you can, and see how high you can get your kite up in the air.

You get your coats now, and I'll hand you your kites. Hold onto them, so that you won't let anybody step on your tail, because what might happen?

CHILDREN: Break. Tear.

MISS LEE: Yes. And just in case we have an accident, I wouldn't get upset or worried about it. We have paste in here, and you can fix it up. Let's get started.

50

With their coats on, and kites in hand, they all went outside to run up and down the sidewalk flying their kites.

❧　　❧　　❧

The next day the children talked about the fun they had had flying their kites. At the conclusion of this discussion, Miss Lee reminded them of the story she had read, *City Springtime*. They talked some more about Lewis and the things he saw. They also talked again about all the signs of spring in their own neighborhood. Miss Lee then suggested it would be nice to make some spring pictures. She also suggested that when they finished their pictures, they might like to write poems about their pictures. She would write their poems on the paper for them.

Here are two of their spring pictures and the poems they dictated to Miss Lee:

Trees are green
Grass is green
Sun is Shining
Boy is pointing to flower
Boat is coming back

Trees are green
Blue in sky
Flowers growing
Flower hat
Grass is growing

Three Days in Mrs. Rychener's Kindergarten

Mrs. Rychener is very warm and affectionate toward her children. Her class is orderly, and she takes great pains to prepare all minute details for any work she has planned. Mrs. Rychener has a rich musical background; she plays the piano very well and sings with ease. Group singing and dance punctuate the activities in her class with regularity. Various possibilities for experiences in the arts are continuously available to her children.

The school in which Mrs. Rychener teaches is located in a suburban community, one of the affluent residential neighborhoods which surround a rather large city. The school is modern though not new. When you enter Mrs. Rychener's classroom, you get the feeling of an abortive architectural effort to achieve the effect of a house. The walls are panelled, and there is a huge fireplace at one end of the room. In spite of the immensely tall and vaulted ceiling, Mrs. Rychener succeeds in creating a warm and comfortable atmosphere in the room. She has forty children in this class.

The children were gathered around Mrs. Rychener on the floor, and they began their activities of the afternoon by checking the day, month, and date on their calendar chart. It was Friday, February 7.

Mrs. Rychener then began to play the piano. The children sang a song they knew about a snowman.

MRS. RYCHENER: Would you like to play like you were a snowman?

CHILDREN: Yes. Yes.

MRS. RYCHENER: Good. Then let's spread out with lots of space. You're tiny now, and you'll need space to grow. Spread out and get your heads down as if you were tiny snowflakes. I'll play something, so you'll grow higher and higher.

Good. Now show me how very tall you can grow. You are a real big snowman now, growing up, up, up.

That was fine. But now the sun is coming out, and it's getting warm, and you are melting down, down, down.

Mrs. Rychener played the music and suggested the dance, because she wanted them to feel the "growing up" and "melting down" of the snowman in their own bodies. After their dance, she read a story about a snowman: some children built him, and then the warm sun melted him away. They talked about the story and their dance, and then it was time for their work period. The various work spaces were already arranged, and Mrs. Rychener had prepared all the materials, so that they were ready. Some

of the children chose to make pictures with crayon and colored paper. Some played in the playhouse. Others painted at the easels, worked with clay, or built with blocks and boards.

One of the boys, who was painting at an easel, re-enacted the building up and melting down of the snowman as he worked on his picture. Look how he made his picture grow.

First he painted the sky.

Then he made three snowmen, and put in the sun.

And when the sun became real bright, he melted his snowmen away.

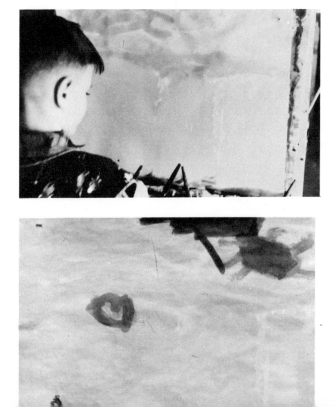

53

Kindergarten Classroom Records

The following day, after they had checked the calendar and counted the attendance, Mrs. Rychener asked the children to listen carefully to something she was going to play on the piano.

MRS. RYCHENER: Do you hear the accents in that piece? How would one of you like to go to the table and get an instrument that would be real good for making accents? Marcia, would you like to go?

MARCIA: Yes. (She goes and returns with a triangle.)

MRS. RYCHENER: Let me play that again for you, Marcia, and you beat the accents on your triangle.

In this manner Mrs. Rychener invited individual children to select their instruments. They came back with drums, cymbals, tambourines, and blocks. Soon all the children had instruments, and they proceeded to play in a rhythm orchestra.

MRS. RYCHENER: Now I'm going to ask you something real hard. You know, music makes us feel a certain way. Some kinds of music make us feel happy. Some kinds make us feel sad, don't they? You know that. I'm going to play something, and you can tell me how it makes you feel—happy or sad. (She plays a gay piece.)

CHILDREN: Happy.

MRS. RYCHENER: Listen to the big accent in this one. I wonder what we could do to that music? What could we do?

JOHN: We could skip.

MRS. RYCHENER: Would you all like to do that?

CHILDREN: Yes.

MRS. RYCHENER: Good. Then get up and put all the instruments away, so that we can skip and dance.

During the work period the children made pictures, used clay, played in the playhouse, built with blocks, and a few of them made finger paintings.

≈≈ ≈≈ ≈≈

54

The next day, while the children were seated on the floor in a circle, Mrs. Rychener began to talk with them about something new.

MRS. RYCHENER: I wonder how many of you saw something different when you came into our room this afternoon? Tommy, what did you see that was different?

TOMMY: New pictures.

MRS. RYCHENER: Yes. What are the new pictures about?

TOMMY: Trains and planes.

MRS. RYCHENER: What do all these things do?

JOHN: They all move.

MRS. RYCHENER: Good. Do you have another idea?

MARY: Tires.

MRS. RYCHENER: Some of them have tires, but not all of them. What does each one of them do?

JEAN: They all run.

MRS. RYCHENER: That's a good idea.

JOHN: They have power.

MRS. RYCHENER: They have to have power to go. That's right.

CAROLYN: People go on them.

MARY: They take people.

MRS. RYCHENER: What's another word for take?

CHILDREN: Carry.

MRS. RYCHENER: That's right—they carry. But do they carry only people?

JOHN: Trains and trucks carry things.

MRS. RYCHENER: Yes. They carry all kinds of things. Trucks, and trains, planes, and cars carry people and all kinds of other things. Do you know what they call a train that carries people?

JEAN: A passenger train.

MRS. RYCHENER: Good. Does anyone know what they call a train that carries things and not people?

CAROLYN: Freight train.

MRS. RYCHENER: I wonder how many of you would like to make some pictures today of different things that have power, and move, and carry people. You might want to make a picture of a train or a truck that carries things. Some of you might prefer to make an airplane. I've prepared some colored paper and crayons and paints, and you can choose any one of these things for your pictures. There is some clay if some of you would like to build a train.

There's another idea too. Some of you might like to build a big train out of blocks. So, you choose the thing you'd like to do during work period.

The children made their choices and went to work in different sections of the room. Here are four of the pictures made that day:

In the first, one of the boys is finishing his picture of an airplane.

The second is a crayon drawing of a freight train.

The little girl who made the third picture used pieces of colored paper for her train, and then she used crayon to draw the tracks, wheels, and other parts.

The fourth picture was by a little boy who wanted to make a boat because, as he said, "boats carry people."

❧   ❧   ❧

These three kindergarten teachers—Miss Joslin, Miss Lee, and Mrs. Rychener—have individual teaching styles which are uniquely their own. Each has her special strengths, and each develops a particular rhythm and quality in her teaching. Yet it is obvious from the record that each encourages, stimulates, and communicates to her children what it means to be alive, to notice, to react, and to create. All these things contribute to making them excellent teachers. Their teaching, and the work of their children are analyzed in the next chapter.

ANALYSIS OF

KINDERGARTEN

3

The kindergarten classroom records presented in the preceding chapter reveal how art was being taught. In each case, the teacher provided her children with abundant opportunities to create and express ideas through various art forms—music, dance, dramatization, poetry, story, and the visual arts. In the visual arts, each teacher provided a variety of art media—finger paint, paint, clay, wood, paper construction, and collage.

Above all, each of these teachers created a background and climate which encouraged her children toward purposeful activities. Ideas were brought to life in discussions with the children, so that they became moving ideas for meaningful expression. Because the children were able to identify themselves with these ideas, they were able to recreate them and express them in their own unique ways.

You undoubtedly noticed that each teacher developed a particular variation and rhythm among the different kinds of classroom activities. Although the specific activities varied from class to class, each of the three

CLASSROOM RECORDS

teachers encouraged her children to move naturally and rhythmically from experiences in listening, observing, and discussing, to activities for the creation and expression of personal ideas.

This rhythmic sequence served two important purposes: it provided shifts in tempo to vary the attention of the children; and it created a natural flow where the content of one activity provided the background for the development of the next one. Alternating activities which differ in tempo—such as dancing to listening to working—allow for relaxation and overcome tension. When the experiences in one activity contribute to the development of the next one, the sequence encourages cumulative learning.

For example, in Miss Joslin's class, the discussion about spring, the buds on the trees, and the many different kinds of leaves served as the background experience out of which the children went to work to create cloaks of leaves for their naked trees. In Miss Lee's class, the listening to and discussion of the story about Raggedy Ann provided the source of ideas for the children to make their pictures of Raggedy Ann. In Mrs. Rychener's class, the song about the snowman became the background experience out of which the dance of the snowflakes was created. This dance in turn led to the story about the snowman. The entire sequence culminated in the painting about the snowman.

At times, the focus of attention was on some activity in the visual arts—painting, clay, crayon, collage, or construction. At other times, special attention was given to music, dance, story, or poetry. Sometimes the teacher suggested a particular art activity. Just as often the children were free to choose the expressive activity that attracted them at the moment. In each instance, however, the expressive activity followed the development of some specific background in the form of listening, moving, singing, observing, or discussing. Consistently, each of the teachers helped the children to crystalize some event in their experiences as background and purpose for their art activities. This made the event as vivid as possible, so that it belonged to each child and served his expression in art.

Events in the experience of kindergarten children are grist for their mill, and they respond to them as sources of ideas for expression. These events take many forms—the discovery of something interesting on a field trip, fascination with a character in a story, or curiosity and interest in the manipulation of an art material. Sometimes, as in Miss Joslin's class, the fascination for the varied textured materials became the event that created interest and stimulated the construction of collages. The nature of an art material itself can thus provide the idea for expression. Sometimes, as in Miss Lee's class, the stimulating event was a story—the story about Lewis in *City Springtime*. This encouraged the children's response to signs of spring in their own environment. Sometimes, as in Mrs. Rychener's class, an act of expression in the form of music and dance became the event in experience which stimulated expression in art. In each instance, the teacher planned for the event to occur; she developed the discussion about it so that the children could discover significance in it.

Every fine kindergarten teacher creates expanding and penetrating experiences for her children, while she simultaneously provides multiple possibilities for them to express their ideas and sensations. A rich environment for development and learning thus is created through the stimulating experiences and the challenging avenues for expression. These are among the earmarks of good teaching. They form the basis for wise education of kindergarten children. They were the means through which art became meaningful to these children.

To children of this age, the distinction between play and work is indeed ambiguous. The five-year-old child plays at his work, and he works to achieve the control to which he aspires in a variety of forms of expression. Through play he uncovers new dimensions in his ideas, and he works to embody these into some tangible form. The distinction between play and work is, therefore, almost imperceptible, and the overlapping of both is evident in the vocabulary of his teachers.

When Miss Lee's children painted their large pictures, they called it "work." But when some elected to paint rather than participate in other possible activities, they called it "playtime." Painting was thus referred to as work or play depending upon the particular situation. In Mrs. Rychener's class, painting, drawing with crayon, block building, or the dramatization of life in the playhouse were all called "work."

Regardless of the name—play or work—the opportunities to explore newly discovered ideas through play in order to work for their embodiment in expressive form provide the kindergarten child with the means to achieve some of his most important developmental goals. The interaction between play and work expands his horizon and focuses his attention and energy.

A very brief review of some of the major developmental achievements in the growth of kindergarten children will contribute to the analysis of both the work of these teachers and their children's art activities. Awareness of the children's developmental characteristics will enable you to utilize the analysis to greater advantage.

Major Developmental Achievements of Kindergarten Children

Physically, most kindergarten children can achieve good general muscular control in their large bodily movements. They can skip, run, and climb securely and skillfully; and their entire bodies are involved in these movements. Their sense of rhythm is well developed, and they enjoy activities of rhythmic dance and play. This was evident in the dancing in Miss Joslin's class, in the movement and gestures to the poetry reading in Miss Lee's class, and in the rhythm orchestra and dance in Mrs. Rychener's class.

At this age, children are highly energetic, but they show fatigue at frequent intervals. They require periodic rests, and alternation of activities with different tempos often provides such needed rest. Miss Joslin showed her awareness of her children's physical needs when she frequently suggested that they stop and sing during a long discussion period. Miss Lee was attentive to her children when she observed their fatigue, concluded the discussion of their Raggedy Ann pictures, and promised to hang the rest of them on the wall. General attention to the need for variation in tempo was apparent in the rhythmic flow of moving from listening to working activities in the programs in each of the classes.

Although five-year-old children enjoy the challenge of demanding physical activities, the level of refinement of their hand and finger movements is limited. A child this age can handle a large paint brush with confidence, but his movements are comparatively broad and sweeping. He enjoys drawing with crayons and pencils, as did the child who drew the airplane in Mrs. Rychener's class. But little crayons or small-diameter pencils are generally difficult for him to hold and manipulate. For all that he can cut and paste paper into a variety of constructions, like the kites in Miss Lee's class, such activity bears the earmarks of his limited finger coordination. He can saw and hammer with small-size tools, and he can work with soft wood, such as white pine, as did the children in Miss Joslin's class; but here again his movements are more of his entire body than the refined arm-hand-finger coordination he is striving to achieve.

Emotionally, kindergarten children need support and patience from their teachers. They require opportunities to do things for themselves in an atmosphere of adequate and appropriate freedom where they can use their own powers. Above all, they need such signs of assurance from their teachers as convey the feeling that they are valued and respected. When the little girl in Miss Joslin's class insisted that branches without leaves were ugly, Miss Joslin respected her feeling by valuing it. Miss Joslin's assurance to the child to have the right to her own feeling showed how able she was to give her children the degree of freedom and support they needed.

Children at this age still require a great deal of attention from others. Although they are growing toward increasing awareness of others, their behavior remains rather self-centered, and many of the things they do are conceived from the point of view of a "me" world. This fact was evident in the many self-centered and attention-getting remarks made by children in each of the three classes.

Five-year-old children anger easily and quarrel rather frequently. Most often their anger seems to be aimed at those who interfere with their belongings, or those who interrupt their plans. In general, girls tend to show less quarrelsome behavior than boys.

Socially, most kindergarten children have strong feelings about their rights and ownership, but this is accompanied by a growing recognition of the rights of others. An increasing readiness to share space, tools, toys, time, and responsibilities is evident in their behavior. They can await their turn, and they enjoy helping a friend—as the two boys did in Miss Lee's class while helping each other make their kites. When their teacher encourages them to understand, they can show real concern for the welfare of the group, as was evident in the way all of these children shared the equipment they used, and acted with responsibility to keep things in order. The wise authority of the teacher tends to elicit positive reactions.

Intellectually, most kindergarten children have achieved conspicuous development. They are curious and inquisitive, and their language is studded with innumerable questions about "how," "why," "what," and "who." With a vocabulary that has developed extensively, they can understand and use over two thousand words. Their expanding command of verbal language is accompanied by increasing ability to discuss ideas. They can relate a story and communicate ideas to each other. The discussions in each of the classes revealed both the extensiveness of the children's vocabularies and the level of ideas these children were able to discuss.

Although their conception of time is rather limited, "a few days ago," "yesterday," "morning," and "tomorrow" have real meaning to five-year-old children. At this age, they are also growing in their ability to perceive size relationships by comparing larger things with smaller ones. Their conception of space, however, is still circumscribed by their image of themselves as the center of the universe. This is quite evident in the pictures they make, with the sun located overhead and most often in the corner, the sky on top, and the ground where one stands. Everything—sun, sky, and ground—is seen primarily from an emotional and kinesthetic point of view.

The aesthetic development of kindergarten children is at a naive level. At the same time, their aesthetic behavior is inseparable from their physical, emotional, social, and intellectual achievements. Their characteristic spontaneity is governed by an inner sense for movement, rhythm, and unity. Repetition of language is a constant source of pleasure, as was apparent in the recitation of poems in Miss Lee's class. These children also have a feeling for the imaginative make-believe of drama; the snowflake dance in Mrs. Rychener's class was an example. They participate freely in dramatic situations.

The unity in the drawings and paintings by these children is intuitive rather than conscious. It is achieved through an innate feeling for things that fit together, accompanied by sensitive response to the requirements of their emerging ideas. They start out with a fragment of an idea, and they add things in the empty spaces they discover in their pictures as they go along. This is evident in the way they go about making their pictures, constructions, and designs.

With these major developmental achievements and tendencies in the immediate background, you can see how they were reflected in the work of the teachers, and how they were evident in the behavior of the children and in the art works the children created.

The Content of the Teachers' Conversations

Various ideas were discussed in each of the three classes, and in some instances different art activities were developed. Some of these differences stem from the fact that Mrs. Rychener's teaching was recorded in February, Miss Lee's in March, and Miss Joslin's in April. The time of year can have important effects on the interests of children, and especially of kindergarten children. Their characteristic and insatiable curiosity about the "how," "why," and "what" of things in their immediate environment sharpens their sensitivity to season, weather, and events in their surroundings. Their self-centeredness magnifies the effects of direct experience on their interests. These teachers were attentive to the developmental characteristics of their children in discussing ideas and in planning the activities in their programs.

Some of the differences in ideas and activities were reflections of the individual teachers. Each had unique interests, abilities, and strengths; each taught in a way that was characteristically her own.

In spite of some differences in ideas and activities in these three classes, there was a series of striking similarities: (1) there were daily provisions for activities to be carried on by the group, and there were things to be done individually; (2) art activities were always accompanied by the development of a vivid background and depth of feeling to enable the children to identify themselves with broad ideas; (3) there were always several possibilities for individual choice within a broad idea or in terms of different ideas, whether the art activity was to be carried on by the group or by individuals; (4) each day, a variety of art materials was provided for individual choice, even though the group may have been working with a particular material; (5) periodically, each of the teachers and their children discussed the art works they had made, in order to share their accomplishments and to profit from each other's discoveries and inventions; and (6) materials, equipment, and tools were prepared and arranged so that individual children could assume the level of responsibility they could manage for getting to work and for cleaning up.

Because the specific ideas and activities in each of the classes were varied, these similarities are apparent in different ways. For this reason, I shall refer directly to sections of the classroom records in the previous chapter to indicate how these similarities are present in the work of the individual teachers.

Miss Joslin generated a vivid background and depth of feeling through her enthusiastic attention to nature. This was accompanied by equally sensitive attention to the people and things found in special places in the community. The science collection and the periodic field trips were direct sources of experience. These were the subjects that dominated the group discussions in her classroom. They became moving ideas through the way Miss Joslin helped her children to look at their experiences. She encouraged them to consider a variety of things they encountered and to examine them "in depth."

For example, contributions for their science collection were not brought to class merely to be shown, named, and put away. They were examined with care, played with, and talked about in detail. Virtually every item was used as a stimulus to look more closely and carefully at things out of doors or at other things in their collection. Each thing talked about was identified as an exciting possibility for someone to use in some form of expression. The children were learning to observe their environment as a source from which they could create their own ideas.

A similar zest for experiencing events was apparent in the discussions which preceded and followed the trip to the airport. Miss Joslin helped the children to recognize the rich possibilities for drama, construction, painting, and clay modelling. They did not just go, and look, and talk. They looked with purpose, because Miss Joslin had helped them achieve some feeling for the things they were going to see. They discovered ideas, because they talked in detail about many different things that intrigued individual children in the experience. Inquisitive looking, followed by the discussion of personal discoveries, provided a classroom climate in which each child was able to become the creator of his own ideas.

The discussions in Miss Joslin's class were punctuated by frequent talk about their art expressions. When they looked at the clay work by the children in the afternoon kindergarten, they were encouraged to respect each other's creations. They were learning to appreciate the personal interpretations which people put into their works of art. When they talked about the paintings they made of the animals in their classroom, they were encouraged to enjoy the uniqueness in each other's expressions. Individual interests and feelings were valued, and the children responded through their willingness to assume the responsibility they could for conducting their work and for choosing the things they wanted to do. They were learning to create their own ideas in their work and to enjoy the individuality in the art works of others.

The rhythm of activities in Miss Joslin's class moved alternatingly from group discussion for the examination of ideas to either group or individual activity for expression. The media available were constantly varied, and except for the days when they worked together on their trees, or with clay, or in the construction of collages, the emphasis was on individual choices in art activities.

Although Miss Joslin's children sang very often, the singing fulfilled a different purpose from that in Mrs. Rychener's class. In Miss Joslin's class, singing served primarily as rest from discussion or as summary and climax of ideas under discussion. Mrs. Rychener used singing to develop an idea and to establish a mood; Miss Joslin tended to use it to relax the tension by creating a shift in tempo, or to bring a phase of discussion to conclusion.

During the first day in Miss Lee's class, she read the story about Raggedy Ann; the group discussed details in the story; they made crayon drawings about parts of the story; individual children selected other activities utilizing various art media; the group discussed the pictures they made; and then they went out on the playground. The rhythm of activities thus moved from group listening and discussion to activity done together, to individually selected activities, and back to group discussion.

Through the introductory discussion, individual children had the opportunity to react to the story, to discuss specific events in it, and to identify themselves with selected parts. This enabled them to see the variety of elements included in the story. When Miss Lee invited them to make their crayon drawings, each child was ready to choose his own idea and go to work. Listening to the story and talking about it provided the background and prepared them for the picture-making activity.

In the discussion about the pictures which followed, two kinds of things were talked about. Miss Lee commented on the way the children made their pictures and the colors some of them used. They told about the particular incidents they selected from the story. Miss Lee's comments helped to encourage their imaginative use of color in subsequent pictures. The children's comments added richness to the experience, because they reinforced the feeling that each person should select the idea he likes best to put in his own picture. Although this was a group activity, in that they listened to the story together and they all made crayon pictures, their pictorial expressions were highly individualized, because Miss Lee put emphasis on individual selectivity. The timing of the discussion helped the children to realize what they had accomplished. The content made them aware of what they had learned through the experience.

When Miss Lee read the poem on the second day about the old woman who swallowed the fly, the children were so intrigued, nothing more needed to be said. The poem itself created a feeling for the idea. Through their dramatic recitation of the poem, they were full with feeling, and were able to go directly to their large paintings.

On the day when Miss Lee read the story about *City Springtime*, she developed the background and stimulus for a whole series of activities. She and her children not only discussed the story itself, but they also spoke about the many signs of spring in their own neighborhood. In addition to constructing their kites, the children achieved a feeling for spring which carried over into other expressive activities that followed. When they had completed their kites, the children were able to go directly to painting pictures about spring and writing poems about their pictures.

Each day there was a single art activity for the entire group; and each day, during playtime, there were more art activities for individuals to choose. In making their individual choices, the children were able to profit from what they had learned through the group activities. The group art activities and the discussions about the works they made provided general background and guidance for their individual selections.

Even though Miss Joslin and Miss Lee both used the theme of spring with their children, each developed background and feeling for the idea in a different manner. Miss Joslin brought leaves into the classroom, and referred directly to branches and buds in their science collection. Miss Lee read the story, *City Springtime*, asked her children to look at the trees through the classroom window, and talked with them about various things which were beginning to grow in their own back yards. In rather different ways, both of these teachers created a feeling for spring, and encouraged their children to observe changes in their environment. Both involved their children with the content and character of spring. In their own ways, each of them brought ideas about spring to life. The aliveness of the ideas enabled their children to create expressions which were meaningful.

Mrs. Rychener developed different kinds of background experiences to feed the expressive activities of her children. On the first day, they began with a song about the snowman, and moved into the snowflake dance. Then they were ready to listen to the story about the snowman. The total experience of singing, dancing, listening to the story, and talking stimulated their imaginations and created the climate in which the children were able to identify themselves with the growth and demise of the snowman in the sun. This personal identification led to the little boy's fanciful re-enactment of the life of the snowman in his painting. Mrs. Rychener used the group activity as the means to call forth the children's feelings so that they would interpret their reactions in their art work.

On the third day, the discussion about different forms of transportation brought together much information the children already knew. Knowledge they had from prior experiences was brought into their immediate awareness, and made actively available for selection in the creation of ideas. When Mrs. Rychener invited them to choose an idea for a picture, many ideas were already in the air, and the choices were varied. Even though several children elected to paint a train, their ideas about trains were unique.

One child painted this locomotive with its many, many wheels.

Another child was obviously impressed by this window pattern on a passenger train.

During the three days in Mrs. Rychener's class, the group activities served to provide the background experiences and moods for the art activities. Depth of feeling was encouraged through singing, dancing, listening, and discussing. Each day there were at least three or four art media available for choice, including paint, crayon, colored paper, finger paint, and clay.

Some of the differences among these three teachers are already apparent. Their particular personal strengths led them to characteristic focal points in their teaching. Miss Lee's love for stories and poems, Mrs. Rychener's musical knowledge, Miss Joslin's enthusiasm for nature and people—these personal strengths and preferences, reflected in their teaching, gave it individual quality. It isn't that any one of these teachers ignored what the other emphasized. Each had her own deep center of interest which she followed in relation to others. Their own feelings permeated their conduct of all the activities, and were communicated to the children.

Even though Miss Joslin encouraged her children to work in a wide variety of activities so that each child selected his own center of interest, she maintained a unified source of ideas, and a continuous group feeling for the admiration and exchange of individual accomplishments. Even though Miss Lee did not bubble with enthusiasm, her sensitive attention to poetry and language elicited enthusiasm from her children. Even though Mrs. Rychener was so warm to her children that she sometimes seemed protective of them, the spirit she encouraged through music and song led them to engage in independent adventures.

The work of each of these teachers revealed her persistent purpose to provide a background and climate where children could become aware of

the things they encountered. All three teachers were attentive to the developmental abilities and interests of their children in creating experiences and in selecting ideas for discussion. The material out of which ideas grow, and the means for expressing them through art, were valued, enjoyed, continuously at hand, and explored in detail. Their children were thus encouraged to create ideas.

The Teachers' Use of Classroom Time

Time is an instrument of teaching, and the manner in which any teacher subdivides time to arrange sequences of activities reveals a good deal about the character of her teaching. Although each of the three teachers followed a time routine, no activity ever suffered from arbitrary time limits. Each day began with checking the calendar and attendance. This was followed with a listening and discussion period. The program then went on to a group art activity or to an activity composed of many choices, with the arts among the several choices.

Such a routine provided essential stability to the program, but never dominated by controlling the activities. It was a framework around which most activities were organized and conducted; but when activities or events required a change in routine, it was changed.

Such changes in time routine are most evident in the records of activities in Miss Lee's and Miss Joslin's classes. When Miss Lee's children had completed their kites and were ready to fly them, the routine for the next day was reconsidered. They began by checking the date and attendance, and then proceeded directly to their free play, instead of having their customary listening and discussion period. This time adjustment gave them enough of a block of time to dress for outdoors and go outside to run on the sidewalk and fly their kites.

The day Miss Joslin's children discovered the cages with the rabbits and ducks in their room, they gathered around to look and play. This was special, new, and exciting, and nothing else was done for over half an hour. Checking the calendar and attendance, and the introductory morning discussion both waited until the children were ready. Readiness meant that they first had enough time to take their turns playing with the ducks and rabbits. Then they had their listening and discussion period before proceeding to individual choice activities. That morning they had no group activity for work.

Thus, although the time routine was followed with general regularity, it was treated with sufficient flexibility to accommodate the needs of certain activities or events as they developed.

Another important element in the time routine in these three classes is the amount of time devoted to art activities. Following the listening and discussion period for the development of background and a feeling for ideas, approximately thirty minutes were devoted to work in art.

The art activity period was usually followed by opportunities for individual choices; and the fact that this was so is significant. The children moved to their free choice activities individually, as they finished their work in art. Some of the children were through with their art work in about fifteen to twenty minutes; some worked as long as forty minutes. Each was able to work at his own speed. The time routine took into account the needs of individual children by making it possible for them to take the time that was necessary for the work in which they were engaged.

The Teachers' Use of Classroom Space and Equipment

Each of these three classrooms was spacious, and each was subdivided into areas so that various activities could be conducted with maximum ease. Each classroom had a large open floor space where the children could sit together for their listening and discussion activities. The same space served in Miss Lee's class for work on the very large paintings. This is the space Mrs. Rychener used for her music and dance activities. In this space, Miss Joslin's children danced on some days, and built their huge airplane the day after their trip to the airport.

This open center area was surrounded by various spaces for special use. One special space was a group of tables and chairs for activities such as modeling with clay, picture-making, collage, and quiet games. The other spaces included: easels, large building blocks, a wood-working bench, a science area, a library table, and a section outfitted like a kitchen with table, chairs, stove, and refrigerator for playing house. All these special places were always ready to use and were available to the children during their playtime activities.

In each classroom the teacher organized her equipment and materials so that the children could use them with maximum independence. Here are four examples of the organization of materials and equipment to enable the children to work freely, and to assume responsibility for using and caring for the things they needed:

(1) Tempera paint with a brush for each color was kept in discarded fruit juice cans all held together in a convenient wooden carrying tray. Different chalk colors were stored in a muffin tin.

(2) Plastic squeeze bottles, manufactured as ketchup dispensers, were used to store and dispense finger paint.

(3) A wire rack, which is common equipment at the news-stand, was converted into a convenient storage place for colored construction paper.

(4) A common shallow pasteboard carton was used to store small pieces of colored construction paper. The children knew they were to look in this box first for the colors they wanted before cutting into a large sheet. They also knew they were to save small pieces by returning them to the box.

Through such simple and ingenious devices, these teachers recognized the developmental abilities of their children and challenged their desire to assume some responsibility. With equipment and materials organized in an accessible manner, the children were free to help themselves to the things they wanted to use when they needed to use them. Responsibility of the children was thus encouraged; materials were within reach of each child. The teachers in turn had more time to talk to individual children, and to help those who really needed assistance.

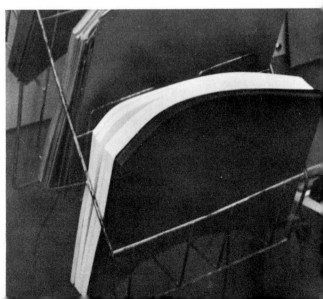

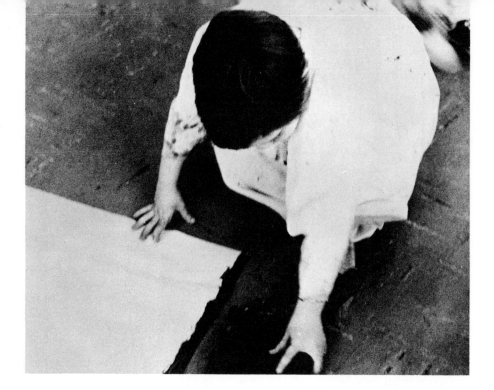

Sometimes the children needed help to get materials for work, as in Miss Lee's class, when they were preparing to make their large paintings. Because the paper was especially large, Miss Lee cut the pieces from the roll for them. But they themselves knew where the aprons, paints, and brushes were kept. They gathered what they needed independently, and went to work. When paint got onto the floor, as some of it naturally did, the children knew how to wash it with a sponge.

The Children's Art Works

A major developmental task in art for children to achieve at this age is a pictorial symbol system with which to express ideas about experiences with people and things in their environment. They strive to create pictorial symbols to represent and interpret the people and things which are part of their experiences. This quest for a symbol system is accompanied by efforts to deal with and control the space and size relationships among the things included in their pictures. Although these characteristics dominate the visual expressions of most kindergarten children, any group includes some children who have not yet reached the anticipated level of development, and some who are surpassing it. Among the pictures made by children in these three classes, you can see the variations in individual development any kindergarten teacher might expect to find in her group.

Here are three paintings made by three different children in Miss Lee's class on the very same day:

The first is primarily a manipulative play with color, repetition and rhythm. It conveys a sense of organization, and indicates a stage of development which is beyond the random drawing and scribbling of younger children. This is the kind of painting which is not surprising to find in a kindergarten or even among some first-grade children. Yet it is generally more characteristic of the pre-kindergarten child.

The second is an interesting example of a typical painting by a kindergarten child in which he combines the pleasure of physical manipulation with his quest for a communicable symbol for a man. In terms of the idea, the left and right sides of the picture are rather unrelated. Visually, however, in terms of the location and balance of the parts on the page, there is an innate feeling for unity.

The third is by a child who has developed beyond the stage of the mere quest for a symbol, because she has painted a person with expressive characteristics. This is not just a picture of a person but it conveys a particular kind of person.

73

Here are three crayon drawings which were made the day Miss Lee read the story about Raggedy Ann. Compare the first and the second from the point of view of the symbols the two children created for Raggedy Ann. Compare them also in the way the first child located his Raggedy Ann on the bottom edge of the paper, whereas the second child demonstrated his active awareness of ground and grass by making a base for her Raggedy Ann. In the first, the symbol itself is somewhat more mature because the figure is drawn in a manner which is less geometric than in the second; and yet the second child created a base line for her figure to stand on, while the first one did not.

In spite of these differences, both the above Raggedy Ann pictures are much more similar to each other, in respect to their level of visual conception than to this third one by another child in the same class. He not only created a characterization of Raggedy Ann, and planted the figure on a base line, but he also shows us the sky above. This child utilized the entire picture area by embellishing and decorating it with his bird-like forms.

The following chalk drawings by two children in Mrs. Rychener's class afford some interesting comparisons: Notice how the snowman and tree in each are related to the ground on which they stand. The position of the objects in each, however, reveals a difference in developmental level.

In the first, the ground is a straight line across the bottom of the picture with the tree, rocks, and snowman standing side by side. This side-by-side relationship is a great achievement in visual organization for a kindergarten child.

The second one, however, is even more surprising, because it contains characteristics which generally do not appear until almost a year or two later in the development of most children. Notice how this child has made his hill, with the snowman and tree standing perpendicular to the line of the hill. He drew the snowman and tree as if they were seen at separate moments in time, and as if he were drawing separate pictures of each. Indeed, these parts appear as if they were seen from different points of view.

Pictures by children of this age often reveal a multiplicity of points of view. The individual parts of their pictures may be related to each other visually in that the whole page is well organized. Yet the parts are often conceived separately to represent parts of the ideas.

Compare the levels of symbolic development in these two paintings by children in Miss Joslin's class. The first is an earlier stage in the development of the symbol as compared with the second. The first presents symbols of people in general, whereas the second expresses particular characteristics of certain people doing something special.

In the next two pictures of rabbits by children in Miss Joslin's class, you can see individual differences in development in respect to the symbols of animals.

The first is an early level quest for a symbol of a rabbit.

The second is a more mature characterization of one of the rabbits the children played with in their class.

The colors these children use in their paintings are generally rich and vivid. Rarely, however, do they mix them; and they are not concerned particularly that the colors they use should represent the objects they put in their pictures. They use and enjoy colors for their sensual delight.

Your familiarity with the visual expressions of kindergarten children will enable you to react realistically and sympathetically to the art work they do. A knowledge of the characteristics of their symbols and their con-

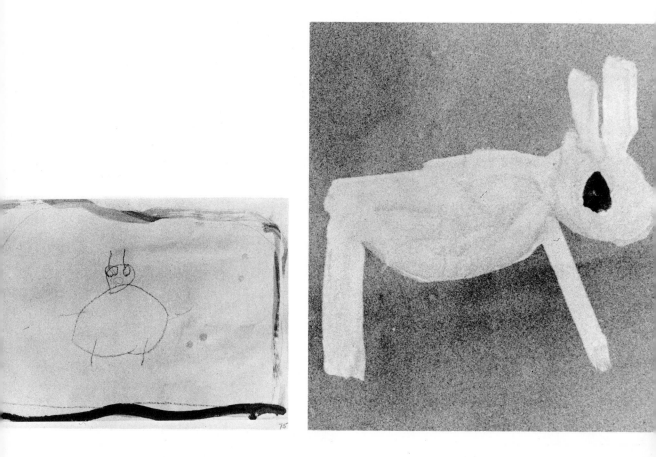

Analysis of Kindergarten Classroom Records

ceptions of spacial organization will provide you with essential understanding about their mode of thought. Knowing the direction of their development, and some of the variations among children within the same age group, you will recognize the kind of encouragement you can give to individual children in your own class.

Many important insights are thus derived from studying the finished art works of children. They are enhanced enormously, however, when accompanied by information about the sequence of stages through which an individual child created his particular painting. When observed from this point of view, you can see what he put into his picture first, how he added things, and ultimately how he developed his idea.

Here are four stages in the development of a painting by a boy in Mrs. Rychener's class:

He began his painting of a man by boldly placing the head and body to the left side of the sheet.

Then he made the right arm small and the left arm large, because of the sizes of the spaces he discovered remaining on either side of the figure.

In the third stage he painted the body.

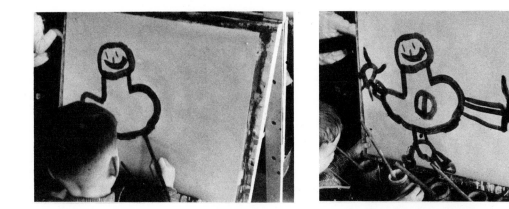

In the fourth, after having painted a line for the sky and included the sun, he discovered an empty space in the lower right-hand corner. His decision to solve the problem by including a smaller version of the original man is typical of the whimsy and unanticipated humor in paintings by children of this age.

Kindergarten children generally begin with a kernel of an idea; and as they express it, they respond to what they have already done by adding more to it. The things they add are most often unanticipated. They draw from their background of ideas in response to each successive thing they include in their pictures. Empty space in a picture calls forth new additions. The child who has a vivid background has a rich fund to draw upon as he makes his picture grow.

Here are five stages in the development of a painting by a little girl in Miss Lee's class:

In the first, she painted the house, the cloud, and sky.

In the second, she began to put birds in the vacant space.

Then it occurred to her to paint circles around the birds in the third stage.

Look how she became fascinated with the circles in the fourth.

Analysis of Kindergarten Classroom Records

Analysis of Kindergarten Classroom Records

Notice how the circles literally took over the idea of the painting in the fifth. Compare the first stage with the fifth, and you can see how the imagination of a kindergarten child stimulates itself. This little girl played with her idea, embellished it, and ultimately recreated it. She not only created an idea, but she did so by treating the idea in her picture as if it were something growing and alive.

In the following sequence of six stages, you can see how another little girl in Miss Lee's class struggled to solve the problem of space relationship in her picture. This was the day when the children made their large pictures.

The paper was huge, and she began by painting the head from an upside-down position.

Rapidly, she added the body, legs, and arms.

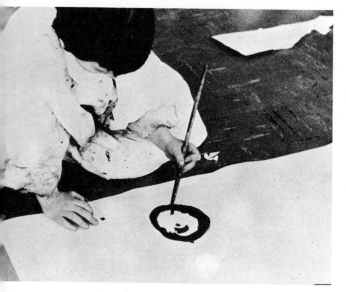

The empty upper right corner was a good place to put the sun, and the bottom of the sheet was where she felt she had to paint the ground line. The fact that the ground line had no relation to the figure didn't bother her at the moment.

The next thing she did was to make the sky line.

And then she discovered the empty space between the figure and the ground line. She proceeded to add some grass.

Finally she invented a way to connect the grass to the ground on the bottom of the sheet.

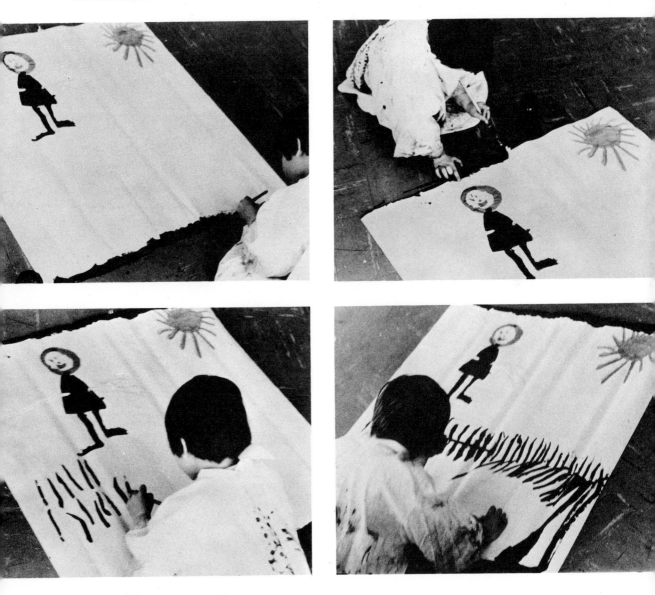

In this sequence, as in the others, the ultimate idea evolved as the child was creating it. Only the beginning was realized when she began. The way she began created problems which she was able to perceive and solve at her own developmental level.

Characteristics in the development of kindergarten children and the variety of their individual levels of maturity are as apparent in their three-dimensional work as in their pictures. The work these children do with clay not only reflects their manner of conceiving and expressing ideas, but it reveals the nature of their hand-finger motor control and dexterity.

The feel of clay in the hands of most kindergarten children is among their more pleasurable experiences. They can squeeze it, pull it, and manipulate it. They can push it in, and draw it out. They can make it react to their will, while they enjoy the sensation of the clay on their hands. It's like the fun of playing with mud with the added challenge of handling a material that responds by staying put. They can shape their ideas in it.

The following four constructions in clay were made in Miss Joslin's class, and I have arranged them in sequence to show the developmental direction of sculpture by kindergarten children.

The first piece represents an effort to control and create a form, but it is primarily manipulative. The child who made it is at a level of development where he is devoting major energy and interest to the pliability of the material and its sensuous feeling in his hands.

The second represents a significant stride in the effort to shape clay into a symbol for an idea.

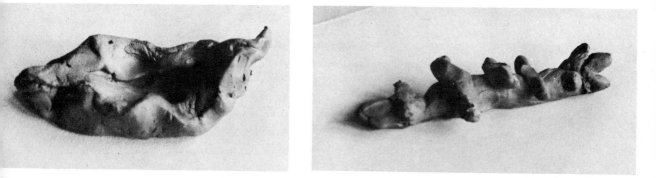

The third is a great achievement in controlling the material. This child created a symbol to communicate the animal idea.

The fourth is beyond the level of symbolic development. This

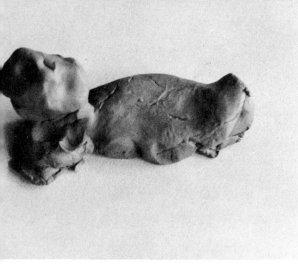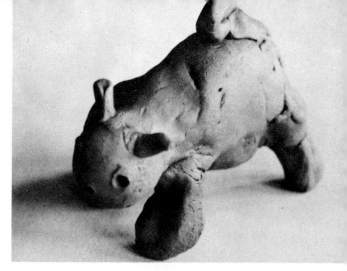

child has achieved a degree of maturity and control enabling him to express particular characteristics about a selected animal.

Although the manipulative piece and the early symbolic efforts are typical of the work of kindergarteners, they can be observed just as often among older children. The subtle characterization in the last piece, however, is much more typical of older children. Yet this broad range of individual developmental accomplishments was present within a single group of children.

Summary

Kindergarten children, like any group, share certain characteristics, but they vary individually in their ability and development. In art, they share the developmental growth direction toward increasing control of materials for the symbolic creation of ideas. Good teaching supports their individual efforts, and challenges their forward movement.

In their own inimitable ways Miss Lee, Mrs. Rychener, and Miss Joslin provided the support and challenge their children needed. They accepted and valued what their children did, while they created the necessary stimulation for expanded perceptive awareness. They taught art well because they created in their classrooms an alive and vibrant climate where ideas were brought to life. Vivid ideas become real experiences for kindergarten children. They can feel them deeply and respond to them personally.

When such a climate is accompanied by a stimulating variety of materials for children to use, and when space, materials, and equipment are organized so that children can share the responsibility for their own behavior, they grow in their ability to create ideas because they have the opportunities to express ideas.

As Miss Joslin said to her children: "You know why we can do so many things in this kindergarten? Because you help each other. You help each other, and that helps me." That helps each of these teachers to do the exciting teaching she does.

CLASSROOM RECORDS

IN THE EARLY

The work of four teachers is presented in this chapter. Mrs. Kessler and Miss Carr are both first-grade teachers. Mrs. Keller teaches a second-grade class; Mrs. Rood teaches a combined second- and third-grade class.

These four teachers work independently from an art teacher. There is an art supervisor in Mrs. Kessler's school system; Miss Carr has one, too. Both these school systems are so very large, however, that the supervisors rarely work with individual teachers. There is an art consultant in Mrs. Keller's school system, but she spends most of her time with new teachers who are brought in to staff the expanding enrollment. There is a traveling art teacher who comes to Mrs. Rood's class for a very short period just once a week. Mrs. Rood recognizes the inadequacy of this one experience, and independently she provides the additional opportunities she feels her children should have for activities in art.

Here are excerpts from the records of the conduct of activities in

ELEMENTARY GRADES

each of the four classrooms, accompanied by additional information about the teachers:

Six Days in Mrs. Kessler's First Grade

Mrs. Kessler is a very soft-spoken person with sensitive feeling toward people. She is intrigued with the character and quality of things in her own environment; in turn, she encourages and values the attentiveness of her children to things in their environment. Her school is located in a semi-rural neighborhood at the edge of a large city; there is a good deal of population movement and transience, reflected in frequent changes in class enrollment. There are thirty-six children in her class.

Mrs. Kessler's school building is old and drab; her classroom is very crowded. The old screwed-down desks have been removed and replaced with small tables and chairs of convenient size. Her room has no sink;

hence, water must be carried from the hall.

In spite of the drabness of the school, Mrs. Kessler does a great deal to brighten her classroom. She uses colorful draperies on one wall; she covers another wall of superfluous blackboard space with wrapping paper as background for her children's poems and pictures. In addition, she creates interesting arrangements of plants, branches, curious rocks, and intriguing pieces of wood for her children to see.

There is a bookcase along the window wall in Mrs. Kessler's room; the top, about fifteen inches deep, serves as useful counter space. She uses this space to arrange displays of books and other interesting things. Among them are four cafeteria trays, each with its own sign card: "It is fun to see," "It is fun to smell," "It is fun to touch," and "It is fun to hear." Mrs. Kessler changes these displays at least once a week and includes such things as: a flower, a prism, and valentine cards to see; cinnamon, mustard, and perfume to smell; fur, coal, and glass to touch; and musical blocks, or maracas to hear.

Here is the display of things to touch this morning.

The children await each new display she arranges. They take turns playing with the things by looking, smelling, touching, and listening.

Mrs. Kessler provides her children with continuous and varied opportunities for expressive activities in the arts.

MRS. KESSLER: We've been talking about satellites and rockets. Did you see the picture of the rocket in the newspaper yesterday?

JOHN: I seen it.

MICHAEL: One of them broke. One part comes off, then another one comes off, and "sputnick" falls out.

MRS. KESSLER: It's such a hard job to make these rockets that even big people have to work very hard and a long time. Where do the rockets go?

PAMELA: Into outer space.

MRS. KESSLER: Do you remember how the earth pulls? It pulls rockets and airplanes down; and they have to have an awful lot of power to fly away from the earth.

Now I'm going to play some records, and I want you to help me find the best rocket music. Let's stop talking now and listen.

NONA: I want to be a satellite.

MRS. KESSLER: (Plays a gay soaring piece of music, and the children sway to the rhythm.) Jimmy, why don't you come into the middle of the room and show us all what you are doing? (Jimmy dances.) Didn't you like how Jimmy was dancing? Mary and John, would you like to dance too? (They join Jimmy.)

Now let's listen to another record I have. (She plays something slow and heavy.) Could this be earth music?

CHILDREN: Yes.

MRS. KESSLER: Let's all dance now, and let's dance from our bodies. Our bodies can swing and sway, and fly away from the earth like a rocket. Oh, I think that's fine now.

Classroom Records in the Early Elementary Grades

When they had finished their dance and rested, Mrs. Kessler announced that it was time for their reading groups.

The class was divided into three reading groups, and while Mrs. Kessler worked with one group, the other two usually worked independently. Sometimes, the second group worked on writing and the third on an art activity. Sometimes, Mrs. Kessler read with one group while the other two worked in art. When the reading group was finished, they traded places with one of the other groups.

Before beginning their group reading and independent work, Mrs. Kessler always talked with the children about the things they might do.

MRS. KESSLER: I thought you'd like to make some paintings of rockets today. Everybody knows what they look like in the newspaper picture, but I thought you might want to make a special kind.

You know, the scientists who make the rockets make things nobody ever saw before. Maybe you can think of a space ship that's different from any others. It doesn't have to be like what you've seen. It could be a "make-up" one that you thought of yourself. You might even want to put people in your rocket.

You know, a lot of people make things that other people got the ideas for. But do you know, some people make things that they have thought up in their own heads. What do you call somebody who works at thinking?

CHILDREN: Inventors.

MRS. KESSLER: They are the people who think up brand new ideas. Maybe one of you will grow up to be an inventor some day, and maybe today you can invent a rocket of your own.

With this introduction and the dance of the rockets in their immediate past experience, the children who were going to paint got their supplies and began their paintings. Mrs. Kessler worked with the first reading group for about fifteen minutes. When she finished, they joined the painters, and one of the other reading groups sat down with her.

Here is one of their rocket inventions with a space traveller inside.

෧ඁ෨   ෧ඁ෨   ෧ඁ෨

On many days, Mrs. Kessler read poems to her children, and often she asked them to write their own poems. Sometimes they would compose

88

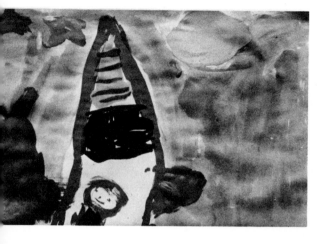

A Friend

A friend is nice to you.
A friend plays with you.
A friend gives you things.
A friend shares with you.
A friend sometimes helps
you with your work.

a poem as a group. Mrs. Kessler helped them choose words that sounded nice and felt good. Valentine's day was coming, and the children had already composed two valentine poems.

Here is one of their poems which Mrs. Kessler wrote on a large sheet of wrapping paper and hung over the blackboard space, together with some cut-out pictures the children had made.

When the class assembled the next morning in a circle to talk, one of the children asked if they could write another poem.

MRS. KESSLER: What would you like to write about today?

PAMELA: We can write a story about somebody to make him our valentine.

MRS. KESSLER: That's a good idea, isn't it? If you'd like somebody to be your valentine, what would you write about?

WOODROW: His valentines could fall out of his sack, and he wouldn't know it, and they'd fall on the floor, and get all kicked,—um—and he wouldn't have any money to go to the store,—and he wouldn't be able to get any.

MRS. KESSLER: Now Woodrow is giving us an idea. We could start our poem with a little boy getting his valentines all torn. What should be the boy's name?

MICHAEL: I know. We can write about the new boy (a boy who just joined the class).

MRS. KESSLER: How many would like to write about our new boy, Danny? Would you like us to write this poem about you, Danny?

DANNY: Yes.

MRS. KESSLER: How shall we begin the very first line?

JEAN: Danny is a little boy with a great big smile on his face and big blue—

JIMMY: Eyes.

MRS. KESSLER: (As Jean and Jimmy talked, Mrs. Kessler began to write their poem on the blackboard). Isn't that a nice way to tell about Danny? What did Danny have?

MARY: A big red valentine.

MRS. KESSLER: Can you think of another word for *big?* What's another word for *big?*

NONA: Large.

MRS. KESSLER: Now what was Danny doing with his large red valentine?

MARY: He was walking.

MRS. KESSLER: He was walking where?

MARY: In his bedroom.

MRS. KESSLER: He was walking in his bedroom? And what happened as he was walking in his bedroom?

WOODROW: They fell out.

PAMELA: He tripped over a toy.

MRS. KESSLER: Would you like him to trip over a toy?

JOHN: He tore the sack.

MRS. KESSLER: Danny tripped over a toy and tore his sack. What do you want to say next?

JOHN: And they all fell out—ah, mm—and broke.

MRS. KESSLER: Do you want to say broke or tore?

JOHN: Tore to pieces.

MRS. KESSLER: What do you think Danny did after he saw that his valentines were all torn?

Classroom Records in the Early Elementary Grades

They continued in this way suggesting and choosing ideas, selecting and deciding on the words. As they decided on each line, Mrs. Kessler wrote it on the blackboard. They spent about half an hour composing the poem.

MRS. KESSLER: Everybody sit up now, and I'll read you our whole poem. But while I'm reading the poem, I'd like you to think about a picture you can make. You think about it while I read the poem.

Danny was a little boy with a big smile and big blue eyes.
He had a large red valentine in a sack.
He was walking into his bedroom and he tripped on a toy.
The valentine fell out on the floor.
Danny ran to his mother.
He said, my valentine got torn.
Can I get some more?
No, no, no, you may not, said mother.
Danny thought and thought.
Then he got an idea.
He got some red paper, some crayons and paste.
He was quiet and busy for a long time.
Then he was happy because,
He had some more valentines.
His friends were very happy.

That's a good poem. Danny, do you like the poem we wrote about you?

DANNY: Yes.

MRS. KESSLER: I wonder now what ideas you have for your pictures. Have you thought about the picture you want to make? Are you ready to get up and get your crayons and some paper?

CHILDREN: Yes.

MRS. KESSLER: You may get your crayons and go to your tables.

The writing of the poem developed the idea, and brought forth a sequence of details. Different children contributed the various parts, and all of them achieved some vivid images about the boy who tore his valentines. The idea was fresh and alive for them, because they had composed it. They were ready to make some pictures.

The children went to their tables and got their crayons. Mrs.

91

Kessler asked one boy to distribute the paper, and they went to work. Some of the children finished in about fifteen minutes; others worked almost half an hour.

Here is one girl just finishing her picture of Danny. She had to show him twice, because he was a happy boy who became sad when he discovered that he had torn his valentines.

❧　　❧　　❧

Two days later was Valentine's Day. After the work with the reading group, Mrs. Kessler began to talk to the whole class:

MRS. KESSLER:　What day is today?

CHILDREN:　Valentine's Day.

MRS. KESSLER:　How does Valentine's Day make you feel?

CHILDREN:　Happy.

MRS. KESSLER: What other words can you use to tell me how you feel inside?

CHILDREN: Good.

MRS. KESSLER: Do you feel good inside? Does it tingle or tickle? Aren't those nice words?

Today, I thought you would like to make something special for Valentine's Day. I thought you would like to make some hats to wear. I've saved a whole box of things and scraps, and I'll show them to you. Look at this pretty ribbon. And what is this?

JOHN: Crepe paper.

MRS. KESSLER: And how is it fixed?

MARY: Ruffled.

MRS. KESSLER: Look at these pieces of lace and beads and buttons. I'd like John and Pamela and Mary and Jean to spread all these things on the window counter. Then each group can take a turn to pick out a few things to use. I'll put some paste on your tables, and you can use the paste to make a special Valentine's Day hat.

The four children took the boxes of scrap materials and spread the things on the window counter. Then the groups took turns choosing what they wanted to use. By the time they had made their selection, Mrs. Kessler had distributed the paste. She also took out some colored construction paper and some small boxes she had collected. The children gathered their materials and went to work. They worked over half an hour constructing their hats. Mrs. Kessler helped those who needed it, and many of the children helped each other to put parts of their hats together.

Here is one of the Valentine's Day hats they made.

೧৯   ೧৯   ೧৯

Because of Valentine's Day, Mrs. Kessler talked with her children about friends; friends send valentines to each other. The children wrote stories about friends and made pictures too. Each child made a book to hold his stories and pictures. A few days after Valentine's Day, Mrs. Kessler talked with them about the pictures they had made for their books.

MRS. KESSLER: Yesterday afternoon while some of the boys and girls were waiting for the last bus, we set up some of your "friends" books. We'll change them around so that everybody has a chance to have his book up.

I saw something real unusual in the colors of one of the books. Did you notice it? I was surprised because I had never seen any colors like that. (She gets one of the books to show how one child had mixed his crayon colors and made a plaid pattern on the dress of one of the figures.) How many of you are wearing a shirt or dress with such a pattern? Look how Michael colored the red on that dress. How does that red look different from any other red you have seen before?

NONA: Blue stripes show.

MICHAEL: There's red in it with blue right on top of it.

MRS. KESSLER: Did you hear what Michael said? And when he made those blue lines on top of the red, it made those light and dark purple colors. Do you suppose when you work with your crayons you could color on top of another color?

Now the day before yesterday you made pictures about your school friends. Did you ever think about friends who are not your own age?

DONALD: A big friend?

MRS. KESSLER: Do you have a big friend?

DONALD: Charles.

MRS. KESSLER: Who is Charles?

DONALD: He's my uncle.

MRS. KESSLER: Why do you suppose you call him a friend?

DONALD: He works in a bicycle shop, and every time he gives me things.

94

MRS. KESSLER: Who else has a big friend?

JACKIE: The teacher.

MRS. KESSLER: Can teachers be people's friends?

CHILDREN: Yes.

JACKIE: They help you read and learn.

MRS. KESSLER: A good friend is a helping kind of person.

They continued this discussion for almost ten minutes about friends among older people.

MRS. KESSLER: I thought you might like to paint some pictures today about friends, but this time I'd like you to paint some of your big friends.

JIMMY: It'll be a big friend.

MRS. KESSLER: Make some big friend of yours. Think what you would want your friend to be doing. You might want to put yourselves in your pictures too, and show why this person is your friend.

Look at some of the paper I have for you today (18″ x 24″ sheets). Here are some real big sheets some of you might like to use. And remember, you could hold the paper this way (horizontal), or this way (vertical). If some of you have a great big picture in mind today, and if you think you can fill this paper up, you may take one of these large sheets.

We'll have to work in groups, because we don't have enough space for everyone to paint. I'll read with the second group, and the rest of you can paint. Then we'll change.

The reading group gathered in a circle with Mrs. Kessler, and the others went to the cupboard for the paints and began to work. A few of the children went into the hall to get water. After about twenty minutes the groups changed. When recess time came, most of the children had completed their paintings.

Here is one of the pictures they made.

After recess the whole class brought their chairs up to the front of the room and gathered together to talk about some of their paintings.

MRS. KESSLER: Let's look at some of our pictures and see what kind of stories we can tell about them. Mary, would you like to tell us about your picture? (Mary was a shy girl, and Mrs. Kessler wanted her to have an opportunity to talk to the class.) I'll hold your picture up for you so you can have a good look at it.

MARY: That's my next-door neighbor.

MRS. KESSLER: Can you tell us something about your next-door neighbor?

MARY: She's a big friend.

MRS. KESSLER: What is your big friend doing?

MARY: She's playing in the snow.

MRS. KESSLER: Look how happy Mary's friend looks. Now I want you to see Donald's picture. He didn't paint a picture of a friend, but he did something else that was very nice.

JEAN: He used all different colors.

MRS. KESSLER: Yes, and how do you like the way he painted his picture? Do you like the colors of the clouds? Doesn't that cloud feel like it looks? It looks heavy.

Let's look at Woodrow's picture, because he did something different too. Everybody take a good look.

JIMMY: He painted all over.

MRS. KESSLER: Yes, he painted the whole background. What do you like about it?

MICHAEL: The colors.

MRS. KESSLER: Look how nice the colors stand out because of the way Woodrow painted it all over.

They continued to talk about a few more pictures and then Mrs. Kessler said: "These are all the pictures we can talk about today. I'll save the rest; tomorrow we'll talk some more about them."

❧ ❧ ❧

97

A few days later while two of the groups were writing stories, Mrs. Kessler showed the third group how they could make people out of paper sacks. The children enjoyed this; those who were writing wanted to make paper sack figures, too. Mrs. Kessler told them that they would be able to do this next day.

MRS. KESSLER: Today, some of you are going to be able to make your paper sack figures. And those of you who made figures yesterday will be able to work on something else. I want to show you something you haven't done before. (Mrs. Kessler called Jane and Pamela to the front of the room because they were wearing dresses of print fabrics.) Look how the designs on Jane's and Pamela's dresses are the same all over. They go over and over again. Here are some things which you can use to make over and over designs (she shows them some pieces of potatoes and carrots, some buttons, spools, and bottle caps).

How many of you have ever seen daddy or mother use a stamp pad? Did you ever see anyone take a stamp and put it on a pad like this (she demonstrates), and print with it like this? Now you use all these other things just like a stamp. Can any one of you show me how?

JOHN: I think you have to dip this (cut potato) in that (small aluminum pie pan with piece of felt on bottom saturated with paint).

MRS. KESSLER: Why don't you try it, John, and show us how it works. Take the potato in your hand, press it on the felt pad in the pan, and then press it on the paper. (John does it.) Does it work easy?

JOHN: Yea.

MRS. KESSLER: And you can stamp this out as many times as you would like to make an over and over design.

Let's spread newspapers on the tables. The group that's going to make paper sack figures can begin their work, and the rest of you can print with the stamp pads.

The children spread newspapers on their tables, divided into the two groups, and went to work. The children who printed were thoroughly fascinated with the things they could do. They used all the scraps Mrs. Kessler had collected (potatoes, carrots, bottle caps, mason jar rings, and various pieces of hardware). They dipped the surfaces in the pie tins and printed them by pressing the things against their papers.

98

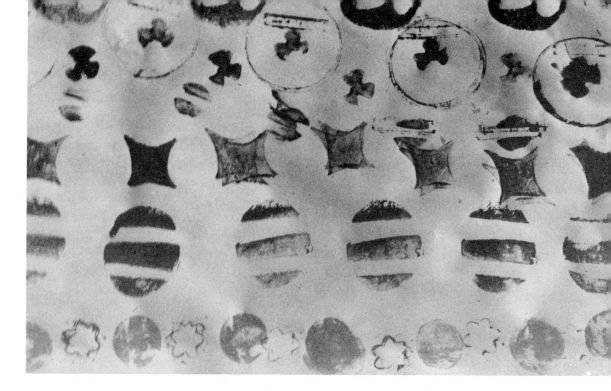

Here is one of the over and over designs they made.

This is one of the paper sack figures made by one of the other children in the class.

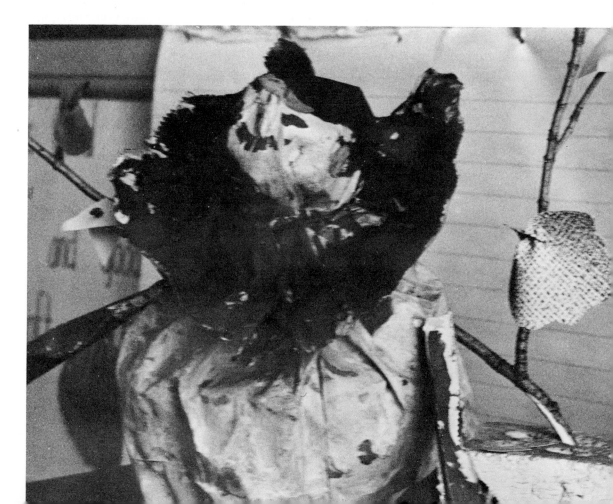

Three Days in Miss Carr's First Grade

There are four first-grade teachers in Miss Carr's school, and during the first semester, all of them noticed an unusually large number of children with significant behavior problems in each of their groups. Consequently, it was decided to form a special class for these children with Miss Carr as their teacher. All of her children are, therefore, somewhat difficult to work with, but Miss Carr responds sympathetically to them—their moods and limitations—and works with them in a sensitive manner. Because this is a special group, there are only twenty-seven children in the class—an extremely small number in comparison with the standard enrollments of thirty-five to forty in the other classes in this school.

Miss Carr's school is part of a very large metropolitan system. The immediate neighborhood was once a comfortable middle class community, but during the past decade there has been a complete turnover in population. The former residents have moved to the suburbs, and a new population has moved in. Most of the houses are well kept, but the neighborhood and the school, too, are much more crowded than they used to be.

The school building is old, but a few things have been done to modernize it. Good lighting has been installed, and the old screwed-down desks have been replaced with comfortable tables and chairs. Miss Carr's room is spacious. Aside from an easel and a work bench, however, the equipment is meager. Storage space is so limited that it is almost non-existent; there is no water in the room. In spite of these difficulties, Miss Carr provides her children with frequent art activities.

The children in Miss Carr's class have great difficulty in sustaining an activity over any extended period of time. Miss Carr is extremely sensitive to the temper of the group and, although she is secure and clear in what she requests of them, she is very careful not to create such pressure as could aggravate their personal difficulties. A great deal of time is spent in individual choice and free play activities, and much of the classroom routine is reminiscent of a kindergarten.

During any typical day, some time is spent in a group art activity. During choosing time, many of the children elect to draw, paint, work with wood, put puzzles together, or play. The easel is a very popular place to work, and those who choose to paint must announce their desires in advance and take their turn.

On this particular morning, when they were planning their activities for the day, the class decided to work with chalks, and to enact a story that one of the boys had made up and told to the group. They were going to do these two things in the afternoon.

MISS CARR: We were going to work with chalks this afternoon. How about doing that now, and then you'll be able to do your play after recess.

CHILDREN: Yes, yes (noise and commotion).

MISS CARR: O.K. Should we get started on what we're going to do? Are you ready to listen now? I think everybody has worked with colored chalks before. What do you do first when you get your paper?

MARY: You sprinkle the paper and you put some water on it. Then you rub it all over, and then—

JIMMY: And then you make a picture.

LARRY: But I want to explain something. You can't do it on both sides, because if you do, it'll get all over your table, and then your picture'll all be spoiled.

MISS CARR: You have to think carefully about the thing you want to make. You remember, we talked about how Frank did this one up here (she points to a chalk picture on the wall). He didn't use the chalk like a crayon. He used the chalk to make you feel like the colors are real strong. He used the side of the chalk, not just the point.

Some people might want to make spring pictures, and they might want to show how things look in the spring. You might want to show how the trees look and the little leaves and flowers. But remember that chalks are different from crayons, and you can use them in a different way.

Now let's see how we're going to arrange things.

JIMMY: I know.

MISS CARR: I fixed the chalk boxes so that—(noise)—I'm sorry but you won't know what to do if you don't listen. Mary is going to get the water for us in the pitcher—(noise)—now you have to listen. There are enough chalk boxes for each person to use one with a friend. There are not enough boxes for each one to have his own. So you'll have to share with a friend. Suppose you'd want to use black and there wouldn't be any black in your box?

WARNETTA: You can use your friend's black.

MISS CARR: Yes, you might have to share a few of the colors.

JIMMY: I'm gonna make Zorro (the current T.V. superman).

101

MISS CARR: All right. Some of you might want to make spring pictures, but if you don't, you may make anything you care to. Now you can come up and get your pan of water, and then you can work on your picture.

Most of the children did make spring pictures.

Jimmy made a picture of Zorro, but when he was almost finished, he smeared it up.

When all the children had finished their pictures, they cleaned up and went out on the playground for recess. Two of the children volunteered to stay behind to sponge the table tops. After recess, the whole class gathered in a large circle to enact the story that one of the boys had made up. It was about hunters, lions, and Indians, and as the boy told each detail, different children played the various parts. This acting captured their imagination, and most of them were very much involved in the activity.

The next day during choosing time, two of the boys decided to work with wood. They used lumber from empty fruit crates.

In the picture, one of the boys is sawing a piece of wood to build something.

This boy finished building his airplane, and he is painting it.

103

Just before recess time, Miss Carr began to talk about what they were going to do when they returned to their room.

MISS CARR: After recess, we're going to do what some of you have been thinking about for the last few days. We're going to talk about what you want to be when you grow up. Then we're going to talk about how we can make pictures of ourselves showing what we want to be when we grow up. When you come in after recess, if you sit at your tables, then we can get out the things we need to make our pictures.

REGINA: Can we make chalk pictures?

MISS CARR: Some people will be able to make chalk pictures.

When they returned from recess, they sat at their tables and began to talk about the pictures they were going to make.

MISS CARR: We're going to talk about what we would like to be when we grow up—(noise). If there are some people who don't want to join us—Jimmy—would you just excuse yourself and find a job at your table!

I'm glad everybody is going to join us. Before we start making our pictures, let's talk about some of the things you were thinking about drawing.

LARRY: I'm gonna be Zorro when I grow up.

MISS CARR: We've been thinking for a couple of days about what you want to be, so let's see now what some of your ideas are. Inez, you said you were going to be a lady when you grow up.

LARRY: I'm gonna be Zorro.

MISS CARR: O.K. You're going to be Zorro. Frank?

FRANK: I wanna be a policeman—(noise).

MISS CARR: If we would talk one at a time, I think we could hear everybody. Warnetta?

WARNETTA: I'm going to be a nurse.

MISS CARR: Yes.

BARBARA: I'm gonna be a nurse.

MISS CARR: You're going to be a nurse, too? Dorothy?

Classroom Records in the Early Elementary Grades

DOROTHY:	I'm gonna be a nurse, too.
MISS CARR:	My, a lot of these girls are going to be nurses.
DONALD:	I'm gonna be a doctor.
JIMMY:	I wanna be a—I wanna be a—I wanna be a fireman.
LARRY:	I wanna be Zorro.
MISS CARR:	All right you want to be Zorro.
FRANK:	You shouldn't be Zorro—(noise).
MISS CARR:	Frank, just a minute. Excuse me. Carol wants to speak.
CAROL:	I want to be a teacher.
JOHN:	I don't wanna be anything.
BARBARA:	Then you'll always be a little boy.
MISS CARR:	Barbara thinks that you'll still be a little boy when you grow up. Nicky?
NICKY:	I want to be a teacher.
MISS CARR:	You want to be a teacher, too?
DONALD:	That's only ladies.
MISS CARR:	No, it's not. There are men teachers, too—Mr. Ramsey, Mr. Mahone. They're teachers.
NICKY:	That's right.
MISS CARR:	Larry, do you think you can sit down over here and listen?
	There are different ways you can show what you want to be, so think how you are going to do it. What do you want to be? What do you think you'd look like? What would you be doing?
	Now I'm going to give you this paper (12″ x 18″ manila) to do your drawing on. You can hold it this way (horizontal) if this is better for you, or you can hold it this way (vertical) if this is better—(noise). All right, Frank. I'm speaking now. When you think of the way you want to make your picture, you may begin.
BARBARA:	Can you have puppies if you're a nurse?
MISS CARR:	Do you want to put a puppy in your picture? Is that the idea?

105

Classroom Records in the Early Elementary Grades

BARBARA: Yes.

MISS CARR: Well, what do you think? When you grow up, can you have little puppies? What do you think?

FRANK: Sure, she can.

MISS CARR: Why sure. Regina's mother works in a hospital. She's a nurse, isn't she? Could she have a puppy at home if she wanted to?

CHILDREN: Yes.

MISS CARR: You can put that in your picture if you want to. Now here comes another important part of what I want to tell you.

WARNETTA: Can we use chalks for our pictures?

MISS CARR: That's what I'm going to talk about now. If you want to draw your picture—(noise)—. I'm sorry. I really can't tell you what we can do if you don't sit still and listen. We can do these pictures in either one of two ways. You may do it with crayons, or if you choose, you may do it with colored chalks.

FRANK: I want chalk.

MISS CARR: Now those people who are going to choose to work with chalks will have to wait a minute, because we have to get the water first.

JIMMY: I'll get the water.

MISS CARR: All right, Jimmy. You can get the water. Those people who choose to work with crayon can get your paper and start right now. Then I'll get the chalks for the other people.

They made their choices, got their materials and went to work. Jimmy, who wanted to be a fireman, quickly made a picture of a fireman and a burning house, but he was dissatisfied with it.

JIMMY: I don't like this picture. It's no good.

MISS CARR: I think you did a very nice job on your fireman and on that burning house.

JIMMY: It's no good. I don't wanna be that. I'm gonna be a pirate.

MISS CARR: You want to be a pirate? That's what you told me the other day, and I thought that's what you were going to draw.

JIMMY: That's no good.

MISS CARR: And now, what you want to do is to make another picture of what

106

Classroom Records in the Early Elementary Grades

you really want to be?

JIMMY: You wouldn't let me do another one.

MISS CARR: You don't think I would? Sure you can.

JIMMY: Oh boy!

MISS CARR: Do you want to put that one aside and make your pirate picture?

Jimmy put his fireman picture aside, and here is the second picture he made that day.

A few of his friends looked at what he had made, and admired it. Miss Carr came to see what he had done and said, "I like your picture, Jimmy. I'm glad you made one you wanted."

Most of the children made pictures of what they thought they wanted to be when they grew up.

Here is Nicky's picture of himself as a teacher.

And here is Barbara's with her puppy dog and herself as a nurse.

❧   ❧   ❧

Because Miss Carr's children are so noisy and their behavior so explosive, it is difficult for them to work independently. Consequently, it is not easy for Miss Carr to find enough time to help them individually. There is a physical education teacher in Miss Carr's school, and the children go to the gymnasium to work with her for about twenty minutes every day. Miss Carr arranged with this teacher for a few children to remain in their classroom for special work while the group came to the gymnasium. The two teachers thus created the opportunity for Miss Carr to give more individualized help to small groups of children. Each day, therefore, she invites four or five children to stay with her while the class goes to the gymnasium. In this way, she can give special help to each child about once every five or six days. The children view this as a privilege, because they get to do something special.

The day after the children made the pictures of what they would like to be when they grew up, Miss Carr invited four of the girls to stay with her while the others went to the gymnasium. She selected these girls because of the way they were making their pictures.

There was one girl in the class who had become rather expert in making a girl's head with bangs, pony tail, and doll-like facial features. Because this appealed to many of the girls, they began to copy her way of doing it. In fact, the pony tail and the doll-like features became their stereotyped way of making a face. The children had evolved a step-by-step formula to produce it.

Here are two step-by-step sequences showing how two different girls used precisely the same system to produce the stereotyped face.

Miss Carr invited the four girls to stay with her today, because they were among the group of girls who were making the stereotyped faces in their pictures. She had collected their pictures of the day before and had hung them on the wall. Miss Carr and the four girls pulled their chairs up in a circle to talk about their pictures.

MISS CARR: How do you feel about the pictures you did yesterday?

CHILDREN: All right.

MISS CARR: What do you like about them? Karen, you made a real interesting one. You were telling me about it yesterday.

KAREN: (Giggles)

MISS CARR: You've got the giggles.

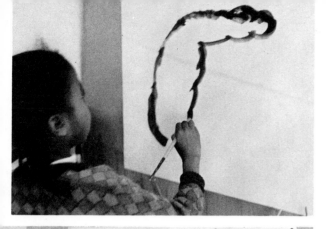

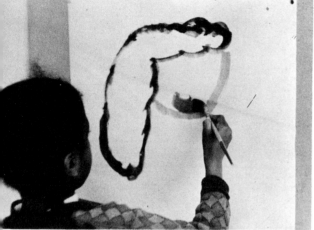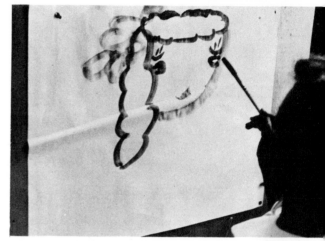

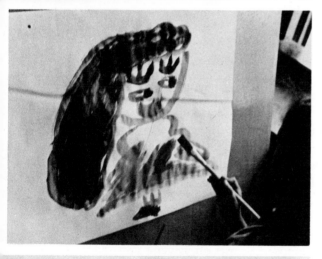

KAREN: That there is my little girl (she points to the middle figure in the picture).

MISS CARR: Oh, it is?

KAREN: That there is my little boy (she continues to point). This is me.

KATHY: I like it.

MISS CARR: So you really followed through on what you said, that you're going to be a lady, didn't you? Which one is yours, Kathy? Would you like to tell us about yours?

KATHY: That's a girl.

MISS CARR: She has a very interesting dress on. How did you think of that? Did you see one like that before?

KATHY: Uhuh—mm.

MISS CARR: Do you want to say something about yours, Ina?

No? Well, it seems to me that you people chose some interesting colors to put in your pictures. You certainly showed different things. There's one thing that interests me about your pictures. There's something that all of you are doing that looks pretty much the same. Do you see something in your pictures that's kind of all alike? You all drew girls, didn't you? You're all going to grow up to be mamas.

CHILDREN: (Giggle).

MISS CARR: You've all got different kinds of dresses on, haven't you? Kathy's girl looks as though her dress is swinging as she's running along.

KATHY: She runs.

MISS CARR: She surely is, and you can tell just by looking at her. That's a new fashion dress, isn't it, Kathy?

Ina, you didn't have room enough to put all yours in your picture.

INA: Yes.

MISS CARR: You don't have to. Sometimes pictures just show parts of people, don't they—just show the top part? All your people look happy. Look at the smile on Kathy's girl.

KATHY: Yes—mm.

MISS CARR: Anna, look at yours. They look so serious. You must have been thinking about something real serious. Were you?

ANNA: No.

MISS CARR: No? There are different ways to make faces, aren't there? Sometimes you can make people looking happy, and you can make them looking angry, or you can make people looking surprised in your pictures. Did you ever try any of those different ways? Did you ever try to make somebody looking angry in a picture? How would you make him look if you were going to make him look angry?

KAREN: I don't know—I'd mess it up.

MISS CARR: You'd mess it up? Ina, do you have any ideas how you would do that? That's something for us to really think about and try out. Did you ever look at different people and see how different their faces and their heads look?

INA: Their hair's all messed up.

MISS CARR: Yes, sometimes it is. When I came in from recess, my hair really looked messed up. My hair was standing out like this (gestures). The wind was blowing outside.

Look how differently all of you fix your hair. Did you ever notice how differently all of you look—the ways you fix your hair?

111

| | Look how Ina's mother fixes her hair. Look at the interesting way she fixes it (parted in the middle with four braids on each side). Does she do that every day, Ina? |

INA: Sometimes.

MISS CARR: That's a job, isn't it? If you were going to make a picture of yourself as you look right now, look how you'd have to fix it. Now look at Kathy. Her mama has an entirely different way to fix her hair (bangs).

KATHY: I'm gonna ask my mom tomorrow. She can't make me no part until she gotta wash my hair.

MISS CARR: See, Kathy has some hair that comes over in the front. And then you can't see any along the side. Anna. How do you have yourself fixed? Let's see. You know, the other day Anna was looking at my hair, and you know what she said to me? She said, "You got a ball (bun) on the back of your head."

CHILDREN: (Laughter)

MISS CARR: Did you see my ball back here? If you were going to make me, you'd have to put a ball back there if you were showing the back of my head.

You know, I noticed that a lot of your girls have their hair hanging down, don't they? You try hard to fix it that way.

INA: When I don't know how to make 'em, I go like that, like Kathy makes hers. I used to make a thing and then color in the hair. And I didn't make it like Kathy.

MISS CARR: Well, you don't have to make it like Kathy; you know that.

INA: I still know how to make it.

MISS CARR: You mean you still know how to make it a different way? When you make it like Kathy, then all the girls look alike, and we can't tell who's who. All of you look different. Didn't you ever notice that? And if you make your pictures so that the girls look different, then you'll be able to tell who you are. But I thought the hair on your girls looks very much alike.

KAREN: My kids and I is runnin'.

MISS CARR: Sure, they're running.

KAREN: We is runnin' after a ball.

112

MISS CARR: Maybe tomorrow you girls would like to make some more pictures, and maybe you'd try to fix the people to look a little more like you. You know, if you're going to make yourself as you will look when you're grown up, maybe you can take a good look at your mama tonight and see how she's got her hair fixed, and look and see how her dress looks.

ANNA: I always look at my mama every time.

MISS CARR: I'll bet you do, because you love her, don't you? She takes care of you. Next time when you draw, maybe you'll think about making yours not like Kathy's, but different. You are different from Kathy right now. Why don't we all go over to the mirror and see how we look.

Thus Miss Carr did not reject the pictures the girls had made, but she did help them realize that they were copying someone else's idea. She did this by encouraging them to recognize what was unique in their own appearance.

❧   ❧   ❧

During the next few days at choosing time, Karen, Kathy, Ina, and Anna made some more pictures.

Karen's is a complete departure from the old stereotype.

Anna's is quite different, too.

Ina's is also different.

But Kathy still made hers according to the old formula, even though it differs somewhat from her first picture. Kathy was the girl who originated the system, and whose work was being copied by the others.

Five Days in Mrs. Keller's Second Grade

Mrs. Keller is always very warm and pleasant toward her children; they respond to her with real affection. She speaks beautifully and is unusually discriminating in her use of language. She directs the attention of her children to the character of events in their environment, thus stimulating them to create ideas for activities in the arts.

Mrs. Keller's school system is located in a very modest and expanding suburb of a metropolitan center. Her school is located in an older section of the area. The homes are generally small and well tended; the population is composed of working people and business and professional families.

Mrs. Keller's school building was constructed sometime during the twenties when it was thought that a small classroom is an efficient size. As a result, the room provides very limited space in which to conduct a good teaching program. Although Mrs. Keller's class enrollment is comfortable with only twenty-three children, her room is crowded. The lighting is new and good. The furniture consists of movable desks with seats attached; these, however, are of inferior quality. The desk tops are not only very small, but they are also in a fixed tilted position.

Storage space is extremely limited, and there is no water in her room. A single table is the only space to arrange supplies for daily use. Mrs. Keller's children do most of their art activities on one of the walls or on the floor. In spite of these limitations, Mrs. Keller provides continuous and varied opportunities for art experiences.

The children were in their seats, and Mrs. Keller began by asking them to close their eyes and listen to "a word picture" she was going to "paint" for them.

MRS. KELLER: Close your eyes now and listen while I try to tell you about something. Can you see outside in your mind's eye? Can you see the bare trees? Can you see the cold ground, hard, frozen?

MARY: I can.

BOBBY: I can't.

MRS. KELLER: Try to imagine it in your mind's eye—a picture of a gray sky, cold frozen ground, brown grass—

CHILDREN: Yes.

MRS. KELLER: Try hard. I think you'll see it if you try. I see a few birds. They're jumping around on the tree. There are not very many of them. The ones that I see have a color—a brownish gray color. I don't see any bright colors. All the trees are bare. I'm looking for some flowers, but I don't see any. Do you see any leaves on the trees I'm talking about?

CHILDREN: No.

MRS. KELLER: No, they're bare. The wind is blowing. Now tell me—what kind of a picture was I painting for you? During what time of the year do you think I made my picture?

JOHN: Winter.

MRS. KELLER: Could you add anything to that picture if you were painting it? Mary, what would you add?

MARY: You can see green shrubs.

MRS. KELLER: Do you know what you call the shrubs? Evergreen. And they stay green even in the winter. Would you say that this was a very happy gay picture?

CHILDREN: No.

MRS. KELLER: What are some of the things that have to happen to that picture to make you feel happy? We're going to talk some more about that, but I'm going to ask you now—

DOUGLAS: Paint a picture?

MRS. KELLER: No, Douglas. We're going to go out for a walk, and I want you to see if what's outside is all gray, and brown, and without much life. But if you can find some signs of life—what do you think you might find outside now? Can you think of one thing? Nancy?

NANCY: Buds on trees.

MRS. KELLER: Yes. Bobby?

BOBBY: Flowers.

MRS. KELLER: Flowers, yes. Mary?

MARY: Maybe some worms.

MRS. KELLER: Yes. Cindy?

CINDY: Grass.

MRS. KELLER: Green grass, Cindy? I'll bet there will be. Janet?

JANET: Birds.

MRS. KELLER: Will we see any birds?

CHILDREN: Yes.

MRS. KELLER: What kind of birds do you think we might see?

JANET: I saw a robin.

MRS. KELLER: You look when we go out. When we go out, I'd like you to stay together and be sure to walk on the sidewalk.

When all the children had gotten their coats, they went out for a walk. While walking Mrs. Keller pointed things out to them, and they stopped along the way to look and talk.

MRS. KELLER: (Pointing to a flowering forsythia bush) They're like yellow stars.

CINDY: We have some of those.

MRS. KELLER: See how they look between the green bushes.

BOBBY: That's a green evergreen.

MRS. KELLER: Come over here. I want to show you something. Look through there and you can see a tree—a drooping tree.

CAROL: Oh, a willow tree.

MRS. KELLER: It is a willow tree, but it is a drooping tree, isn't it? Is it brown?

116

Classroom Records in the Early Elementary Grades

CHILDREN: No.

DOUGLAS: Look at the willow tree.

BOBBY: Oh boy.

MRS. KELLER: Look how yellow and fuzzy it looks.

As they walked along, the children found a budding tree with a low branch. They pulled it down to examine it closely.

Then they returned to their classroom to talk about all the things they had seen.

MRS. KELLER: If I asked you right now to imagine something you saw on our walk, I'm sure each one of you would have a picture in your mind.

JANET: I can.

MRS. KELLER: All right. Now, when I painted the word picture for you—do you remember—were there lots of colors?

CHILDREN: No.

MRS. KELLER: Mostly what colors did you see in your mind's eye from my word picture?

DOUGLAS: Brown.

MRS. KELLER: Yes.

CINDY: Gray.

MRS. KELLER: Did you see any bright colors?

CHILDREN: No.

MRS. KELLER: Then later, when we went out, what did the sky look like?

NANCY: Light blue.

MRS. KELLER: Carol?

CAROL: Gray sorta—, blue sorta—, and light sorta.

MRS. KELLER: Is the sky ever bluer than it is right now?

CHILDREN: Yes.

MRS. KELLER: As you looked around when we walked, did you see the dress the earth was wearing? Was it all brown-gray? What colors did you see?

JOHN: Green.

MRS. KELLER: The same green as when I made the word picture with the evergreens in it?

CINDY: No.

MRS. KELLER: Was there any other green?

CINDY: Yellow.

BOBBY: Yellow-green.

MRS. KELLER: How many saw yellow-green? I saw yellow-green, just like when I look out of this window. I can look out, and I can see yellow-green. Can you?

JANET: I see.

MRS. KELLER: Besides yellow-green, what else did you see?

CAROL: The little grass.

MRS. KELLER: Were there any other colors as we walked down the street?

JOHN: Pink.

MRS. KELLER: What was pink?

JOHN: The trees.

MRS. KELLER:	The trees were budding. Are you thinking of the fruit tree we saw? How many of you have an idea in your minds? Do you think you have?
	Suppose we imagine now that today would have been a sunshiny day, and the sun had come out real bright and warm the way it was yesterday. What was the air like yesterday?
CAROL:	Nice and warm.
MRS. KELLER:	Was there any wind yesterday?
LANA:	A little.
MRS. KELLER:	How did the wind feel to you, when it touched your face?
LANA:	Nice.
BOBBY:	Cool.
MRS. KELLER:	Can you use another word other than nice?
NANCY:	Pleasant.
MRS. KELLER:	Pleasant, yes. Did it blow against your face hard?
JANET:	No, soft.
MRS. KELLER:	Softly? What other word can you use?
JANET:	Gentle.
MRS. KELLER:	Gentle. That's a good word. Who can give us a nice sentence that would tell something about how things felt to him today as we went on our walk? Give me a nice sentence. Let's try to write a poem about our walk.
MARY:	The air was fresh, and the flowers were out.
MRS. KELLER:	The air was fresh, and the flowers were out. I think I'll write that on the board, and maybe somebody else will have another good idea in a minute. (She writes.)
	I'm going to ask you to think about what flowers were out. What flowers were out, Janet?
JANET:	Forsythia.
MRS. KELLER:	What other flowers were out that you saw on our walk?
JOHN:	Daffodils.

MRS. KELLER: Yes, the daffodils were out. Would you say they were just out, or could you say that in a nicer way? Think about how they looked.

JOHN: The daffodils were swaying.

MRS. KELLER: Good. Now can you tell us a little bit about why they were swaying? Who can add a little bit? Listen to the beginning of this sentence. The daffodils were swaying—

BOBBY: In the nice fresh wind.

MRS. KELLER: Good. The daffodils were swaying in the nice fresh wind. Would you like to change that, or should we leave it just that way?

CHILDREN: That way.

MRS. KELLER: The daffodils were swaying in the nice fresh wind.

They continued writing their poem a short while longer, and it was almost time to go home for the day. They had already spent over an hour and three-quarters talking about how things looked outside, going on their walk in the neighborhood, and beginning to write their poem.

MRS. KELLER: It's almost time to put our things away and get ready to go home. We'll finish our poem tomorrow, and we'll paint some pictures, too. How many of you have ideas in your minds of a picture you would like to make?

CHILDREN: Yes.

MRS. KELLER: Tomorrow, we'll finish writing our poem, and I'll ask you to remember what we did today. I'll ask you, too, to tell me what you would like to put into your pictures. Could you think about the different colors you would have in your pictures? You be thinking about that, and we'll try to do it tomorrow.

❧   ❧   ❧

The next day they finished writing their poem:

The air was fresh and the flowers were out.
The daffodils were swaying in the nice fresh wind.
A last year's nest looked cold and bare.
The wind was bouncing the pretty daffodils from side to side.
The chilly breeze played catch with the dainty daffodils.
Fat robbins darted here and there on the green grassy lawn.
Pink buds were trying to break out of their little brown houses.

120

Classroom Records in the Early Elementary Grades

They were waiting for spring to open the door.
The pussies on the willow tree were crawling up the branches.
The "hanging tree" looked yellow against the gray sky.
A rabbit was taking his spring walk.
Some crocuses had stripes like soldiers.

The walk out of doors, their discussion, and the poem they wrote sharpened their senses about the feelings of spring. They were anxious to paint some pictures.

MRS. KELLER: Let's get our paints ready now, so we can paint those pictures we wanted to do.

Mrs. Keller had a special table for paint preparation. They used dry powder colors, and they prepared them in glass jars and empty milk cartons. They had aluminum plates to use as palettes for mixing their colors, and they carried water from the hall in milk bottles.

There was a bucket of water for washing their brushes, and an empty bucket for dirty water.

MRS. KELLER: Let's move our desks out of the way and spread newspapers on the floor to work on. Let's move one row of desks at a time.

You may start now, and if I were you, I'd keep the paint on the newspaper. Then if you do have an accident it won't hurt anything

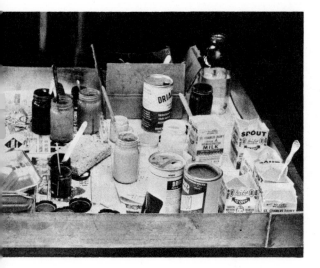 

Carol, do you remember what you said about the willow tree?

CAROL: It's like hair hanging from the branches.

MRS. KELLER: That's how you said it—like hair hanging from the branches.

DOUGLAS: Mrs. Keller, I need purple.

MRS. KELLER: If you want some purple paint, come over here, and let's see if we can make it. Tell me what color should we start with?

DOUGLAS: Blue.

MRS. KELLER: And let's add some red.

DOUGLAS: A little bit of white.

MRS. KELLER: All right. Do you like it now?

DOUGLAS: It's good.

While they worked on their paintings, Mrs. Keller walked around the room looking at what the children were doing and talking to them.

MRS. KELLER: If your paint is too thick, be sure to tell me because we can always thin it. Those daffodils are fine, Mary. I like them.

MARY: Ooo, this yellow is good. It's a nice color.

MRS. KELLER: You know, Sharon, your hanging tree has such pretty hanging branches. And those blossoms you're putting on them are so nice.

They painted for about an hour, and most of the children were able to finish their pictures.

Here is one of them.

Another child painted an indoor-outdoor picture with spring on the outside and spring cleaning on the inside.

The children who got through early began to clean up while the others were finishing their work. They moved the furniture back into the center of the room and arranged the rows. They spread their wet pictures to dry on the floor in back of the room. Then they continued with some of their other studies. That afternoon a few children stayed late to help Mrs. Keller hang their pictures.

∾   ∾   ∾

The next day, Mrs. Keller talked with the children about their spring pictures.

MRS. KELLER: Do you notice anything different in our room this morning?

CHILDREN: Yes.

MRS. KELLER: What is it?

RONNY: You got our new pictures up.

MRS. KELLER: Yes, we hung up the new pictures yesterday afternoon. Do you like them?

CHILDREN: Yes.

MRS. KELLER: Look at your pictures and see if they say—

RONNY: Spring.

MRS. KELLER: Yes. They do say, "Oh, it's spring!" Tell me about some of them.

JANET: Carol's.

MRS. KELLER: What is it about Carol's picture that says spring to you?

JANET: Well, the flowers and everything.

MRS. KELLER: Carol, which picture says spring to you?

CAROL: This one, mm—the flowers and trees. It has spots on the flowers.

MRS. KELLER: Don't you boys like any of those pictures?

BOBBY: I like the hanging tree, and mm—that squirrel in the hanging tree.

MRS. KELLER: I like that one, too. John, which one do you like?

JOHN: Bobby's.

MRS. KELLER: What do you like about it?

JOHN: The flowers, the buds on the trees, the stream.

123

Classroom Records in the Early Elementary Grades

CHILDREN: (Laughter)

MRS. KELLER: Isn't it a stream, Bobby?

BOBBY: No.

MRS. KELLER: What did you want it to be?

BOBBY: A path.

MRS. KELLER: A path and a stream sometimes do the same kind of thing, don't they? What does it do to that picture?

JANET: It makes it look better.

MRS. KELLER: Yes. It makes the picture interesting, doesn't it? Whether it's a path or a stream doesn't really matter. What it does is add nice color. I like it, too. We can call it stream-path. Shall we?

Do you want to say anything else about the pictures? There are so many things I like about them. I'm thinking of the whole picture now. I'm not thinking about any one thing you put in your pictures. I'm looking at all these pictures, and I'm thinking that every single one has one thing that's especially nice—something we've talked about before. When I look around, I don't see a single picture with great big empty spaces. Don't you think we've done pretty well with our space-filling?

CHILDREN: Yes.

CINDY: I like that picture.

MRS. KELLER: And what do you like about it?

CINDY: The dainty little things.

MRS. KELLER: That's a good word you just used. I want to ask you something. Would you say that your pictures make you feel something?

CHILDREN: Yes.

MRS. KELLER: What do they make you feel?

PAMELA: Cheerful.

MRS. KELLER: When the sun is out in the spring and everything begins to bloom, it does make you feel cheerful, doesn't it? And your pictures do look cheerful.

Now, I thought you'd enjoy making something together about

124

Classroom Records in the Early Elementary Grades

spring. Do you remember the collage pictures we made a few weeks ago? Well, I thought it would be nice to make a collage mural, and we can all work together on it.

Do you remember how we used cardboard, and string, and shiny paper on our collages? Come up here and look at all the materials I have in these cartons. There's corrugated cardboard, and wallpaper. There's string, yarn, absorbent cotton, wire mesh, and burlap. And there are some paper and fabric scraps. I think it would be a good idea if about four of you would prepare the background for our collage mural. The rest of us can make some crayon pictures just to get some ideas.

Before we get started, let's move all the desks into the middle of the room, so we'll have space to work on the floor and on the wall.

Four children volunteered to prepare the background. Mrs. Keller helped them cut and hang the paper over the blackboard. They painted the sky; the other children made crayon drawings to get ideas for their mural. After about twenty minutes Mrs. Keller asked them to stop and see what they had been able to do.

MRS. KELLER: Let's see what we have done so far.

PAMELA: We fixed the paper for the background, and we painted the sky.

MRS. KELLER: Good. We need to talk about what we want to have in our mural. We have all kinds of things out here to use, but we're not sure how we should start. I see some people with ideas. As soon as you think you have an idea and you can use something up here to make it with, then you come up and choose whatever you want.

John, bring your tree up. Hold it up here, and see if the size is what you want.

JOHN: I think I'll make another one—a different feel to it.

MRS. KELLER: Janet, let's try yours.

May I suggest something? Do you think you could try to make your tree out of some material?

JANET: You mean make the branches?

MRS. KELLER: You decide what you'd like to use. I just meant for you to make the tree of a material that has a feel to it.

JANET: You mean make a tree on there?

MRS. KELLER: How do you think that would work?

JANET: Fine.

MRS. KELLER: Is there any other way you can think of? Would you cut out this tree and paste it on?

JANET: It wouldn't look good.

MRS. KELLER: Well, this was just an idea. You know what you had in mind. Go try and put it on the wall.

JANET: O.K.

Janet went off to make her tree of a material she could feel. She soon came back to try it on the mural.

In this way, the children began to paste trees, clouds, and houses onto their collage mural, and by the end of their work period the whole idea was well under way.

❧　❧　❧

The next day, they worked on the mural individually in their spare time, and added bushes, trees, branches, and blossoms. The following day, Mrs. Keller asked them to look at it before they did more work on it.

MRS. KELLER:　Let's take a look at our mural now. I wonder if everything looks all right to you?

CAROL: We want a pond in the mural.

MRS. KELLER: Where would you like the pond to be? Bobby, would you like to show us where you think it should be? (Bobby walks up to the mural and points to the lower right hand corner.)

NANCY: Could we have a lake?

MRS. KELLER: A lake?

NANCY: Yes.

MRS. KELLER: Well that's what a lake is.

NANCY: It's bigger.

MRS. KELLER: Oh, I see. A lake is bigger than a pond. I think you're right. How would you make your lake?

NANCY: We could make some paper, maybe light—I mean dark blue, or light, or maybe paint it, or else take some material that we have and cut it and then glue it on.

MRS. KELLER: You said paper or cloth.

NANCY: Paint.

MRS. KELLER: Do you mean just paint it on there? I'm going to show you several things we have. Here is some blue shiny paper, and here is some aluminum foil.

BOBBY: The lake I've seen has brown water.

NANCY: It could be blue.

MRS. KELLER: Well, for the sake of the mural would it have to be brown, Bobby?

BOBBY: No, we could change it.

MRS. KELLER: Maybe you would like to make two lakes out of the blue shiny paper and out of the aluminum foil, and then we can try them both.

Nancy and Bobby did just that. They took the materials and each made a lake. Then they held them up to the mural to see which they liked better.

In this way, the children tried out their ideas, adjusted them, and worked them out to suit different parts of the mural. They would get together in small groups with Mrs. Keller to talk over what still needed to be done and changes they felt they wanted to make.

GARY: That one doesn't look like a tree to me.

MRS. KELLER: Which one doesn't, Gary? Show us. (Gary points to one of the trees.) You made that one, didn't you? Do you have an idea what to do to it? Jackie, do you?

JACKIE: It should have some feel to it.

MRS. KELLER: Could you get any feel in that tree, Gary?

JACKIE: He could put some brown stuff—take some cardboard and paint it brown. He could paint something else brown.

MRS. KELLER: It is brown.

JACKIE: But he could put something on his trunk.

MRS. KELLER: Like what?

JACKIE: He could use the brown stuff—just little pieces of it.

MRS. KELLER: That's a good idea. Gary, do you think you know what you'd like to do?

GARY: It should swerve like—you know like the trunk of a tree has a swerve.

MRS. KELLER: Now you're talking about putting some feel into that tree. Could you do it?

GARY: Yes.

By the end of this work period they had accomplished a great deal. The trees, branches, leaves, and blossoms were now made of different textured materials. The lake was in, and they had built a wire mesh fence around the house.

❧   ❧   ❧

The next morning, a few of the children put some people they made on the chalk ledge alongside their mural, and the whole class looked at what was accomplished to see what still had to be done.

MRS. KELLER: Let's take a look at our mural.

DENNIS: We gotta put people in.

MRS. KELLER: Is there anything else besides the people?

PAMELA: We could have a few more butterflies.

DOUGLAS: To paint one of the trees.

MRS. KELLER: That's right; Johnny still needs to paint his tree. Is there anything else we can do to our mural? You can feel the flowers; you can feel the red bud tree; you can feel the fence. Is there anything that you can't really feel?

DENNIS: Oh, I know.

MRS. KELLER: What, Dennis?

DENNIS: Some grass.

MRS. KELLER: How about that? We don't have any grass. We have grass color but you can't feel it. How would you show the grass?

CINDY: You can put one stripe of paint after another.

MRS. KELLER: That would be all right, but would you feel that?

SHARON: Well, maybe we can make it hang over a little bit.

MRS. KELLER: How would you make it hang over a little bit?

SHARON: Grass from out of your Easter basket.

MRS. KELLER: That might be all right, but is there anything else you could use?

MARY: Use some yarn like on the hanging tree.

MRS. KELLER: Yarn might be good.

JANET: Green string.

MRS. KELLER: That would work.

DOUGLAS: We could fix paper, and just put it here and there.

They reached their decisions and went to work to finish their collage mural. John painted his tree. They selected some figures and decided where to put them in the mural, and they made some grass "here and there" with some "feel." Now they were satisfied, and the mural was finished.

Four Days in Mrs. Rood's Second- and Third-Grade Class

Mrs. Rood is a very warm and friendly person with a calm and relaxed manner toward her children. She values their ideas, and is always ready to follow their constructive suggestions.

Mrs. Rood's school is located in a very modest neighborhood of a small city. A new wing has just been added to the building, and her classroom is spacious, bright, and quite well equipped, with adequate storage space and running water. Although some of the old movable desks with seats attached are still in use, she does have several good tables with enough comfortable chairs.

In order to solve two special problems, Mrs. Rood was asked to teach a combined second- and third-grade class. One problem was caused by the size of the second-grade enrollment in the school. The other stemmed from the needs of some of the children who were in Mrs. Rood's class the previous year.

131

The second-grade enrollment was heavy and unbalanced, and the school wanted to avoid having more than twenty-five children in any class. A number of the more able second graders, therefore, were selected for Mrs. Rood's combined class. The third-grade children in the combined group had been with Mrs. Rood the previous year, and it was felt that they would profit by moving with her from the second to the third grade. In this way, the combination of the two grades became a workable solution to the two problems, with a total enrollment of twenty-four children in her group.

Just a few days before, there had been a tea for the mothers of the children in Mrs. Rood's school, and part of her room was still decorated from that event. A little earlier in the year the class had studied about reptiles and insects, and the snakes, butterflies and spiders they had made were still exhibited on the wall.

Now they were in the midst of a study about transportation and trains. Mrs. Rood had read poems to the class about freight trains and steam locomotives. The children had seen several film strips of railroads, cars, and engines, and they were in the process of building trains out of shoe boxes, small cartons, corrugated paper, and construction paper.

The children were working independently at their desks and tables, and Mrs. Rood circulated around the room to help those who needed assistance.

132

Classroom Records in the Early Elementary Grades

ROSIE: What is this for (stiff cardboard)?

MRS. ROOD: You can use that for your wheels if you want to.

ROSIE: What do you do with it?

MRS. ROOD: You would have to cut the wheels. Don't you remember all the things we talked about the other day—how we were all going to figure out for ourselves the way we wanted to build our trains? Don't you remember? These bottle caps may not be large enough for wheels. You may want to make larger ones. George, how are you coming?

GEORGE: How do you put this on (wheel)?

MRS. ROOD: I think you may have it a little too small. You might try a larger one.

GEORGE: Maybe.

MRS. ROOD: Maybe if you use some of that stiff cardboard you could manage it. (Noise) Look, girls, I think you're going to spoil things. You looked so nice before when you were busy working.

JANET: I want to make a train with a balcony on the back.

MRS. ROOD: That sounds good—a balcony on the back. That would be good if you made one like that.

DAVID: I can't make a hole.

MRS. ROOD: Could you use your scissors? Let me help you. I'll punch one, and you punch the rest.

In this way, Mrs. Rood walked around the room looking at what the children were doing, answering their questions, helping them when they needed help, and suggesting ideas for them to try.

One of the boys was building a modern diesel engine.

One of the girls was building a steam locomotive with a cow-catcher in front.

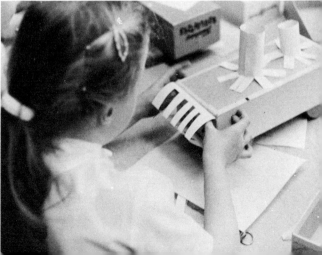

By the end of the week they had concluded their study of trains; most of the children had finished building their locomotives and railroad cars.

❧   ❧   ❧

In their informal conversations, the children had been talking about animals and pets, so the following week Mrs. Rood began a study of mammals. This had special meaning for them. They were interested in animals, and they had already spent a period of time earlier studying reptiles and insects. To begin their study about mammals, they collected books from the school library and were reading.

MRS. ROOD: This morning we read our books, and we talked a lot about mammals. Now, I have two film strips I want to show you, so you can see more about some of the animals. Then I thought you would like to make some animals out of clay. Let's all take our chairs to the back of the room. I have the screen and projector ready to show you the film strips.

Although the room is bright and without window blinds, Mrs. Rood prefers to show the film strips in her classroom rather than take the children to the school's projection room. She prefers this in order to be able to use the reference material while the children are working, as well as before they start. In order to show the film strip in the light classroom, Mrs. Rood put the screen in the corner of the room and against the window wall so that the light from the window hit the back of the screen. She also put the projector close to the screen so that the projected image would be as bright as possible. This made the image small but reasonably brilliant and usable without a darkened room.

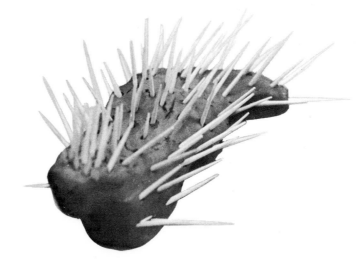

MRS. ROOD: Here's a porcupine. Look at his nose.

JAY: I found a dead porcupine, and I took out all the thorns.

MRS. ROOD: Look at this cougar. He looks like a cat, doesn't he?

Now, some of these animals would be much easier to draw, but when we do them in clay we need to choose one that's good for clay. You know that if you make parts of your animal too thin, the clay will crack.

After viewing the film strips the children took newspapers and covered their tables and desks. Mrs. Rood asked two of the children to distribute balls of clay which she had prepared in small pliofilm sacks.

MRS. ROOD: You can choose any animal you like, but I would stop and think which kind of an animal would be good to do in clay. Some animals have very thin legs and that would be very difficult to do in clay.

As the children began to work, Mrs. Rood talked to them individually to help some of them get started.

MRS. ROOD: You can start with sort of a ball, and then you can add more clay to it. Look at Mary's. She isn't trying to make real slim feet, or anything like that. She's making quite a heavy base, and then she's pinching some ears. She has a real good start.

Jean, would you like to come back with me and look at the film strip again? That might help you get a good start.

They worked for almost an hour. The boy who had told about the dead porcupine made one by sticking tooth picks into his clay form.

When they had finished their pieces, they put them on the window sill to dry. Then they rolled up the dirty newspapers and cleaned up the room.

When they were all finished, there was a surprise. Jay had talked to Mrs. Rood that morning and arranged to give a puppet show with some puppets he had made at home. Jay's parents had bought a record for him of "Peter and the Wolf," and he got the idea of making puppets of Peter, Grandfather, the wolf, cat, and bird. He also used a board to make a tree, and he covered it with linoleum. He had brought his record and all his puppets to school; his friends, Jerry and Larry, were going to help him give the show.

The children arranged their chairs for the show, and the three boys fixed a table in front of the room for the stage.

Mrs. Rood played the record on their player, and the boys manipulated the puppets to the accompaniment of the music and narrative. The class was excited about the performance, and all the children wanted to make puppets, too. Jay told them how easy it was to make puppets, and what they would need to use. Mrs. Rood knew that the kind of hand puppet which Jay had made was in fact somewhat complicated for second- and third-grade children. The enthusiasm of the children was so high, however, that they decided to begin work on their puppets the next day.

༺ ༺ ༺

The next day, the children brought many things they needed for their puppets, and they were ready to begin.

MRS. ROOD: This morning we discussed our characters, and we decided which plays we wanted to do with our puppets. Now let's think about some of the things we have to remember in making a puppet. Jay told us a little bit about how to start, and about some of the problems he ran into. Let's just think about them a little bit more. First of all, Jay, what do we need to do?

JAY: Well— (he laughs).

MRS. ROOD: I thought you were teaching me this morning.

JAY: You blow up your balloon.

MRS. ROOD: All right. Go ahead and explain it. You have to explain it carefully.

JAY: You blow it up and tie it, and you put the paper on and the paste (paperhanger's wheat paste).

136

MRS. ROOD: You need to tear the paper, don't you? We found when we tried it this morning,—and Jay was showing me how to do it—Jay and I tried some of that sticky paper (brown gummed tape). I think that's good to connect the balloon to the little cardboard roll. If you don't have a roll, you can use one of the paper cups. We found if you use the sticky paper to attach the tube to the balloon, it makes a good strong collar. Then you can use strips of newspaper or paper toweling with the paste.

Janet, do you have any suggestions? You were helping us this morning.

JANET: I don't have any other suggestions.

MRS. ROOD: Jay, do you?

JAY: Yes, one thing—ah—you gotta hold the sticky paper, or it'll fall apart.

MRS. ROOD: That's right. It's better to take your time and hold it till the sticky paper sticks. It's better not to hurry.

JAY: We don't want it sloppy.

MRS. ROOD: I also think you might find it easier to work together, and help each other to get the roll attached to your balloon. Once you get it attached, then it's easy to work by yourself. So, we could choose partners to help each other on that.

Another thing—it's going to be very difficult to manage the paste at the desks, so you had better work at the tables. Let's clear the tables and move some of the chairs around them. If we're careful, then we'll have a very successful afternoon, because this takes a lot of hard work.

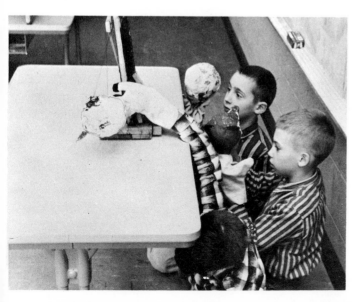

The children rearranged the furniture and began their work on the puppet heads. First they blew up their balloons and tied the ends. Then they attached the paper tubes to the balloons with the gummed tape to make a collar.

And then they began to cover the balloons and the collars with strips of paper and paste.

After they had built up about five or six layers of paper strips, the heads were good and solid, and they were ready to build out noses, ears, and other features.

They worked for about an hour and a half, but by the end of their work session some of the children still had more to do to their puppet heads. Many others, however, were ready to let their heads dry, so they could paint them.

෨ඏ ෨ඏ ෨ඏ

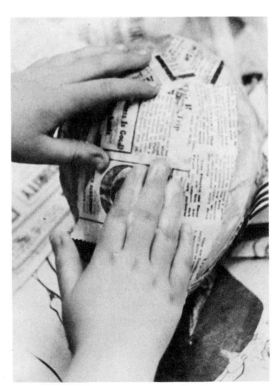

The next day, they began their work on the puppets by talking over their plays.

MRS. ROOD: I think we need to talk about what we would like to do in our plays. We need to get ourselves grouped according to the ideas for our plays. If you would put your things down for a few minutes, we can talk things over and decide what to do. Mary, why don't you tell us about the idea you and your friends want to work on.

MARY: We want to do Cinderella.

MRS. ROOD: Do you have enough characters among you?

MARY: We need some help.

MRS. ROOD: Weren't you going to borrow the prince from one of the other groups?

MARY: Yes.

MRS. ROOD: Now, do you people want to get together and talk over what you need to do? We do have more work on the puppet heads, and we do need to make the other parts of the bodies. So if you talk over your plays now, you will know how your puppets ought to be finished. Then you can do a good job on the character you have selected.

JANET: Let's get together in groups and talk it over.

MRS. ROOD: Let's gather all the people who are going to work on Cinderella at the table in that corner, so they can talk for a few minutes.

In this way, they arranged their groups to talk over the important details for finishing their puppets and planning their plays. There were five groups, and each went to a different part of the room to talk about their ideas, and to reach their decisions.

One group decided to write down all they were agreeing to do.

139

Classroom Records in the Early Elementary Grades

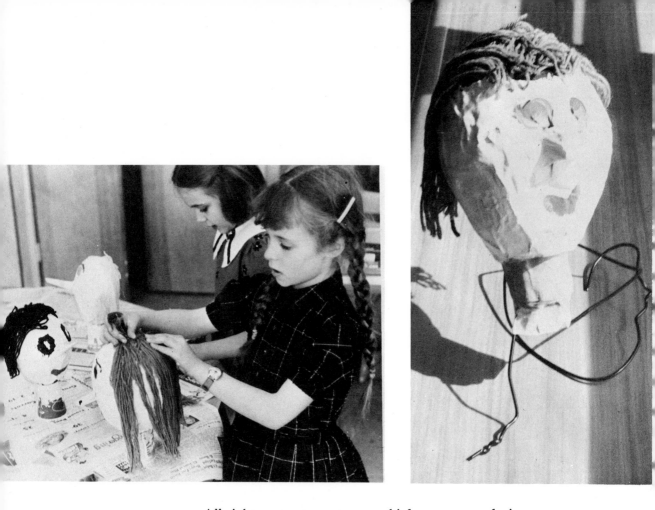

MRS. ROOD: All right now, as soon as you think you are ready in your committees, you can go right to work to do the necessary things to your puppets. While all of you are talking, I'll begin to get the work tables and materials ready for you.

While the children were talking in their groups, Mrs. Rood began to arrange the room for the various things they would need. The desks would be used as places to cut and sew the costumes. One table was arranged for pasting paper and hair onto the puppet heads. The counter near the sink was laid out with paints and brushes for painting. Another table was prepared with strips of paper and wheat paste for those who still needed to make additional puppet heads.

The children took about fifteen minutes to make their decisions, and then they were ready for their various jobs. Some painted their puppet heads. Some of the heads were ready to have hair put on; a few of the children were busy at the job.

One head was all finished and standing on the window sill while the boy who made it was sewing the body and the clothing.

140

Classroom Records in the Early Elementary Grades

It took several more days to complete their puppets, and to get ready to present their plays. A few of the groups used recordings, just as Jay had done, to provide the accompaniment and narrative for the movement of their puppets.

Mrs. Rood found a puppet stage in the building that they were able to borrow and use for their show. When they presented their plays to the class, the children backstage had as much fun and satisfaction from giving the performance as the whole class had in watching.

❧   ❧   ❧

These four lower elementary grade teachers—Mrs. Kessler, Miss Carr, Mrs. Keller, and Mrs. Rood—have the capacity to teach their children how to observe and discriminate; they have a quality of excitement that communicates to their children to encourage them to create ideas. Each has her own unique strengths and interests, but all four share the characteristics of excellent teaching. Their work and the work of their children are analyzed in the next chapter.

ANALYSIS OF

IN THE EARLY

5

If you compare the classroom records of the early elementary grades in the preceding chapter with the kindergarten records in Chapter Two, you will notice important differences in the manner of teaching. The kindergarten teachers taught more informally than do the early elementary grade teachers. Except for Miss Carr's class, where there was a special problem, the daily programs on the early elementary grade levels included more organized attention to language, numbers, and social studies. This fact brought about a somewhat more formal programming of art activities.

By comparing the classroom records of the first and second grades, you will also detect some important differences in the behavior of these children, with corresponding differences in the work of the teachers. Although first-grade children are more mature than kindergarteners, they are much less mature than second-grade children. You were probably impressed by the relatively smaller differences between the first-grade and the kindergarten groups, in comparison with the greater differences between the first- and second-grade groups.

CLASSROOM RECORDS

ELEMENTARY GRADES

Children exhibit greater spurts of growth at some points than they do at others. The degree of growth from the first to the second grade seems to be more dramatic than that from the kindergarten to the first grade. This difference was evident in the behavior of the children, and it was reflected in the work of their teachers.

In spite of the effect of developmental differences on the work of these teachers, the perennial characteristic of excellent teaching in art was always apparent. Each teacher—Mrs. Kessler, Miss Carr, Mrs. Keller and Mrs. Rood—created a climate in which ideas were brought to life in discussion with her children. The ideas became moving ideas, because each of the teachers directed attention to intriguing details about the things they were discussing, to capture the imagination of the children. Their enthusiasm resulted from identification with the ideas. They made them their own and created new ones from them.

Each child was encouraged to choose the idea that interested him most, and to interpret it in his own way. You should recognize, however,

143

how each teacher developed and illuminated the general idea with her children. The children were never asked to draw, or paint, or build just any idea they wanted. They were taught to experience—to see, to feel, to consider—and to choose in order to express their ideas artistically and meaningfully. Through the help of their teachers they were taught to experience by becoming aware of a variety of possibilities. In their discussions, they did more than just name the things they wanted to make; they talked about the things; they moved their bodies as they imagined the things might move. Their teachers helped them capture the spirit of the things they wanted to make. This is what created the "moving spirit" in the ideas they selected for work.

In Mrs. Kessler's class, the discussion about satellites and the people who invented them, coupled with the dance of the rockets, created the spirit out of which her children painted their own conceptions of rockets; Miss Carr's sympathetic discussion of the paintings by the four girls, coupled with her understanding manner in helping them to recognize the different ways they combed their hair, encouraged them to be themselves and to depart from stereotypes. Mrs. Keller's attention to nature, and her sensitive use of language prepared her children for their walk out of doors, thus encouraging the experience out of which they painted their spring pictures, and constructed their collage mural. Mrs. Rood's willing response to her children's enthusiasm for the unexpected puppet show provided the impetus for their involvement in creating their own puppets.

As a result, the art activities of these children were purposeful. They were not merely given materials and time for work. The background of experiences out of which their art activities grew provided the incentive. The children were ready and wanted to shape their ideas through art.

Purposeful art activities are the products of active teaching. They do not occur by accident. Even though Mrs. Rood did not plan for her children to make puppets, she responded to their desire, because one of her teaching goals was to build upon the interests of her children. It did not matter whether the children worked independently, as in Mrs. Kessler's class while she was reading with one group; or whether all the children worked in art at the same time, as in Mrs. Rood's class. The point of significance was the mood that had been created and the background developed by these teachers. The mood and background enabled each child to achieve a personal purpose for his work.

The specific ideas discussed, many of the activities, and the ways of conducting them varied from class to class. As among the kindergarten classes in the earlier chapters, some variations stemmed from the different times in the year when the work of these classes was recorded—Mrs. Kessler's in February, Mrs. Rood's in March, Miss Carr's and Mrs. Keller's in

April. Current events, seasons, and holidays continue to be of interest to children on the early elementary grade levels.

Some variations stemmed from the physical limitations in some of the classrooms. Mrs. Rood's and Miss Carr's classrooms were spacious. Although one was rather well equipped and the other meager, both had comfortable spaces in which to arrange various activities. The fact that Mrs. Kessler's and Mrs. Keller's classrooms were so very crowded required them to follow a more formal kind of space and time organization to manage certain activities.

One of the most important reasons for some of the variations stemmed from the developmental differences among children in the early elementary grades. A review of the growth characteristics of first- and second-grade children will reveal some important reasons for the work of these teachers, and the art activities of their children. It will also provide the basis for further analysis of the classroom records.

Major Developmental Achievements of Children in the Early Elementary Grades

First- and second-grade children have a great deal of physical energy. They move expansively; they walk and run with abandon and determination. They cannot sit still for too long; and prolonged sedentary activity is the most reliable way to produce the proverbial wiggles. Although they do get tired, frequent changes in tempo by alternating quiet and moving activities are generally more important than periods of rest. Periodic changes in tempo were evident in the sequence of activities in each of the four classes.

The ability these children developed during their kindergarten year to run and climb is growing into more extended body control. Although their body coordination is still partial, they now have the skill to do stunts and to create ingenious body movements.

During this age, there is a tendency toward gradual refinement of arm-hand-finger coordination. Most first-grade children handle paint and brush with greater assurance than kindergarteners, but their movements still tend to be rather broad and sweeping. In comparison, second-graders paint with much greater physical dexterity, and exhibit a marked degree of detailed control. First-graders can cut and paste paper, model with clay, and saw wood, as was evident in the activities in Mrs. Kessler's and Miss Carr's classes. Their arm-hand-finger coordination is more precise than that of kindergarten children, but infinitely less refined than that of second-graders. The second-grade children in Mrs. Keller's and Mrs. Rood's classes demonstrated how they can create relatively complex constructions of paper, cardboard, clay, and wood. Even though the hand puppets in Mrs. Rood's class were somewhat complicated to make, the children's enthusiasm coupled with their growing dexterity enabled them to carry through this activity with high success and satisfaction.

Emotionally, first- and second-grade children show progress toward self-sufficiency. They desire some independence—wanting, enjoying, and taking pride in doing things for themselves, like the boy in Mrs. Rood's class who made his own puppets, thereby inspiring all the children in the class. At the same time, they still seek and require the security of adult approval, encouragement, and support. They are boastful, sometimes jealous, and often quarrel with each other. Girls tend to fight less than boys, but there is a general tendency to settle arguments verbally rather than physically.

This is an age of fantasy accompanied by highly imaginative play. First- and second-grade children love to dramatize. They "make-believe" and create imaginary roles. They literally live their parts. As was apparent in the dramatization in Miss Carr's class and the puppets in Miss Rood's class, these children identify themselves with animals, cowboys, robbers, fair ladies, and princesses. They *are* these characters, physically and verbally. Mrs. Rood's children derived as much learning and value from acting out their ideas through their puppets as they did from making the puppets themselves.

Although first-grade children still tend to live in a self-centered world, it is different from the world of the kindergartener. It is becoming a world of "me and" someone else—"me and my dog," "me and my friend," "me and my mother." It is becoming more inclusive toward the realization of a "we" world. The social-emotional horizon of the second-grader shows a marked inclusion of others in relation to himself. His interests and concerns, however, are still closely circumscribed by his immediate environment.

As is to be expected, most first- and second-grade children show increasing awareness of group life. They play more together with each other, rather than alongside each other. They organize group games, even though they often make up their own rules. Second-graders begin to engage in team activities, and to see themselves as members of a social group. They can work together on a common enterprise by contributing their thoughts and integrating their ideas into the development of a group project, as was evident in the making of the collage mural in Mrs. Keller's class and in the work on the puppet play in Mrs. Rood's class.

The general social behavior of these children demonstrates their growing realization of group membership and personal responsibility. They require sympathetic assistance and encouragement by teachers and other adults, but at the same time they show increasing ability to await their turn, to listen to each other's ideas, to share the attention of their teacher, to use materials and equipment together, and to manage some limitations of time.

The intellectual development of first- and second-grade children reveals insatiable curiosity for explanations about virtually all things in their environment. Compared to kindergarteners, who tend to emphasize "what" and "who" questions, early elementary grade children grow more concerned with "why" and "how"—"why does it get dark?" and "how does it work?" They are moving from mere questions of identification toward questions of cause-and-effect relationship.

These children are growing better able to think about and to discuss complicated ideas. Their intellectual development, coupled with their social growth, enables them to begin to think together. This fact was evident in the group poetry writing in Mrs. Kessler's and Mrs. Keller's classes. Through the patient guidance of their teachers, first- and second-grade children were learning to contribute to ideas the groups were developing.

Conceptions of time and space are growing more extended. The first-grader can talk meaningfully in terms of "when I was in kindergarten," or "we took a trip in the summer." The second-grader's conception of ground, sky, and space, as revealed in his paintings, begins to convey some beginning realization of depth in space. Although he is still strongly guided by his direct emotional and kinesthetic experiences, he is developing the early awareness of some of the objective relationships in the visual world. The paintings of most second-grade children begin to reveal a growing awareness of big, little, and middle-size things in their environment.

Aesthetically, early elementary grade children are still guided by their intuitive feelings. Their level, however, is less naïve than that of children in the kindergarten. They enjoy repetitive play and are able to create

charming rhythmic patterns in their paintings. They are fascinated by words that sound good, and they love repetitive sounds. As was apparent in the poem about spring by the children in Mrs. Keller's class, they can combine words to convey interpretive moods.

Much aesthetic growth occurs during these years. When compared to the kindergartener, the second-grade child has a more controlled grasp of his whole idea. Whereas the kindergartener intuitively develops his pictorial idea piece by piece, the second-grade child seems to be more aware of its totality at the outset. He tends to use the space of a sheet of paper in a more conscious manner. He is less prone to leaving blank areas, and he is less likely to run out of room for things he wants to include.

Second-grade children are growing more discriminatingly aware of characteristic details, like spots on a flower or buds on a tree. They are not only able to differentiate color subtleties, but they also begin to strive to mix those colors that will best suit the ideas in their pictures. When Mrs. Keller's children talked about the color of the sky, they did not just say it was blue. It was "sorta blue." They qualified the mere name of the color; they showed awareness of color differences.

These major tendencies in the development of early elementary school children are reflected in the work of the teachers and in the art works created by the children.

The Content of the Teachers' Conversations

The sequences of art activities in each of these four classes were unique to the local developments in the classes. The programs were organized, but there were no unalterable plans. Each art activity grew out of some event, some point of interest, or some current problem. The activities were neither isolated nor fragmentary. They had continuity, flow, and direction. As a result, they achieved cumulative significance and produced profitable learning.

The various ideas for their art activities stemmed from two distinguishable sources. One source included current affairs, holidays, seasons, things children sometimes talk about, and the current unit study. The other source was in the art activity itself. While the children worked in art, the teachers discovered problems; the children discovered new interests. The fact that both these kinds of sources are evident in the classroom records is one important indication of excellent teaching. To show you the interplay of ideas from both sources, I shall refer directly to sections of the records from two of the classrooms.

During the first day in Mrs. Kessler's class, she talked to her children about satellites and rockets. This was news at the time, and it captured

148

the interest and imagination of the children. Their discussion led first to the dance of the rockets soaring from earth, and then to painting. A current event thus became the source of the idea for their paintings.

The firing of the rocket, however, occurred at Valentine's Day time, and naturally the children were also interested in the holiday. They had already written some poems about Valentine's Day, and then they wrote another poem about the new boy in their class. It is interesting to note that aside from their reference to red valentines, their poem did not include the usual stereotypes associated with that holiday. Their interest in Valentine's Day, and the experience of writing the poem, provided the idea for their crayon pictures. Because the poem was free from the customary stereotypes, the pictures they made were also devoid of stereotypes.

The third day was Valentine's Day, and Mrs. Kessler arranged for the children to make holiday hats to create a festive occasion. This activity fascinated them.

During all this period of time, Mrs. Kessler talked with her children about friends. Friends send valentines to each other, and they help each other. The children read and wrote stories about big and little friends, and on the fourth day, they painted pictures about friends. Their classroom study was the source for this activity.

Then two things happened: some of the children kept talking about how they had made their Valentine's Day hats, which was a clue for Mrs. Kessler that they had enjoyed the construction activity; and one of the boys made a plaid repeat design on the dress of the person in his picture. These were outcomes of two previous art activities. The interest of the children in the construction activity and the repeat design in the boy's picture thus became the source of the next two art activities. Mrs. Kessler responded to the interests of the children in planning the activities for the fifth day. Some of the children built paper sack figures, and some made repeat design prints with vegetables and scrap materials.

During the five days, Mrs. Kessler's children worked on six different art activities. Each had a particular source which was significant to the children. The sequence of activities evolved in direct relation to progression of major events in the ongoing classroom program. One idea came from a current news event; two stemmed from a holiday; one grew out of the classroom study and topic of discussion; and the sources of the other two were special interests discovered in previous art activities. The sequence was orderly and meaningful, because each activity was relevant to things the children were talking about, reading, or doing. As a result, each activity contributed to the totality of the children's experiences.

During the five days in Mrs. Rood's class, her children worked in only three art activities. Though their sources were somewhat different

Analysis of Classroom Records in the Early Elementary Grades

from those in Mrs. Kessler's class, they were equally meaningful in terms of the particular classroom context.

On the first day, the unit study was the source of the idea for the art activity. The class was concluding a study of trains, and they were building locomotives and railroad cars. This activity developed parallel to the study, and they completed both at the same time.

When they began their new study about mammals, they also began a new art activity. Animals became the subject of interest, and clay sculpture was a fine medium to deal with such ideas. Although this activity also had its source in the unit study, the following one did not. Unexpectedly, the puppets, which one of the boys had made at home, became the new center of attention for work in art. The study about mammals continued its course, but it was no longer the source of ideas for the art activity. The children's excitement about puppets was dramatic enough for Mrs. Rood to allow it to take over. The one boy's unexpected contribution to the class provided the idea for their next art activity.

The three art activities in Mrs. Rood's class thus grew out of two different sources: the units of study and an unexpected event of special interest. In Mrs. Rood's class, as in Mrs. Kessler's, the art activities followed in an orderly sequence. Both sequences evolved out of the particular set of circumstances in each of the classes—current events, studies in process, and special interests of the children. Some activities in the sequences were anticipated by the teachers and planned in advance. Some emerged during the immediate developments in the two classes and were incorporated into the teaching plans. The orderly planning and the flexible incorporation of unforeseen points of interest gave the sequences their flow, direction, and educational significance. For the children, they provided cumulative learning and meaning.

Another distinctive characteristic in the work of these teachers is evident in the things they talked about while developing background for their children's art activities. They not only described the various ideas by identifying interesting details; they also dwelt on the emotional feelings and the visual qualities related to the ideas, to encourage their children to create visual images of them. They helped their children to create the kinds of ideas that could be expressed well through the visual arts. The children thus learned to focus their attention on those qualities which were distinctively relevant to the visual arts.

The arts are interpretive activities. They convey people's ideas, feelings, and attitudes. They do not merely represent or illustrate, nor do they convey what is seen superficially. The visual arts interpret in a particular manner, because they deal with visual sensations—the colors, rhythms, shapes, and positions of things. Good teaching of art encourages children

150

to interpret their ideas by reacting to things of interest. Children then learn to perceive visual qualities in their ideas to the limits of their developmental capacities.

The day Miss Carr talked with the four girls in her class about their pictures, she helped them become more keenly aware of the way each of them combed her hair, the expression on their faces, and the clothes they wore. She helped them to observe and to identify the characteristics that were unique to each of them. She helped them to look with care and to develop a feeling for the things they saw. The effects of her discussion were evident in the subsequent pictures they made. The children learned to observe independently, to interpret what they saw, and to rely less on stereotypes.

Mrs. Keller's introductory discussion about spring provided a series of verbal poetic images by creating a feeling and mood. She not only described trees, colors, and weather; through her words, these things came alive. On their walk out of doors, her children were ready to search beyond the surface and to experience the quality and character of springtime.

When they returned to their classroom, the things they saw were further reinforced through the poetic images they developed. They thought about the things they saw and described them imaginatively. When they began to paint, they were so attuned to the visual potentialities in the idea, that their pictures developed with sensitivity and with ease.

Still another distinctive characteristic of the work of these teachers is apparent in the classroom records. Each was guided by the developmental capacities of her children. This was revealed in a number of ways— the kinds of ideas developed and the nature of detail that was emphasized; the relatively informal program in the first grade as compared to the somewhat more organized activity in the second; the individual art activities in the first grade compared to the tendency toward some group activity in the second.

The ideas developed by the first-grade teachers were largely within the immediate environmental experiences of the children. The ideas in the second grades had more extended scope. This difference revealed the teachers' sensitivity to the social, emotional, and intellectual horizons of early elementary grade children.

In the first-grade classes, ideas were discussed together, but the children worked on their art activities individually. They engaged in similar activities at the same time, but each child worked independently from the others. In the second grade, some of the activities were individually developed, but some were group projects. The teachers thus demonstrated how aware they were of the capacities, limitations, and progress of children of this age for group experiences.

It is important to notice the nature of the group activities in the second-grade classes. Even though the puppet activity in Mrs. Rood's class was a group project, each child built his own puppet. He coordinated his efforts with the efforts of a group, but he did not make any single thing with other children. Even though the collage mural in Mrs. Keller's class was a group activity, each child made something which was later attached to the mural. Things which did not seem to fit very well were looked at, discussed, moved, or changed. The important point here is the fact that the puppet and the collage mural activities not only permitted easy adjustments but indeed encouraged them.

A good teacher encourages the growing capacities for group activity in her children by challenging them to work together. Such a teacher, however, is careful to select activities which do not frustrate the efforts of the children. Young children who are beginning to learn to work together are learning to give and take. Art materials whose form and position can be changed and adjusted easily, in a give and take manner, can encourage profitable group experience. Materials which do not allow the kind of give and take that second-graders can manage tend to frustrate rather than assist them.

Puppets which could easily be brought together into different combinations, and a collage mural where parts could be shifted with relative ease were excellent group art activities. Mrs. Keller knew second-grade children well enough to provide the flexibility the collage mural could insure. She knew that had she chosen paint, the children would have encountered difficulties in moving and changing the parts of their mural in the process of developing it. Such difficulties could have led to frustration, or she would have had to direct all the important choices and decisions in the work. Neither of these results would have produced the educational values she desired. The flexibility of the collage materials encouraged the children to try their ideas. They were able to put up their pieces, look at them, reach their decisions, and adjust them as they felt necessary.

Finally, among the things the teachers talked about were the art works produced by the children. These were regular topics for discussion. The teachers talked about them in terms that had meaning for the children. They discussed the interpretations of the ideas, and remarked about the colors, rhythms, moods, and feelings. They challenged the forward development of the children, but at no time did they impose standards of judgment which were beyond the maturity level and comprehension of the children. They respected the artistic efforts of their children.

The Teachers' Use of Classroom Time

Among these teachers, as among the kindergarten teachers, classroom time was treated as an instrument for effective teaching. Time was divided into units to serve best the various activities in the total program. Each teacher followed a routine which was at once regular and flexible. The regularity not only insured attention to the growing variety of organized studies. It also provided essential stability to the program. Yet there was sufficient flexibility in the utilization of time to serve the needs of certain activities and to pursue unforeseen interests when they appeared.

One very important clue to the division of time can be seen in the attention these teachers paid to two time problems: the allocation of time to various activities in a single day, in relation to total time spent in these activities during a week. By thinking in terms of each day in relation to a week, they were able to maintain time stability, while providing fruitful flexibility. The nature of the current art activities dictated some of the variations in time. When a certain activity required a great deal of time for effective development in one day or even in a sequence of days, more class time was devoted to other studies during other days in the week.

In general, these teachers devoted the equivalent of about three-quarters of an hour each day to art activities. Sometimes this time included discussion in advance of the art work itself. Sometimes all of this time was devoted to work—generally when the unit study or another expressive activity like dance or the writing of a poem had already provided the necessary background. In the first-grade classes, there was a higher degree of daily regularity. In the second grades, the time blocks for work in art were more varied and longer.

As a rule, Mrs. Kessler's first-grade children worked on their art activities in the mornings. After she had discussed the ideas with all the children, the whole class divided into their three reading groups. While she read with one group, the other two worked in art or wrote. This combined routine took about one and one-quarter hours, and each child worked in art for about twenty to forty minutes. Sometimes Mrs. Kessler took an additional ten or fifteen minutes to talk with the children about the pictures they made.

The morning they made their Valentine's Day hats, and the day when some of the children worked on their paper sack figures while the others printed, they devoted about one and a half hours to their art activities. Such complex activities occurred about once a week, and they required extended periods of time.

Mrs. Keller's second-grade children generally worked on their art activities in the afternoon. Their morning was devoted to work in arithmetic, language arts, and social studies. They didn't work in art every day, but when they did, they always devoted at least an hour. On days when they painted pictures, they completed their work in about an hour. When their

Analysis of Classroom Records in the Early Elementary Grades

collage mural was in process, they devoted at least one and one-half hours to a working session.

There were three important reasons for the time arrangement in Mrs. Keller's class: (1) When second-grade children become involved in painting, they need a good block of time if their work is to be satisfying. (2) The difficult space in Mrs. Keller's room required the rearrangement of furniture for effective work. Not so frequent, but longer periods helped solve this problem. (3) Because the classroom space was difficult, individual children were rarely able to do independent work in art when they had finished other studies. Longer periods gave them more of the time they needed.

The time routines in Miss Carr's and Mrs. Rood's classes were similar though not identical to Mrs. Kessler's and Mrs. Keller's. Their management of time, however, was guided by similar considerations. The frequency with which all their children worked in art and their intelligent utilization of time contributed to the richness of their children's art experiences.

The Teachers' Use of Classroom Space and Equipment

Good teaching of art requires careful and ingenious use of space. A teacher cannot create space when there is none, but a thoughtful teacher can utilize available space for its maximum advantage.

Both Mrs. Kessler's and Mrs. Keller's classrooms were crowded for the number of children enrolled. They were old rooms with huge, drab expanses of excessive blackboard space, and with hardly any wall space on which to hang things. Mrs. Keller used scotch tape to hang her children's pictures on the surplus blackboards. This practice at once brightened their room, and gave the children an opportunity to enjoy the pictures they painted. Mrs. Keller used this same blackboard wall to hang the large sheet of wrapping paper on which they made their collage mural.

Every bit of surface space in Mrs. Kessler's room was at a premium. She took advantage of the window counter to display things at times, and to arrange materials for distribution and choice at other times. When her children were making their Valentine's Day hats, all the materials they needed were laid out on this counter.

There was no table space for work in Mrs. Keller's room, and the children's desks were so poor that it was impossible to do much work on them. To create space for art activities, she had to move the furniture in order to use the floor and wall. The children learned to do this in an orderly manner. When they were working on their collage mural, they pushed all their desks together into the center of the room to get them out of the way.

Children can learn to take care of classroom furniture when their teacher provides some simple precautions. When Mrs. Kessler's children made their paper sack figures and did their printing, they covered their tables with old newspapers. Clean-up was swift and simple.

While Miss Carr's children worked with wet chalk, they had little aluminum pans of water and small cellulose sponges on their tables. Since they did not have to walk around with water, they avoided the most obvious reason for spilling it. They used their sponges to wipe up any mess as soon as it happened. When they had finished, a quick sponging left the tables clean.

While children work in art, they need easy access to materials. When they paint, many colors have to be within easy reach. When they begin to discriminate subtle differences between colors, they need the opportunity to mix the colors they want. Mrs. Kessler kept her paints in small fruit juice cans. Several of these were put in a shoe box or in a wooden tray with a wire handle. While the children painted, these were in the center of the table for all to share.

Analysis of Classroom Records in the Early Elementary Grades

When Mrs. Kessler's children were through painting, the boxes were stacked one upon another to close the tops of the cans.

Mrs. Keller's children used inexpensive light-weight aluminum picnic plates as palettes on which to mix the exact colors they wanted.

When Mrs. Rood's children were working on their puppets, several different phases of the activity were in process simultaneously. She was able to manage efficiently and with ease because she organized the classroom space carefully and well.

Pasting was done at a table which was covered with newspapers.

The puppet heads were painted at a different table where the paints and brushes were arranged for use.

The puppet costumes were being made at the small desks.

In short, since the best uses were made of the different kinds of spaces that were available, the children were able to do their work conveniently.

Mrs. Rood was the only one among these four teachers who had running water in her room. The others had to create some way of using water from the hall. Mrs. Kessler's children used mason jars; they learned to fill them only half full, and to carry them with care. Miss Carr used a large aluminum pitcher, from which the water was distributed into shallow pans. Mrs. Keller used mason jars and two metal buckets—one for clean and the other for dirty water.

Through such procedures, each of these teachers arranged their physical facilities for effective teaching. They planned with care, and developed essential housekeeping routines which they taught to their children. The children shared the responsibility for distribution, use of materials, and clean-up when work was done. Each room had its limitations and presented its own space problems. Each was utilized to its maximum advantage.

The Children's Art Works

The quest for a pictorial symbol system, which is the developmental task of the kindergarten child, is generally brought to a beginning and workable level by the time most children enter the first grade. This achievement is accompanied by simultaneous efforts to organize the space in their pictures, and to discover ways to relate the symbols of people and objects to each other.

Most first-grade children have learned to create pictorial symbols for people, houses, trees, and flowers. This is largely a "self-taught" kind of learning which is directly related to the individual's maturational development. A good teacher can assist by providing materials and opportunities to

156

make pictures. The creation of the symbol, however, is achieved by the child "all by himself." He cannot be told how to do it. Unless he creates his own symbol, he cannot understand it, and he is inhibited from developing beyond it.

The symbols most first graders learn to create are "shorthand" representations which bear their personal imprints. Once having mastered his beginning symbol, a child will tend to repeat it in a systematic manner.

Here is one child's symbol for people, and note how he has painted all three figures in almost the identical manner.

Here are the symbols by another child for a house and flowers. He used the same symbolic scheme to paint all the flowers.

These first symbolic achievements are not only "shorthand" representations; they are also generalizations of the objects they symbolize. The people and the flowers in the two pictures you have just seen are people and flowers *in general*. At this age, the child is limited in his ability to discriminate particular qualities in the things he puts in his pictures. Consequently his systematic symbols do not convey the unique characteristics of certain people or selected flowers. As the child repeats his symbol, because of the security he has achieved in his accomplishment, it becomes his own stereotyped representation. He tends to copy himself.

When the experiences out of which these children derive their ideas for pictures are sufficiently dramatic, they recreate their symbols. They

158

begin to pay attention to particular details, depart from their own stereotypes, and invent new ways to communicate the essence of the ideas that excite them. They often make certain parts especially large, they leave out unessential parts, and they include significant detail. These are some of the ways through which they make their pictures expressive.

There can be no mistake that the boy is smiling in this picture.

The girl in this picture has a strong hand to hold her umbrella.

A bird needs a special branch in order to be able to sit in a tree.

There is an inherent logic in the expressive symbols created by these children.

Although children generally develop a symbol system while in the first grade, individual differences in maturity level continue to be apparent within any group. All first-grade children are not ready to read, nor are they all able to create pictorial symbols.

Miss Carr's first-grade class included children with an unusual range of developmental problems. The following four pictures indicate the variation in pictorial development in this group.

The scribbles in the first are more characteristic of the manipulative efforts of the three- or four-year-old.

The second is an early effort toward symbol achievement, which, however, is even less mature than the level of most kindergarten children.

The third is rather typical of the "shorthand" pictorial symbols of many first graders.

The fourth has moved beyond the systematic symbol to a beginning emphasis on significant detail. The careful painting of the shingles on the roof and the ribbons in the girl's hair are indications of significant growth toward communicating unique qualities in an idea.

The art works of individual children vary not only according to their ability to achieve symbol systems; they vary also according to the relative richness and poverty of their conceptions of ideas—their imaginative play with the ideas. Here are two paintings from Mrs. Keller's class. The symbolic development in each is evident. Even though the first includes rather well-developed symbols for a person, a tree, flowers, birds, and clouds, it is somewhat meager in comparison with the dramatic richness of the tree, person, dog, and sky in the second one.

Beginning efforts to communicate the relationships among things in space are achieved through the discovery of a base line on which to locate all the objects in the picture. The child of this age perceives the base line as the ground, and he uses it as the unifying force. Instead of locating objects in a picture in random position, as younger children tend to do, most first

Analysis of Classroom Records in the Early Elementary Grades

graders begin to place the parts of their pictures on the ground. Although the base line and the accompanying sky line generally appear in the pictures of first-grade children, you will recall these accomplishments by some kindergarteners in Chapter Three.

Here is a chalk drawing by one of the children in Miss Carr's first grade. The tree and flowers are on a base line and the sky is a line on top.

The following three paintings by children in Mrs. Keller's second-grade class demonstrate further developments in the conception of space:

The objects in the first picture are organized on the base line, but the line of the sky has disappeared to convey the infinity of space beyond.

The second utilizes the bottom of the sheet of paper as the base line, and introduces a line beyond to convey the beginnings of depth in space.

The third is a relatively complex overlapping of figures and objects which is generally indicative of the pictorial development of older children.

Children at this age begin to discriminate color subtleties; especially is this evident among second graders. They talk in terms of yellow-green and brownish-gray, and qualify their description of the character of particular colors. In their paintings, they begin to mix colors to achieve the tones they desire.

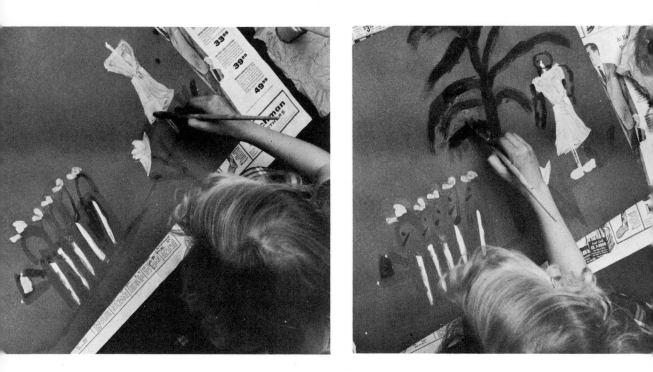

To understand further the levels of achievement of children in the early elementary grades, you need to observe how they go about developing their pictures. You will recall from Chapter Three how kindergarten children reconstructed and embellished their ideas as they painted them. You will also recall how the kindergartener tended to complete separate parts of his picture and to insert objects in the empty spaces that were left.

Many second-grade children reveal a rather dramatic change in the way they conceive and develop their pictures. They begin to show more awareness of the totality of their ideas at the outset. Although they embellish their ideas as they proceed, they grasp many parts simultaneously. They depend less upon adding things in the empty spaces they discover. They know more in advance what they intend to include. Their intellectual development is intimately related to their pictorial growth.

In this sequence by a girl in Mrs. Keller's second grade, you can see four stages in the progressive development of her painting:

In the first, she started with the ground line, and painted the five little people at the left. The flower came next, and then she painted the large figure.

In the second, she painted the tree, went back and did some more

painting on the large figure and on the little people.

In the third, she painted the ground area, began the sky and re-painted the little people, the large figure, the tree, and the flower.

In the fourth, the entire picture, except for the flower, was re-painted. She added clouds, birds in the sky, and a bush. She transformed her row of little people into birds sitting on a fence, and she redeveloped the tree and the figure.

This picture was not painted in the same piece-by-piece manner which is typical of younger children. This girl kept repainting the parts of her picture to accommodate the new parts she introduced. She continued to work all over the painting throughout its development. The stage-by-stage coordination of her idea indicates a new level of achievement in per-ceiving relationship and organizing them.

Many of the characteristics in the pictures by early elementary grade children are evident in their three-dimensional work. Clay responds to their desire to manipulate, and to their capacity to control and shape materials into symbolic form.

Here are three clay constructions by children in Miss Carr's first-grade class which show their range of development:

The first is primarily manipulative, and it evolved through the

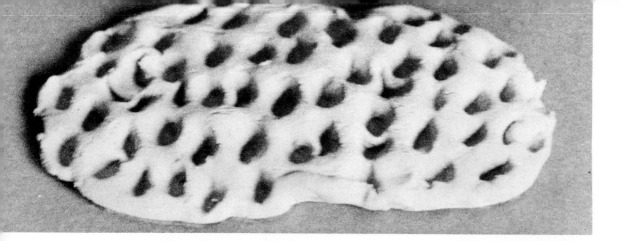

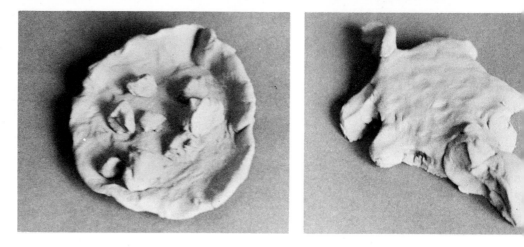

child's sensuous satisfaction from squeezing, patting, and poking the clay.

The second demonstrates a child's early efforts to manipulate the clay to achieve control and to create a particular form.

The third represents an important achievement by a first-grade child to shape the clay into a symbolic form in order to convey an idea.

The following three clay constructions are from Mrs. Rood's second-grade class:

The first is an effort to create a three-dimensional symbol of a head which is reminiscent of some of the beginning symbol formations in pictures.

The second represents a significant achievement in the ability to control the material to differentiate the various parts of a form.

The third is a more mature control of the material in which this child is able to express subtleties about the character of a selected animal.

Now, compare the three pieces of sculpture from Mrs. Rood's class with the three from Miss Carr's class. Also compare these pieces with the kindergarten sculptures in Chapter Three to see the general level at each grade, the individual differences in each grade, and the range of abilities with their apparent overlapping among all three grades. Good teachers know

164

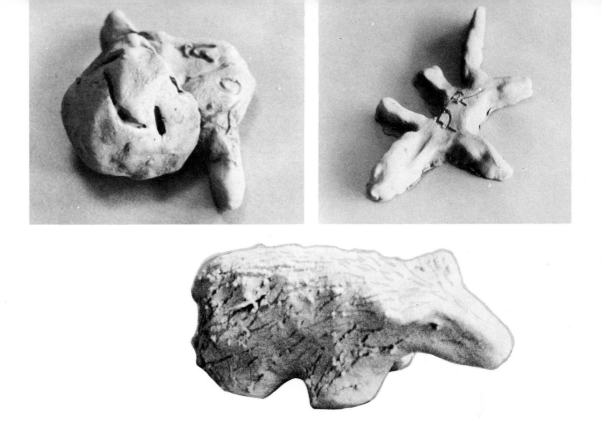

what is generally characteristic of children in their own age group. They also know the range of development below and above. This knowledge enables them to distinguish among individual developmental differences and to help their children accordingly.

Summary

The early elementary school grades represent a broad sweep in the development of children. The differences between first- and second-grade children are often dramatic. In art, they grow from the beginning achievement of a pictorial symbol to variation of the symbol for the expression of particular ideas. The organization and control of space becomes evident in their pictures. Their way of working becomes less fragmentary and more comprehensive. They begin to grasp more complex relationships.

Good teachers know the limitations and abilities of their children. They are aware of the developmental directions of their growth. They value their efforts and achievements, and they challenge their further development. In teaching art, good teachers help their children to become more discriminatingly aware of the visual qualities in the ideas that interest them.

Mrs. Kessler, Miss Carr, Mrs. Keller, and Mrs. Rood each used her own personal strengths in her teaching. Each encouraged the kind of inquisitiveness and awareness which her children were able to grasp. Each created a climate where feelings were valued and individual expression was enjoyed. These qualities permeated all of their work and infused their teaching of art. The arts were integral to their entire teaching programs.

CLASSROOM RECORDS

IN THE MIDDLE

6

This chapter presents the work of six teachers—five classroom teachers and one art teacher. Mrs. Brooks and Mrs. Retzlaff teach the third grade; Mrs. Abele, Mrs. McParlane and Mrs. Shrosbree are fourth-grade teachers; Miss Cupelli is an art teacher.

There is an art consultant in Mrs. Brooks' school system, but her duties are many and varied. She is responsible for assisting the classroom teachers in a very large school district, and consequently she must limit her work with individual teachers. Mrs. Brooks can call upon her from time to time, but direct contact between the two is at best infrequent. Mrs. Brooks plans and teaches art to her children quite independently.

Mrs. Retzlaff has very good assistance from an art consultant, who spends half-time working with the twenty-six classroom teachers in her building. Mrs. Retzlaff plans and teaches art to her children; the art consultant is available for frequent help and advice.

There is an art teacher in Mrs. Abele's school system who works

Classroom Records in the Middle Elementary Grades

ELEMENTARY GRADES

in her building every other week. The art teacher's room is fairly well equipped, but her time is limited. When she comes to Mrs. Abele's school, the classes meet her in the art room for a regularly scheduled brief period. Mrs. Abele considers these bi-weekly art periods inadequate, and independently she conducts a program of abundant and continuous art experiences with her children in her own room.

Mrs. McParlane, Mrs. Shrosbree, and Miss Cupelli teach in the same school building. The services of the art teacher, Miss Cupelli, are shared by about twenty-five classroom teachers. In this school, the teaching of art is carried on cooperatively between the classroom teachers and Miss Cupelli. Although Miss Cupelli works primarily as an art teacher, she conducts her work so that she also functions as an art consultant to the classroom teachers. She teaches art to the children in all the grades, and she consults with the individual teachers to assist them in the art teaching they themselves do.

Miss Cupelli is an alert person with a great deal of vitality. She not

Classroom Records in the Middle Elementary Grades

only knows the arts well, but she also knows a great deal about a good elementary school program. She works very well with other teachers, and much of her effectiveness hinges on that important quality. She teaches children well, because she conveys to them a real feeling for the work in which they are involved.

Miss Cupelli has no art room. Her headquarters is a centrally located supply room which she uses as an office and as a place to store the school's stock of art materials. She teaches classes, but she does not follow any routine schedule. Her work is planned from week to week and from day to day. She will visit a class to listen to and participate in the discussion of a book that is being read, or to hear about a study that is in process. Through such close contact she is able to plan and develop particular art activities for the greatest significance to each of the groups with which she works. She often works with the same class for several days in succession, and it is not at all unusual for her to visit a class twice in a single day. At other times, she may do nothing with a particular group for a week or more.

Most of the art activities in this school are a direct outgrowth of the background of studies and ideas developed by the classroom teachers with their children. When background is being developed, less time is spent in art. When art activities are in process, they work in a concentrated manner.

Very often Miss Cupelli initiates an art activity, and then the classroom teacher carries it forward with Miss Cupelli's advice and assistance. Just as often, however, the classroom teachers initiate their own art activities, and consult with Miss Cupelli when they need her assistance. Mrs. McParlane and Mrs. Shrosbree work very closely with Miss Cupelli, as do all the other classroom teachers in their building. The teaching of art in their classes is frequent, continuous, and richly varied.

Here is some further information about each of the five classroom teachers together with excerpts from the records of the conduct of activities in their classes.

Three Days in Mrs. Brooks' Third Grade

Mrs. Brooks is an enthusiastic and energetic person whose infectious exuberance and vitality communicate to her children. Her own enjoyment of life creates a buoyant feeling in her class. The arts are important to her, and she provides continuous opportunities for her children to write imaginative stories, to sing, dance, and to work in various visual arts.

Mrs. Brooks teaches in the same school system as Mrs. Keller, the second-grade teacher whose work was reported in Chapter Four. The neighborhoods where their individual schools are located, however, are decidedly different. Mrs. Brooks' school is in a working class community in a suburban area. The homes are somewhat crowded, and the railroad that runs through the community spreads its noise, and spatters its smoke and dirt among the little houses and the people.

The school building has one section which is fairly old, and a new wing which was added in recent years. The smoke and grime from the railroad have given both parts a uniform coating. On the inside, however, the old part has been remodelled; the new rooms and the old ones are bright and spacious. Equipment is meager and limited. There is hardly any storage space in Mrs. Brooks' room; there is no running water. The desks are tiny, with a fixed tilt and with seats attached. Mrs. Brooks does have two large tables which she uses as needed for supplies, to display the children's work, for library materials, or for work space. There are thirty-five children in her class.

Mrs. Brooks' children had been reading many books about animals. They borrowed these from the school library, and they had them arranged on one of the tables in their room. Their interest in animals led to discussions about ideas for a spring festival. They were thinking about doing a circus, and they talked about writing songs, making up dances, painting pictures, and making animal masks.

Among their ideas for a circus, they decided to make elephant masks, so that they would be able to have an elephant dance. To make the masks they had collected large brown paper sacks and discarded silk stockings. On this particular morning, after recess, they planned to begin making their elephant masks.

MRS. BROOKS: We're all ready to begin our elephant masks today. All you people did a fine job collecting these paper sacks and old silk stockings.

GEORGIE: The elephant has a trunk.

MRS. BROOKS: He sure does. Do you have any idea how we can make a trunk out of a stocking?

JUANITA: Well, we can stuff it with paper.

MRS. BROOKS: Do you have any idea how we can get it attached to the sack? What do you think?

KENNETH: You could paste it.

MRS. BROOKS: Do you think that'll be strong enough?

VIRGINIA: Clasp it together.

MRS. BROOKS: You think we might clasp them together. But, how do you think

169

Classroom Records in the Middle Elementary Grades

	we can do that? How does your mother fix your pants sometimes when you tear them?
CHILDREN:	Sew them.
MRS. BROOKS:	Yes, we could sew the trunks on. Don't you think they would hold much better if we would sew them on?
CHILDREN:	Yes.
MRS. BROOKS:	Now, do you remember we were talking about the elephants in your stories? What's an elephant's trunk like?
BOB:	It's long.
MRS. BROOKS:	Yes, it is. Do you have any more ideas? Is it stiff or floppy?
BOB:	Floppy. It swings.
MRS. BROOKS:	Sure, it's floppy and it swings. Then you wouldn't want to stuff the stocking too full, because that'll make it stiff.
GERALDINE:	Can we paint the trunk pink?
MRS. BROOKS:	That depends on how you want to make it. You can paint it any color you want. You can even put dots on it if you want.
	Now, let's see about these paper sacks (and she slips a sack over the head of one of the children). What do you think about it?
VIRGINIA:	Too long.
MRS. BROOKS:	Yes, it's much too long. What do you suggest?
VIRGINIA:	Cut it off.
MRS. BROOKS:	Where do you think we should cut it?
VIRGINIA:	At the neck.
HARRY:	To his shoulders.
MRS. BROOKS:	Then you will have to measure it before you cut it off. What else will your elephants need?
KENNETH:	Ears.
MRS. BROOKS:	Yes, ears. Do you remember the elephant's ears we saw in the pictures and the ones when we took that trip to the zoo?
LEON:	They were long and floppy. They were on the sides of the elephant's head.

170

MRS. BROOKS: You're right Leon. The elephant's ears are long and floppy. What do you think we can use to make the ears?

LEON: Colored paper (construction paper).

MRS. BROOKS: O.K. That's a good idea. We can use our colored construction paper for that.

You'll have to use your own imagination about painting your elephant, but when you paint your sacks, be careful not to get them too wet and floppy. You can decorate your elephants with pretty colors. Do you think we're ready to work now?

CHILDREN: Yes.

MRS. BROOKS: Fine. Then let's get the room ready. Let's move the desks out of the way, and spread newspapers on the floor, and fix up our paints. Let's have this group move the desks; this group can spread the papers; and this group can mix up the paints (pointing to the groups to do the three jobs).

Much talking and thinking about elephants—how they looked and how they moved—had already gone into the writing of their stories. With this brief introduction to recall a few details and to talk about the materials they were going to use, they were ready to go to work.

The desk movers pushed all the desks into a single line against all four walls, and cleared the floor of the room. The paint mixers moved one of their tables into the middle of the room. One of the children went out for a bucket of water, and they began to mix their dry powder colors in small jars and fruit-juice cans. The paper spreaders got a stack of newspapers from the closet, and spread the sheets all over the floor. The desk movers and paper spreaders were ready in about five minutes.

MRS. BROOKS: That was a good and fast moving job. Most of us are ready to work now. You can go right ahead and start your masks.

The children spread out all over the floor with their paper sacks. They measured and cut them to size, and then began to paint them.

When they had finished the sack parts of the masks, they put them on the desks to dry and began the trunks.

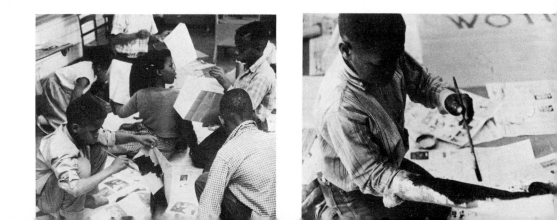

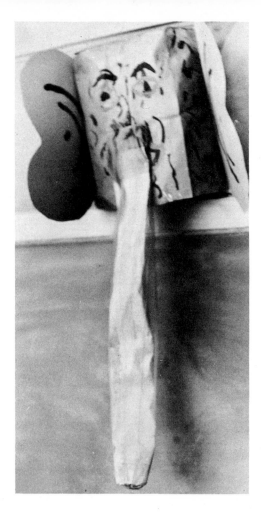

By the end of the morning most of the children had finished making the sack, trunk, and ear parts of their masks. During the next two days, they worked on the masks individually at various times during the day when they were through with some of their other studies. As they finished their masks by sewing, taping, and stapling the parts together, they hung them on the narrow cork strip above the chalkboards in their room.

Here is one of the finished masks.

❧　　❧　　❧

During the days when they were making their elephant masks, they also began to work on songs and dances for the circus. They listened to a record of circus music which Mrs. Brooks was able to find, and they tried to identify the parts which sounded like elephant music, clown music, and lion-tamer music.

The day after they finished their masks, they spent about an hour working on a song and making up a dance.

172

Classroom Records in the Middle Elementary Grades

MRS. BROOKS: Kenneth and Bob have been working on a song to get everybody in the mood for the circus. They took the words from one of the poems we've been reading in our books, and they found out they could actually put it to music. All of you know the words of this poem, so they made up a tune. If you like it, we can use it for our circus song. Kenneth and Bob have done a pretty good job of getting this song together. How about you two boys singing it for us, so we can all learn the tune? Virginia and Mary, you know the music. You do it with the boys.

Now they're going to give us just a little come around, so we'll all be able to sing it. After they start the song, then we can all try to sing it with them.

KENNETH, BOB, VIRGINIA, MARY: (They sing the music they composed to the poem about the circus coming to town with drums booming, clowns falling, lions, elephants, tigers, and a real kangaroo like in the zoo.)

MRS. BROOKS: How do you like it? Do you think we have a tune?

CHILDREN: Yes.

MRS. BROOKS: O.K. Let's try it altogether.

CHILDREN: (They all sing in chorus.)

MRS. BROOKS: Now let's put something to it. How about you four people going back to your seats now, and let's get some suggestions from other people, too. How do you think we should act while we're singing the song?

GERALDINE: We should clap our hands when the song goes boom.

MRS. BROOKS: Like that (and she gives her hands a spirited clap)? Is that what you think?

GERALDINE: Yes.

MRS. BROOKS: All right. But what do you think about the first part, at the beginning of the song? What else can we do?

HARRY: We could dance like elephants.

MRS. BROOKS: Do you want to show us? I think we should have a lot of rhythm to it, don't you?

HARRY: (He dances like an elephant.)

MRS. BROOKS: That looks good. Are there any other suggestions?

173

Classroom Records in the Middle Elementary Grades

JUANITA: When it says, "lions, elephants just like a zoo, tigers and maybe a real kangaroo," where you sound exciting and where it says "real kangaroo," we jump up and clap.

MRS. BROOKS: Good. Let's try it.

CHILDREN: (They sing the part, and try the movement.)

MRS. BROOKS: Good. That sounds very good, and it's beginning to look good. Let's rock from side to side to the rhythm of the music. Let's try it again. Let's go.

CHILDREN: (They sing the song with spirit and movement.)

MRS. BROOKS: Now we're really at the circus. I'll be standing here wishing that the circus will come to town. Let's act real happy. Do you want to try it one more time?

CHILDREN: Yes.

MRS. BROOKS: All right. Let's whoop it up and make it real good. Let's go.

CHILDREN: (They sing and dance again.)

MRS. BROOKS: Very good. That was fine. We need to take a rest now. While we're resting, I'll play that circus record again. It has lots of rhythm, and you might have some suggestions for some more dances.

Mrs. Brooks played the record, and they listened. Some of the children suggested things they could do to parts of the music. Individual children demonstrated their ideas, and the whole group tried them.

Through the singing, dancing, and listening to the recording, the children were achieving another dimension of the feeling of circus. Their enthusiasm was mounting, and they were eager to get on with the job.

❧ ❧ ❧

174

Classroom Records in the Middle Elementary Grades

The following morning, while planning their activities for the day, they decided it was time to begin work on the big pictures of animals for their circus menagerie. This was a big job, and it would take a long time. Five of the children volunteered not to go out to recess; they would stay in the room with Mrs. Brooks to rearrange the desks, to cover the floor with newspapers, and to get the paints ready. All the children would then have more time to work.

When the class returned from recess, everything was ready. The children sat down at their desks around the sides of the room to talk over their ideas before getting started.

MRS. BROOKS: Before we get started on our pictures, we need to talk just a little bit about the things we did before we went out to recess.

BOB: We wrote a story.

MRS. BROOKS: Yes. What kind of stories did we write this morning?

BOB: We wrote—we wrote something about the circus, about the animals, what color he was, and the bears and the monkeys, and we tried to make our stories excitin'.

MRS. BROOKS: Exciting?

BOB: Because we want it to look true.

MRS. BROOKS: Did your stories have to be true stories, or could they be make-believe stories?

HARRY: Make-believe.

MRS. BROOKS: Would anyone like to tell us about the animal he picked to write about? Georgie, what did you write about?

GEORGIE: Kangaroo.

MRS. BROOKS: You wrote about the kangaroo. Did any other people write about kangaroos? Any more kangaroos here? Are you a kangaroo? What was your story about Herbie?

HERBIE: My friend, the kangaroo.

MRS. BROOKS: What did you say about him?

HERBIE: I like the kangaroo. She makes eyes at me.

MRS. BROOKS: She makes eyes at you? That's why you liked the kangaroo. Now if you were to draw your friend the kangaroo, how do you think you would draw her? Since she made eyes at you, what would you want to show most of all?

HERBIE: Blinking eyes.

MRS. BROOKS: All right. That would make a very good kangaroo. Did anyone write about an elephant? Didn't we have a lot of elephants? What did you say about your elephant, Garry?

GARRY: The big elephant.

MRS. BROOKS: The big elephant. What did you say about it?

GARRY: He put his trunk in the water and squirted it.

MRS. BROOKS: He did!

In this way, they described the animals they wrote about in their stories—what they did and how they looked. The experience of writing about the different animals brought many ideas into direct focus. The children were ready to deal with these ideas in pictures.

MRS. BROOKS: Well, boys and girls, you've been telling about the animal stories you wrote. I thought that you could use your story ideas to make the animal pictures for our circus menagerie. You can paint the animal you wrote about. These pictures are going to be very big. Look at these large sheets I was able to get (30″ x 45″ sheets of brown wrapping paper). That's going to be a lot of work, and I thought that maybe you could work in pairs, or maybe even three, on one picture. You can have partners for this. Do you like the idea?

CHILDREN: Yes.

MRS. BROOKS: Good. Now what's the first thing you'll need to do to make a picture like this? Do you just start painting, or do you do something else first?

MARY: Draw it with chalk first.

MRS. BROOKS: Why do you think we should draw it with chalk first?

MARY: If you get mixed up with the paint, you can't get it off. With the chalk, you can erase it.

MRS. BROOKS: That's right. With the chalk you can try out your ideas first. You can erase it, and change it if you want before you paint it. Now, this is a very large piece of paper. What do you have to remember when we draw and paint on large pieces of paper? Kenneth?

KENNETH: Draw big.

MRS. BROOKS: Yes, draw big. And what do you try to do with all the space?

GERALDINE:	Fill it up.
MRS. BROOKS:	Yes, fill it up; and the circus is the main thing.
STANLEY:	Circus animals.
MRS. BROOKS:	Yes, circus animals. Now, if you should happen to choose the kangaroo, the kangaroo would be what type of an animal?
JUANITA:	Tall.
MRS. BROOKS:	Yes, tall and you can hold your paper the tall way.
JUANITA:	You gotta make it big for the menagerie.
MRS. BROOKS:	Yes. The menagerie has to be big enough so the animals can be seen by the spectators. What do you think you could put in your pictures in the space that's left around your animals?
HARRY:	Tents.
MRS. BROOKS:	All right. What else?
PATRICIA:	Swinging on the trapeze.
MRS. BROOKS:	All right.
MARY:	People in the parade.
MRS. BROOKS:	Yes, that's a good idea.
GARRY:	There are people that sell things.
MRS. BROOKS:	That's right. There are people that sell things. And what do they sell?
GARRY:	Popcorn.
LEON:	Pop and peanuts.
MRS. BROOKS:	Very well, then you could have people that sell things. But remember, your animals must be real—
CHILDREN:	Big.
MRS. BROOKS:	Right. And then you can put other things in to fill the spaces.
	Now you can choose the people you'd like to work with. You may work with your friend, but let's remember not to talk too much. Then we won't have to change any of the groups—that's if you and your friend don't do too much talking about things other than the circus.

177

Classroom Records in the Middle Elementary Grades

You know, you have to work real hard if you want to get this done. It would be nice if you could get this all drawn and even start to paint today. The circus isn't very far off, and we still have a lot of work to do. Here's your paper and you can begin as soon as you've chosen your partners.

The children selected their partners. Some chose to work in pairs; others formed groups of three. They spread their large wrapping paper sheets on the floor and worked on their drawings.

As they worked, Mrs. Brooks walked around the room looking at what they were doing, making suggestions, and answering questions.

MRS. BROOKS: Look at that fine elephant squirting water on his back with his trunk. You boys are almost ready to paint.

Stanley. Hold yours up. Look, boys and girls. Look at that fero-

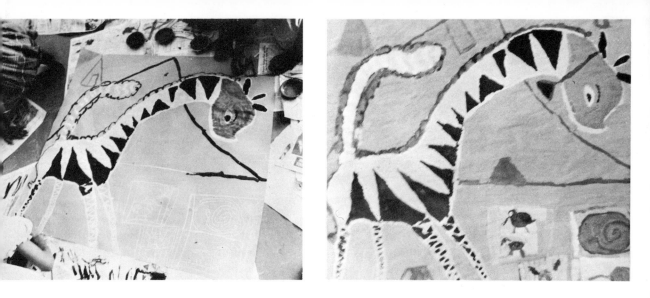

cious lion Stanley and Herbie are making. They're ready to put in the background now. That's a fine-looking animal. He's a beautiful thing.

Here are three stages in the painting of a giraffe by three of the girls in the class:

First, when they began their chalk drawing.

Second, when they began to paint it.

And third, when they were all finished.

The children made many animals for their menagerie. At the end of the morning they still had work to do, so they hung their pictures on the wall until they could finish them the next day.

The boys who painted the squirting elephant put a baby one into their picture.

Three other boys made this gorilla in his cage.

❧ ❧ ❧

The following week they talked a lot about the circus performers: trapeze artist, fat man, hobo, clown, ring master, strong man, cowboy, acrobat, snake charmer, and lion tamer. In talking about all these people, Mrs. Brooks encouraged the children to emphasize the colorfulness of the circus performers. During their discussions they dramatized and acted like the circus people.

They decided to make some more large pictures to decorate the walls of the room where they would have their circus festival. These pictures would be of the circus performers. They worked in small groups as they did on the menagerie pictures; and it took about two days to paint these.

Here are two of their circus performers: three bareback riders on their horses, and a clown.

When they had finished the circus performer pictures, they were almost ready for their circus. They still needed to rehearse their acts, but they were ready to set the date, to invite other classes from the school, and their parents. Altogether, they spent about a month preparing their circus. When the big day came, there was real excitement. One of the girls led the group in a rhythm band. A group of boys did the elephant dance wearing the masks they had made.

Another group of boys did a clown dance. Between the acts, one of the boys walked among the audience shouting his wares and pretending to sell balloons.

Four Days in Mrs. Retzlaff's Third Grade

Mrs. Retzlaff is a warm and sensitive person. She is inquisitive and adventurous; she seeks to create ever-expanding experiences for herself and her children. Knowing how important it is for children to create and express ideas, she enlivens the experiences of her children to develop the background out of which they can create ideas. Continuous and varied activities in the arts are the means through which she helps them develop and express their ideas.

Mrs. Retzlaff's school is located in a prosperous suburban community adjoining a large city. Virtually all of the children come from comfortable professional and business homes. The school building itself is modern. Most of the classrooms are spacious and well equipped.

Mrs. Retzlaff's room is large and bright. There is good storage space and running water. The furniture consists of comfortable tables, which are large enough for four children. They all have regular chairs. From time to time the furniture is moved around, sometimes to facilitate a particular activity, and sometimes merely to create a bit of variety. Mrs. Retzlaff has twenty-five children in her class.

180

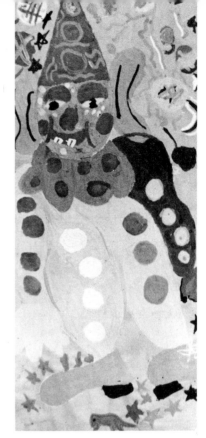

Mrs. Retzlaff's class was studying "Things that Live"—birds, animals, and fish. They had borrowed a collection of books from the school library. Each child selected something special to investigate, and they were reading independently and writing reports of all the information they were collecting.

The art consultant had already been in to talk over with Mrs. Retzlaff and the children the things they were studying about, and some ideas they had for possible things to do in art. In addition to planning with the art consultant, Mrs. Retzlaff had also talked with the music and physical education teachers. They also had some ideas to suggest. Mrs. Retzlaff arranged with the physical education teacher for the children to come to the gymnasium this afternoon to do some work there.

PHYSICAL EDUCATION
TEACHER: I know you have been studying and reading a lot about birds. Who can tell me about some different kinds of birds?

JOHN: Some fly, but some don't fly.

PHYSICAL EDUCATION
TEACHER: That's right. What about some of the birds that don't fly?

KIM: Penguins and chickens.

PHYSICAL EDUCATION
TEACHER: Does a chicken ever fly?

MELANE: Yes. It just goes up, and it comes down again.

PHYSICAL EDUCATION
TEACHER: You mean it doesn't fly very far?

MELANE: Yes.

PHYSICAL EDUCATION
TEACHER: What other birds have you read about?

MARTHA: Thrushes.

KIM: Sea gulls.

PHYSICAL EDUCATION
TEACHER: Does a sea gull do a lot of flapping or gliding?

KIM: Gliding.

PHYSICAL EDUCATION
TEACHER: I'm going to play some music for you. It's very short, and you'll have to listen very carefully. (She plays a brief soaring, swinging

passage.) Do you think you can glide to that music? Let's try it just with your arms.

The physical education teacher talked with them further about other birds, and she played more music. They moved their bodies to the rhythm and feeling of the birds, and the music.

PHYSICAL EDUCATION
TEACHER: You've been very good birds today and I thought you would enjoy flying on the trampoline.

CHILDREN: (Cheers)

PHYSICAL EDUCATION
TEACHER: I thought you'd like that. Let's all go over to the trampoline and stand around the edge, so you can take turns flying.

They spent about half an hour in the gymnasium, and after they had all had a turn on the trampoline, Mrs. Retzlaff and her group returned to their classroom.

MRS. RETZLAFF: That was fun in the gym, and you were all very good birds. Now do you remember we began talking yesterday about some things we might like to do in art?

CHILDREN: Yes.

MRS. RETZLAFF: I know you enjoyed the bird dances we did in the gym, and I wonder. Did that give you any idea for something we might do in art? How did the music make you feel?

KAREN: Nice.

MRS. RETZLAFF: What did the gliding music make you want to do?

JOHN: Kind of float.

MRS. RETZLAFF: It did, didn't it? It had such a nice rhythm, and it was so smooth. Was all the music like that?

CHUCK: No. Some was jumpy.

MRS. RETZLAFF: That's right, Chuck. Some of the music was sharp and jumpy. When you danced, you moved very well to the jumpy rhythm. Chuck, does that give you any idea for something you might do in art?

CHUCK: Well—

MRS. RETZLAFF: Would you like to hear some of that music again? I have the records here, and we can play them on our player.

CHILDREN: Yes.

MRS. RETZLAFF: (She played short parts of several records with gliding, jumping, and swaying passages.) Listen to the different kinds of music— gliding, jumping, swaying—and let's beat the rhythm on our tables.

When you beat and sway, it's almost as if you were making a design.

NANCY: Couldn't we kinda paint like that?

MRS. RETZLAFF: I think you could. What would you try to paint?

KIM: Well, we could make lines and spots.

MRS. RETZLAFF: You could make different kinds of lines. You could make gliding lines and swaying ones, just like the rhythm in the music. What colors do you think you might use?

MELANE: Different ones.

DAVID: Bright colors.

MRS. RETZLAFF: You could combine some bright colors with darker ones. You could make a design like the rhythm you beat on the tables. Would you like to try that today?

CHILDREN: Yes.

MRS. RETZLAFF: All right. We can put our smocks on, and get our paints and brushes. Mike, will you get the paper? I'll play the records again. Let's try the one with the gliding music first.

The paints were in jars on the sink counter in their room. They took their turn ladling the colors into shallow mixing pans, collected their water jars and brushes, and returned to their tables. Mike distributed sheets of 12″ x 18″ manila paper to each table, and they were ready to begin.

184

MRS. RETZLAFF: I'll play the record now, so you can listen to it while you paint. Listen to the glide and sway of the music, and paint what the rhythm tells you to.

They listened to the soaring glide of the music and began to paint. Many of their pictures conveyed the sweep and the mood of the passage. Mrs. Retzlaff played the record a second time, and they worked rapidly.

MRS. RETZLAFF: You are moving to the music, just as you did in the gym. This time you're dancing on the paper.

CHILDREN: (Laughter)

MRS. RETZLAFF: Let's look at some of your pictures. Kim, show us yours. How do you like it?

MARTHA: His glides nice. The spots are like we beat on the table.

MRS. RETZLAFF: That's a good idea. It does look as if Kim combined the music and the beating on the table.

All of you have done real well. Do you want to try another one?

CHILDREN: Yes.

MRS. RETZLAFF: Now I'll play some music that jumps. It hops, just like a bird.

Mrs. Retzlaff played another record, and the children painted again. When they had finished, they talked about some of these pictures, and then they did one more. Altogether, they spent about forty minutes in talking, listening, painting, discussing, and cleaning up. Here is one of the girls in the midst of listening and painting.

The work they thus concluded was more than painting to the accompaniment of music. Through this activity, they brought to a climax the total experience of dancing in the gymnasium and listening to the music. The rhythm was in their bodies, and they transformed it into color and pattern on their papers.

෧෭ ෧෭ ෧෭

185

Classroom Records in the Middle Elementary Grades

A few days later Mrs. Retzlaff arranged for her children to see the movie, *The Loon's Necklace*. They liked the story, and they were fascinated by the beautiful masks of the people and the animals.

MRS. RETZLAFF: Wasn't that a beautiful movie?

CHILDREN: Yes.

MRS. RETZLAFF: What did you like about it?

MELANE: How the loon got his necklace.

MRS. RETZLAFF: That was interesting, wasn't it? What else did you like?

HERBIE: The masks.

MRS. RETZLAFF: Weren't they wonderful? Which ones did you like?

DAVID: All the wolves.

MRS. RETZLAFF: They were ferocious-looking with their sharp teeth. Which other ones did you like?

NANCY: The old man, and the people.

CHUCK: I liked the idiot. He was funny.

MRS. RETZLAFF: He certainly was funny. I thought you'd like that movie. I thought you would get some good ideas for things to do.

KAREN: We can make a bird and attach a little string to the wings, so when you pull the string the wings move.

MRS. RETZLAFF: You mean like a puppet?

KAREN: Yes.

MELANE: That will be too hard.

KAREN: No, it won't. I know how you do it. You make a papier-maché puppet, then you have two strings to the wings and one in the middle, then you pull up and down to make the wings move.

KIM: We can carve birds.

MRS. RETZLAFF: What can you carve it out of?

KIM: You can carve it out of wood, or soap.

MRS. RETZLAFF: That would be interesting. We haven't done any carving yet.

DAVID: Why can't we make a mask like in the movie? Then we can wear them.

186

MRS. RETZLAFF: What do you think of that idea?

MARY: How can we make it?

MRS. RETZLAFF: I know how. We can use paper bags and make some fine bird masks.

MARTHA: Can we paint on them?

MRS. RETZLAFF: Sure you can. You can make the beak and the feathers out of colored paper, and you can paint. Do you think you'd like to do that? Would you like to make a mask of your favorite bird?

CHILDREN: Yes.

MRS. RETZLAFF: All right. I'll see if we have enough paper bags in the storeroom, and if we do, we can work on our masks this afternoon.

When the children returned from lunch that afternoon, Mrs. Retzlaff told them about the bags she had found. There were enough for all of them, and they would be able to make their masks after recess.

After recess they began talking about how they could make their masks.

MRS. RETZLAFF: How are you going to see out of these masks?

JOHN: We can cut holes.

MRS. RETZLAFF: Where?

JOHN: We can put our bags on, and find our eyes, and then draw.

MRS. RETZLAFF: That's a good way to do it. You can make a little mark with a crayon. Then you'll know exactly where to cut the holes.

HERBIE: But how can I make a beak?

MRS. RETZLAFF: You can make it out of paper. You can fold it, or roll it. The beak you will want to make will depend on the kind of bird you are making. How many of you have made papier-maché birds before?

CHILDREN: We did.

MRS. RETZLAFF: Do you remember how you put the head on, and attached different things like the beak, and the wings, and feathers?

I don't think you're listening Nancy—you're not going to know what we're talking about.

And how did you make all the feathers curl around? Do you remember how you cut them and pasted one over the other?

DAVID: Well, we had to do—we had to curl it with our scissors.

MRS. RETZLAFF: That's right. You had to use your scissors. How did you cut the beaks? Do you remember, Kim?

KIM: Well, we cut at an angle, you know, so we could hook it right to the thing.

MIKE: Oh, I know how else you can get it on. You can cut a hole through and then have a little part of the beak stick through and fasten it on there.

MRS. RETZLAFF: You can do it that way if you'd like to. There are several ways you can do it. Do you think you can work on it now?

CHILDREN: Yes.

They went to work with their scissors and paper bags, first fitting the bags to their shoulders, then marking and cutting holes for their eyes and nose. Then they began using the colored construction paper and paste to make beaks, feathers, and other decorations for their masks.

After about twenty minutes of work, Mrs. Retzlaff asked them all to stop and to look at each other's masks and to see how they could help each other with some good ideas. Some of the children made theirs entirely out of construction paper pasted onto the paper bag. Some painted theirs, too. By the end of the afternoon most of the children had finished their work. A few still had some things to do; they would finish when they had free time from other work.

Here is one of the bird masks on the girl who made it.

As part of their study about "Things that Live," Mrs. Retzlaff read many poems about animals to her class. They enjoyed the rhythm of the language and the poetic characterization of the animals.

One day during the following week Mrs. Retzlaff arranged to take her class to the gymnasium, where they would have lots of space. They wanted more space than they had in their classroom so that they could move as the animals do. Mrs. Retzlaff was going to read the poems, while they would act like the animals in the poems.

MRS. RETZLAFF: Let's sit down on the floor. We have lots of space, so spread out with enough space around you. Then you won't bump into each other. I'm going to read the poems for you. Listen to this one.

188

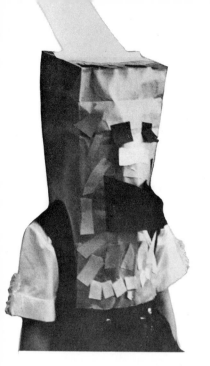

"I saw a proud, mysterious cat,
I saw a proud, mysterious cat,
Too proud to catch a mouse or rat—
Mew, Mew, Mew."

How do you think this proud, mysterious cat walked? How did she move? Would one of you like to show us? Mike, do you want to try?

MIKE: O.K.

MRS. RETZLAFF: I'll read it again, and you walk real proudly like a mysterious cat.

(She reads the poem again and Mike crawls proudly.)

That was wonderful, Mike. Did you see how proudly he held his head, and how mysteriously he walked? Let's all try it while I read it once again.

Mrs. Retzlaff read the poem several times. Some of the children made up other cat-like movements, and they all acted as proudly as they could. Then Mrs. Retzlaff read two other poems. One described how a sea gull curves his wings; the other one was about frogs that jump, caterpillars that hump, worms that wiggle, and bugs that jiggle. While she read aloud, they moved their bodies as if they were all these live things. They spent about twenty-five minutes in this activity, and then they returned to their classroom.

❧   ❧   ❧

As they proceeded with their study during the week that followed, much of their interest and attention turned to fish. They returned their bird books to the library, and borrowed many new ones about undersea life. Again they did much reading, and they divided into committees to investigate the different kinds of fish, undersea plants, and the sand and rocks. They wrote reports on their reading, and shared them with each other.

In talking about what to do in art, they had many different ideas. Some wanted to make a mural showing the depth of the sea, and things that grow in the water. Others wanted to make various fish out of different kinds of materials. After a good deal of discussion they decided they could do both. They agreed that one group could make a mural in chalk of the water and the things in it. The rest of the children could make different kinds of fish. The mural would be long, to fit the cork strip above one of the chalkboards. Then they planned to hang the fish they made in front of the mural so that the fish would move and look as if they were swimming in the water. They spent about an hour one afternoon on the beginning of this project. The next day, before continuing, they reviewed their plans and talked about how to proceed.

HERBIE: I got the sea horse and starfish, and I don't know which to make.

MRS. RETZLAFF: Why don't you make both?

NANCY: I'm making two.

JOHN: I can't find a brush.

MRS. RETZLAFF: Sit down, John, and we'll help you find one.

We need to talk a little bit, so we'll know what we want to do today. What did we get done yesterday?

MARTHA: We got into committees for plants, and sand and—rocks—the sand and rock committee, and the plant committee, and the water committee.

MRS. RETZLAFF: How did you decide what to put in your mural?

NANCY: Well—we looked in our science books and fish books. We saw all these clams and fish. And we thought, if we could put our mural up there (she points to the cork strip above the chalkboard), we could have our fish hanging around it.

MRS. RETZLAFF: That's exactly what you did. Otherwise you wouldn't have known what kinds of committees you needed. How did we decide what to do with the water in the mural?

190

JOHN: Well—mm— the top part, more light gets to it so we made it a light color, and in the middle it's just about half and half, and then near the bottom the water is pitch black down there.

MRS. RETZLAFF: That's right. The deeper the water, the darker it is down below.

How about the plant committee; how did we decide what plants to put in the water?

MARTHA: Well—we drew a sketch.

MRS. RETZLAFF: What about the colors. Martha, can you tell us?

MARTHA: We chose the colors that would go into the mural.

MRS. RETZLAFF: You chose your own colors?

MARTHA: Yes.

MRS. RETZLAFF: What about the coral? John, how did you find out how to draw the coral?

JOHN: I found it in the—my science book, and I found—uh—I forget where I found it.

MRS. RETZLAFF: Did you use any of the pictures we have hanging around the room?

JOHN: Yeh.

MRS. RETZLAFF: Well, I think that the people who are working on the mural can go ahead with their jobs. The rest of us need to talk a little bit more about our fish.

The group divided. Those who had been working on the chalk mural pushed a row of tables together and unrolled their long sheet of paper. They got the chalk from the cupboard, and went to work. The children who were working on the fish came together at the other side of the room with Mrs. Retzlaff.

MRS. RETZLAFF: Have you decided which materials you want to use for your fish?

KIM: Cardboard.

MRS. RETZLAFF: David. What are you going to use?

DAVID: Colored paper.

MRS. RETZLAFF: That ought to be good. Chuck, Karen, what are you going to use?

KAREN: I want the aluminum foil.

191

MRS. RETZLAFF: You're going to have to put it on something stiff, because it isn't strong enough all by itself. What do you think you can use?

KAREN: Cardboard?

MRS. RETZLAFF: That should work. How are you thinking of making your jelly–fish, Melane?

MELANE: Maybe, I was thinking with ribbons and pieces of aluminum.

MRS. RETZLAFF: That's a good idea.

MIKE: I can't hold the wire.

MRS. RETZLAFF: Let me show you how you can bend it around. How are you go–ing to make your octopus?

MIKE: Well—I don't exactly know, but I'm going to shape the body like that (and he gestures with his hand), and have the tentacles hang–ing down.

MRS. RETZLAFF: What are you going to use to shape the body?

MIKE: I don't know.

MRS. RETZLAFF: Don't you have any idea?

MIKE: I know what I'm going to make the tentacles out of.

MRS. RETZLAFF: What?

MIKE: This wire, and paper, and paste.

MRS. RETZLAFF: I'm anxious to see what you make. Chuck, that's a fine sea horse you are making. I think we're all ready to work now.

As all the children went to work, Mrs. Retzlaff answered more of their questions and talked to them individually.

Karen found a piece of corrugated cardboard to use with the aluminum foil. She got the idea of pressing the foil into the cardboard, and she liked the texture it made.

Mike was hard at work on his octopus trying to find a way to put the wire tentacles together.

Monday, Feb 25, 1958

When the children talked about the fish, they remarked how they glisten in the water. One of them found a box of sequins at home and brought them in to use. Here are two of the girls putting sequins on the fish they were making.

This was a complicated project, and they worked on their mural and fish in three long sessions that week. When they were finished, the school custodian came in with a ladder to help them hang the things. He mounted the mural first. Then they showed him where to put thumb tacks into the acoustic block ceiling for strings on which to hang their fish. When the fish were hung, they moved in front of the water. Here is a section of their construction.

Five Days in Mrs. Abele's Fourth Grade

Mrs. Abele is a very calm and sensitive person, who encourages the independent efforts of her children through her warm and attentive attitude toward them. She speaks in a quiet tone with sincerity and ease. The arts are important to her for the attention they direct to the quality and subtleties in the experiences of children. She encourages her children to write beautifully, to dramatize sensitively, and to work in the visual arts imaginatively. She makes all these activities integral parts of her teaching program.

The community in which Mrs. Abele's school is located is the suburb of a large city. All the children come from prosperous professional and business homes. Although on the whole the school building is modern, it was not all built at the same time. The newer rooms are rather spacious; the older ones are cramped.

Mrs. Abele's class is in one of the older rooms. It is crowded; storage space is very poor, and there is no running water. Each child has an individual tilt-top desk with chair attached. These are very comfortable and portable; they are moved frequently. With a class enrollment of thirty-two children in relation to the size of the room, Mrs. Abele must utilize unusual ingenuity, and her children must assume a great deal of responsibility, in order to participate in the variety of art activities they enjoy.

The current unit study in Mrs. Abele's class concerns dinosaurs. In addition, and quite apart from their unit study, they have been working on a marionette project for over a month. Two stories they had read—"Jack

193

and the Beanstalk" and "The Frog Prince"—suggested the characters for their marionettes, and they have constructed them like cloth dolls. A good deal of the work had been done in school. Because their marionettes were complicated and hence very time-consuming to make, some of the work was also done independently at home.

Most of the marionettes were already finished and strung like these.

The children were learning to manipulate the controls.

They were beginning to rehearse their plays; and a few children were still building some necessary props for their stage.

On this particular afternoon, they had several jobs to do: rehearse one of the plays, work on programs, gather information about sound effects, work on props, finish a few puppets, and fix some scenery. They began by planning what each person was going to do.

MRS. ABELE: We need to be sure that everyone has a job this afternoon. But Jack, pounding doesn't work well with planning. They don't seem like things that work well together.

STEVEN: I need some screw eyes.

MRS. ABELE: Could you hold that till we finish planning what we need to do? Is there anyone who isn't clear on what to work on?

PAUL: I got all my work done.

MRS. ABELE: How many ideas have you given us for our program cover designs? You remember we wanted to be able to use several.

PAUL: A couple.

MRS. ABELE: Can you have some more?

PAUL: Mm, I'll try.

MRS. ABELE: Jimmy, how about your doing some reading for us today? We need a lot of suggestions for sound effects and lighting effects. We really need someone to go through these library books for information.

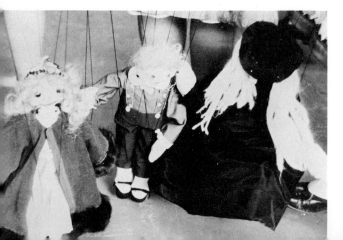

Is there anyone else now who needs to be clearer on some things to do? Good, then we can all go to work on our jobs. Those of you who are not in "The Frog Prince" know what to do. The rest of us can begin our rehearsal. We'd appreciate it if you could be as quiet as possible. I realize that you must do some things, but please do them as quietly as possible.

Now, some of you watched how the other group put their marionettes on the stage the other day. Raymond, you were here last time.

RAYMOND: Yes.

MRS. ABELE: Then you already know some of the things we talked about. The stage hands—what is your job?

BOBBY: Change the scenery, and take care of the curtains.

MRS. ABELE: What were some of the problems you saw the last time?

MARLENE: Keep from getting mixed up.

DAN: We didn't get mixed up. We were wondering which scenery to use.

MRS. ABELE: Maybe we ought to be clear on what scenery we want today. We weren't sure that the witch's cave was going to be finished. If we get on to the garden scene,—we haven't made that scenery yet. Do you suppose we could use just the tree? Roger can you take care of that?

ROGER: Yes.

MRS. ABELE: What else would there need to be in the second scene?

MARY JO: The well.

MRS. ABELE: What else?

CLAUDETTE: The frog.

RICKY: The frog can't fit in the well.

MRS. ABELE: We'll have to think of a way to fix that. The well is too small. What's the princess doing near the well?

CARL: Playing with her ball.

MRS. ABELE: Now, how about the third scene, if we should get that far? Roger?

ROGER: We'll need the furniture.

MRS. ABELE: Do you know the third scene well enough to know where it takes place? Can you help him, Mary Jo?

MARY JO: They are eating their dinner.

MRS. ABELE: Our furniture isn't ready, so we'll have to do without it today. Now, who are the characters in the first scene?

CLAUDETTE: The prince and the witch.

MRS. ABELE: Right. Where is the place or setting, Claudette?

CLAUDETTE: In the witch's home.

MRS. ABELE: All right. Bobby, will you come sit here and help us with our discussion? What's the situation, Bob?

BOBBY: The prince has lost his way.

MRS. ABELE: Let's skip the introduction and begin at the point where the prince comes in. Stephanie, what kind of person is the prince? How is he feeling as the scene begins? How would you feel if you were lost in the woods?

STEPHANIE: Scared.

MRS. ABELE: I think you'll all have to try to get out of your own skin and talk as if you were somebody else.

Now, what are some of the things you need to think about in doing your performance successfully?

MARY JO: We have to talk clearly.

MRS. ABELE: Yes. You have quite a lot to think about. Manipulating the strings is quite a responsibility. The gestures need to mean something. Some children just jiggle the marionettes. Let's try the first two scenes.

The children who were in the first two scenes went backstage with the stagehands. They were ready to project themselves into the puppet characters they had created. The others sat in front with Mrs. Abele to watch the performance. After the two scenes, they all gathered in front again to talk about the way it went.

MRS. ABELE: Now what did you like about the performance?

CARL: The way they talked and gestured with their hands.

MRS. ABELE: Who else liked something about the performance?

MARY JO: The witch had a very good expression.

MRS. ABELE: That was pretty good expression for the first time.

BOBBY: I liked how the witch talked, but I think she overdid it.

MRS. ABELE: You do? Do you think she sounded too much like a witch?

DAN: They talked plainly.

MRS. ABELE: You could understand all the words. Let's think now. How could it be even better?

ROGER: They could hold the marionettes nearer the center.

MRS. ABELE: I believe that would help. Are there any other suggestions? Do you want to try it again?

CHILDREN: Yes.

After they had tried the play again, they talked a while longer about things that went well, and a few things that still needed to be done. The whole class then assessed what they had accomplished that afternoon, and noted the jobs that still needed work.

෧ ෧ ෧

A few days later, Mrs. Abele brought a new book to read to the children.

MRS. ABELE: I have a new book that I want to read to you. I think you'll enjoy it. It's called *Sparkle and Spin,* and it was written by Ann and Paul Rand. It's all about words, and it really helped me think about words.

First of all, I like the dedication. Listen to see if you're included: "To all children who like ice cream."

CHILDREN: (Laughter)

Mrs. Abele read, and then they talked about words in the book that sound like their meaning. They tried out words that make you feel the way they sound. After reading and some discussion, Mrs. Abele asked if they would like to try some oral composing to "paint" some word pictures.

MRS. ABELE: How about clouds? Who can paint them with words?

STEPHANIE: Look at them, pretty and fluffy, and white.

MRS. ABELE: Now that's a good start. Who can sharpen them up?

197

STEVEN: See those clouds fluffy and white, spots of gray here and there?

MRS. ABELE: That's getting better all the time. Let's try thunder. Let us hear what thunder is really like with words.

ROGER: Thunder, thunder rolling around.

MRS. ABELE: Do you remember what we heard in *Sparkle and Spin?* Do you remember how the thunder disappeared? It rolled away, and roared, and thundered.

STEVEN: Thunder, thunder rolling around,
Won't you ever hit the ground?

They tried a few more ideas together for a while, and then Mrs. Abele suggested that they each write something of their own. Here are two things they wrote—a poem and a descriptive paragraph:

"Oh Dinosaur, you are so large
That the earth shakes when you walk.
You could kill at once,
If only you were living."

"Clouds are crawling across the sky—faster, faster, faster! The sky is darkening. A storm is brewing. Thunder is roaring across the earth, and lightning is striking at trees and houses. The rain is falling. Now it is falling down. Suddenly, it is stopped, and everything is quiet once again."

❧   ❧   ❧

The following week they took time out from work on their marionettes. Some of the children had mentioned that they hadn't painted for a long time. One of the children suggested an idea he got from a Dr. Seuss book to make some imaginary pictures. From this they developed the plan of making some very large pictures with imaginary characters. They planned to cut holes in the paper for the faces of the characters; then they would put their own faces through the holes, and act out what the characters have to say. They decided that they would need to work on this project in groups of four, and that each group would make up its own idea. They were going to talk about the ideas for their pictures today, and then they planned to arrange for the materials in order to begin the paintings tomorrow.

MRS. ABELE: Are there some things that you yourself do that would suggest an idea to you? Don't some of you go to dancing school? Do you suppose you could paint about that?

ROGER: We could use story characters.

198

MRS. ABELE: I just heard an idea over here to use story books. That's a good idea.

DAN: We could use some of our own stories and the characters we put in them.

MRS. ABELE: Fine. Some of the characters you have written about might be fun doing. I wonder if you've read some family stories?

MARLENE: I know. The Peterkins.

MRS. ABELE: The Peterkins would make wonderful characters.

CARL: What about Dr. Doolittle?

MRS. ABELE: Dr. Doolittle would be fine. We've been talking about characters from stories, and we've talked about drawing from our own experiences.

JACK: We could do a family from outer space.

MRS. ABELE: Remember now about these characters and how you would want them to look, and how they are going to speak.

MARY JO: Mary Poppins is an idea.

MRS. ABELE: These are all book characters. Does anyone have another kind of an idea?

RICKY: The circus.

MRS. ABELE: Yes. We haven't thought of the circus. Think of all the possibilities.

RICKY: Snake charmer.

STEPHANIE: Family of lions.

MRS. ABELE: A lion tamer, too.

BOBBY: The fat lady.

MRS. ABELE: The fat lady and the thin man. Good. I think we have a lot of good ideas now for you to consider. We can work in our groups for a while to decide what you want to paint about, and then we'll be ready to begin tomorrow when we have our materials. I'll have to get the large sheets of paper for you.

They decided who would work together, and then they moved into their small groups. Among themselves they talked over what idea to choose, and what they would put into it. Some of the children used their notebooks and pencils to sketch their ideas.

The following day they were ready to begin their paintings. Mrs. Abele had prepared large sheets of wrapping paper (36" x 72"), which she cut from the roll in the school storeroom. The children had pushed the desks together to clear as much floor space as possible. They hung four of the sheets over the chalkboards and locker wall with scotch tape. Four of the sheets were spread on the floor. They prepared their paints in shallow pans, and arranged them on cafeteria trays for easy carrying. One boy went out into the hall to fill a bucket with water; they distributed the water into large tin cans. They placed the loaded cafeteria trays and the water cans on the bookcase under the windows until they were ready to paint.

MRS. ABELE: Let's talk over what we need to keep in mind before we begin to work on our paintings. We talked about the ideas yesterday, and I think that all of your groups have already decided what you want to do.

Now, these are all going to be imaginary characters, and that will make your characters look more interesting. Some of your ideas are really humorous, and I think we're all going to enjoy this.

What do you think is the most important thing to try to do in your paintings? What do you think is the most important thing to keep in mind?

CARL: Show how the people are.

MARY JO: Not to make them all real little.

MRS. ABELE: What else?

RICKY: Don't crowd it all in one corner.

MRS. ABELE: You won't be able to do that, because these places where your faces are going to be have already been planned on the sheets. You remember we decided that yesterday. The faces have to be in a certain position to fit the frame we plan to use. Then we'll be able to get behind the pictures to stick our faces through.

I think the most important thing to remember is to figure out a way to put the figures in. If we're going to put the bodies of the characters into the picture, they will have to be rather humorous. They will have to be a little exaggerated. We don't have to worry about having them look exactly as the people do look, because that could spoil the humor.

BOBBY: Blend our colors.

MRS. ABELE: What do you mean by blending colors?

BOBBY: Combine them.

MRS. ABELE: Color combinations are often very personal, and we need to remember that. But, using different amounts of different colors can be very helpful. And you can repeat some of the colors so that they will look well.

Planning is very important in this, and some of us may not get much painting done today. Don't worry about that, and use as much time as you need. Do you think we're ready to start?

CHILDREN: Yes.

The groups went to work, and began to plan their pictures. They decided how to fit the bodies of their characters into the pictures, and they proceeded to sketch the details. By the end of the afternoon work period all the groups had their ideas on the paper, and most of them had begun to paint.

They had a little trouble cleaning up that afternoon, so when they were finished, they talked over some ways to avoid this difficulty.

201

Classroom Records in the Middle Elementary Grades

MRS. ABELE:	You got quite a bit of work done on your pictures today, but we did have some trouble cleaning up. Some of the jobs didn't get done very well. Why do you think that happened?
JIMMY:	We were all mixed up. Everybody didn't have a job.
MRS. ABELE:	I think you're right, but how can we avoid that happening again?
JIMMY:	Make a list of the jobs.
MRS. ABELE:	What are the important clean-up jobs?
JACK:	Wash brushes.
MRS. ABELE:	Yes. What else?
MARLENE:	Sponge the floor.
MRS. ABELE:	That's another thing that needs to be done.
ROGER:	Wash the paint pans.
MRS. ABELE:	Is there anything else? You think that would take care of it? Well, how can we get these things done?
MARLENE:	Make a chart with a committee for each job.
MRS. ABELE:	Do you think that will work?
CHILDREN:	Yes.
MRS. ABELE:	All right. Let's do that, and then let's try to do a careful clean-up job the next time.

They volunteered for their clean-up committees, and when they worked the next time, they did do a careful job of cleaning up. They also completed their paintings in one more work period, and they began to plan their skits to dramatize their ideas. They decided only to plan the ideas and not to write them out. They preferred to give their skits extemporaneously; and they set a date to be ready on the following week.

❧   ❧   ❧

On the day of the performance, all the groups were ready. They had fixed a wooden frame, covered it with corrugated cardboard from a huge carton, cut holes in the cardboard to match the holes in their pictures, and fixed a curtain below to hide their feet. Each group took a turn to mount its picture and give its skit.

Four of the girls painted this picture of mermaids and made up a story about them.

202

"I'm four and a half."

"S'cuse me, she can't talk very well. She's four—"

"And a half, Mommy. I'm older than—"

"And I'm—Oh, oh, who am I, Mommy?"

"Mommy, I'm four and a half, and please talk plainly."

"Honey, why don't you comb your hair? It's so pretty when it's combed."

"You should see little beauty. She swims just like a little swan."

"Oh, mother, I don't mean to interrupt, but I just wish we can find a beautiful treasure chest."

"We might find one at the bottom of this very sea."

"Oh honey, you have found a beautiful treasure."

"And think of it. It's all ours."

"All yours!! I brought up the idea first, so you just haven't any right!"

"Yes, my mother started talking about the subject."

"Well, I found it. It's ours."

"Yes, it's ours."

"It's ours!"

"Let's not argue. Since we both don't have one, let's split it."

Three girls and one boy made the next painting about Mrs. Shorty's Dancing School.

Their skit was brief, but it struck a note with many of the children who attended the local dancing school:

"Good morning, Mrs. Shorty."

"Hello, Shorty."

"What right have you to talk like that? Do all the positions in front of the class."

"Good morning, Mrs. Shorty."

"Good. Let's do all the positions together. One, two, three, four, five. One, two, three, four, five. Good girls. Now let's practice our dance. Music please (music). Not that way, Mr. Clamshell."

"Ha, ha. I can do it better than you can."

"Oh, you pushed me."

"No, I didn't."

"I did."

"Stop arguing, girls, and let's do our dance. Dancing class is over now. You may be excused."

Four Days in Mrs. McParlane's Fourth Grade

Mrs. McParlane is calm, attentive, and deeply interested in her children. Her group is a difficult one, since some of her children are of below average ability, and some are emotionally disturbed. Mrs. McParlane works patiently and supportively to encourage her children to come forth with their ideas. She utilizes the arts as important avenues toward this end. There are twenty-five children enrolled in her class.

The school system in which Mrs. McParlane teaches is located in a small prosperous industrial city adjoining a very large metropolitan center. Her school building, in a comfortable neighborhood, is relatively new, very well planned, and well equipped. Each classroom is bright and spacious with good storage facilities and running water. There is a generous amount of wall space, where things can be hung for exhibit with ease. The

children have individual desks with seats attached. These are comfortable, portable, and of good design. They are arranged in clusters to facilitate classroom discussion and the variety of other activities Mrs. McParlane conducts with her class.

You will recall that Miss Cupelli, who was introduced earlier in this chapter, is the art teacher in Mrs. McParlane's school. The excerpts from the record of activities in Mrs. McParlane's class, therefore, include some of the work Miss Cupelli was doing with her children.

Mrs. McParlane's class has been studying "The Jungle," and the children have been doing much reading to gather information about the people, climate, animals and vegetation.

MRS. MC PARLANE: We've been reading a lot, and writing about the people in the jungle. Can you think of some words that make you think of the jungle?

RANDY: Trees.

MRS. MC PARLANE: Yes. The jungle is full of trees.

KAREN: Vines.

SKIPPY: Viney.

MRS. MC PARLANE: That's good. Can you think of others?

JOAN: Steamy.

MRS. MC PARLANE: Good.

DAN: Thick.

MRS. MC PARLANE: Those words really feel like the jungle. I wonder, now. Do you think we can "paint" some word pictures about the jungle? We've painted pictures with colors. Do you think we can try to paint some with words?

CHILDREN: Yes.

MRS. MC PARLANE: Who can get us started?

JERRY: I see a man with a machete.

MRS. MC PARLANE: That's a good start. Who can paint us a picture of a pygmy? How does he look?

MARY: I can see a little boy that looks real sweaty, because of the hot sun beating down on him.

MRS. MC PARLANE: Real sweaty because of the hot sun. Good. Gary, do you want to add to that?

205

GARY:	Well, I see a boy not much taller than four feet.
MRS. MC PARLANE:	Who else would like to add something?
MIKE:	Well, they have pretty big bellies.
MRS. MC PARLANE:	That's pretty good. Pygmies do have big bellies.

MRS. MC PARLANE: Now let's see whether we can describe what the plants, trees, and vegetation look like. Who can help us paint a word picture about what's growing in the jungle?

SUSAN:	Vines twisting and twirling.
MRS. MC PARLANE:	Vines twisting and twirling. Isn't that a nice picture Susan painted?
BOBBY:	The trees are tall and thick, and the branches are up at the top.
MRS. MC PARLANE:	Jim, can you tell us something about the leaves in the jungle?
JIM:	They use them as plates.
MRS. MC PARLANE:	The pygmies use leaves for a lot of things. Do you remember, we talked about writing different kinds of stories? It can be real, or it can be imaginary. What were some of the ideas we thought about?
JOAN:	We'd move to a jungle.
MRS. MC PARLANE:	Yes. You might imagine you moved to a jungle. What's another possibility?
SKIPPY:	Well, maybe spiders, or snakes.
MIKE:	We can write about the wild animals.
MRS. MC PARLANE:	That's another idea you can use. Do you think you can start your stories now? How many of you think you have a pretty good idea how to get started?
CHILDREN:	Yes.
MRS. MC PARLANE:	O.K. Let's try it.

❧   ❧   ❧

The following day, Miss Cupelli, the art teacher, came in to work with the children. She had already talked to Mrs. McParlane. Consequently, she knew what the children had been doing, and she read some of the stories they had written. Late on the previous afternoon, she had come into the class for just a short while to talk with the children about some possibilities for work in art.

MISS CUPELLI: I enjoyed reading some of your stories about the jungle, and I thought we had some good ideas for some work in art when I talked to you yesterday. Your idea of making some paper sculpture is a good one. Do you still want to do that?

CHILDREN: Yes.

MISS CUPELLI: Have you talked any more to decide on what we can use?

CAMILLE: Colored paper.

MISS CUPELLI: That would be good. We can make paper sculpture with colored construction paper. Tell me some things you know about the pygmies. Can you describe them to me?

DAVID: They have dark skin, and they look real sweaty.

MISS CUPELLI: What else do you know about them?

JOAN: They're short.

BONNIE: Their stomachs are real big.

MISS CUPELLI: What kinds of things do you think you'd like to make today?

BARBARA: Pygmies.

MISS CUPELLI: That would be fine. What else could be possible?

WENDY: We could make leaves and jungle trees.

MISS CUPELLI: Those would be very good.

Now, sculpture stands out. It isn't flat like paper. How do you think we can use the construction paper to make things stand out? Do you have an idea?

JUDY: Fold it.

MISS CUPELLI: Well, you could do that. What else?

KAREN: You could roll it up.

MISS CUPELLI: That could be a good way.

DAVID: Curl it.

MISS CUPELLI: Yes. You can curl the paper, too. All those ways would make the paper stand out. You would need to cut your paper first, and then

207

curl it, or roll it, or fold it. You know, you don't have to do just one of those things. You can use all of those ideas together to make your piece of sculpture. Do you think we're ready?

CHILDREN: Yes.

MISS CUPELLI: Then get your scissors, and I'll get the construction paper and paste. I'll get some scotch tape, too, and the staple machine. They might be useful to put the paper together. Gary and Skippy, would you like to help me?

They got their desks ready, took out their scissors, selected the construction paper in the colors they wanted, and began to work.

While the children worked, Miss Cupelli talked to them individually as they needed help. Through the word pictures they made and the stories they wrote, they had many ideas to draw upon for their paper sculptures. Miss Cupelli helped them with the construction problems.

MISS CUPELLI: Feel your head. That might give you an idea how you could make something stand out. In sculpture things stand out.

Look how Susan is doing the hair on her pygmy. She made hers real short and then curled them just a little bit. See how good it looks. That's one good way to do it. Maybe you can think of some other good ways.

I think you people are making some fine things, and you are thinking of some very good ideas.

They worked on their paper sculptures for about an hour. When most of the children had completed their work, and it was time to clean up, they stopped to talk about what they had accomplished and what they should do next.

MISS CUPELLI: Most of you are about finished now, and the things you've made look real good. The pygmies look nice and fat, as you wanted them to be, and I like the jungle leaves and trees some of you made.

MRS. MC PARLANE: I wonder what we can do with your paper sculptures so that we can all enjoy them? Can you think of anything?

DAVID: We can spread them out on the round table.

MRS. MC PARLANE: We could do that. Can anyone think of something else we can do?

SKIPPY: We can hang them on the wall like a pygmy village.

MISS CUPELLI: What do you think of Skippy's idea? Do you like it?

CHILDREN: Yes.

MRS. MC PARLANE: We could take some of our pictures down, and later in the afternoon when you have some free time, a few of you could hang all your sculptures on the wall and arrange them like a village.

They cleaned up, and spread their paper sculptures on the big round table. In the afternoon, when a few of the children had some free time, they removed their pictures from a wall section and mounted their pygmies and foliage. They added a few huts for their village.

❧   ❧   ❧

During the days that followed, there were a number of developments in Mrs. McParlane's class. She collected several records of jungle folk music with native rhythmic chants. They played these on their record player, and the children enjoyed listening. Some of the boys got the idea of sitting in a circle and swaying to the rhythm, while a few did a dance in the circle. One of the boys brought spoons from home to beat out the rhythm.

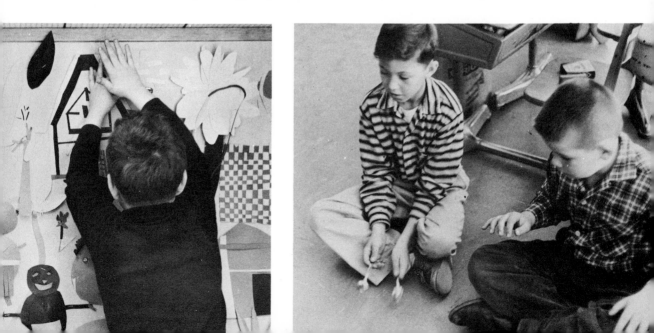

Mrs. McParlane arranged with the music teacher to come in for some work at this time. The music teacher brought a cart loaded with sticks, snare drums, tom toms, and small bongo drums. They listened to the records again, chanted, and orchestrated the rhythms.

In consultation with the physical education teacher, Mrs. McParlane planned a period in the gymnasium. The children gathered on the floor in tribal fashion to talk about the music they had heard and made. Some volunteered to show the physical education teacher their dances. Four of the girls beat a rhythm on the floor, while the teacher helped them put together some slow and quick dance movements.

When they returned to their classroom, Miss Cupelli worked with the group again. They talked about the designs in the rhythm of the music, and the designs in the steps they made up for their dances. The music had loud and soft sounds, fast and slow rhythms. Their dances had slow and quick movements, harsh and delicate ones. As they talked, Miss Cupelli helped them see that designs in art are similar, but different.

MISS CUPELLI: You have been listening to jungle music, and you have been dancing. I wonder. Can you tap on your desk and make a hard sound? Mike, can you?

MIKE: (He raps his desk sharply.)

MISS CUPELLI: Dan, can you make a soft sound?

DAN: (He taps lightly.)

MISS CUPELLI: Now there were loud and soft sounds in the music you heard, but what made the rhythm?

CAMILLE: They repeated.

MISS CUPELLI: They certainly did. But did they just repeat the same way?

WENDY:	Some went faster.
MISS CUPELLI:	Some did go fast, and some went slowly. That's what made the design in the music you heard, and in your dances, too.
	When you make designs in art, do you make them slow or fast?
CHILDREN:	(Laughter)
MISS CUPELLI:	Do you think that's funny?
BONNIE:	They don't move.
MISS CUPELLI:	Well, not in the same way. But how do you make designs in art?
DAVID:	Use bright colors.
MISS CUPELLI:	Wouldn't that be like making music with loud sounds only?
BARBARA:	You combine.
MISS CUPELLI:	Yes. You combine bright and dull colors, or big shapes and little ones, or sharp ones and smooth ones. One sound, or one color doesn't make a design. You have to combine and repeat them. Would you like to make some designs today?
CHILDREN:	Yes.
MISS CUPELLI:	What would you like to use to make your designs? Which materials?
SKIPPY:	Can we use chalk?
MISS CUPELLI:	That would be a very good material, and you can use colored paper if you care to.

The children went to the cupboard for the chalk and paper, and began to work. Miss Cupelli left to go on to another class, and Mrs. McParlane talked to the children as they worked. They spent about another half-hour on this activity before most of them were through.

Those that hadn't yet finished their designs used their free time to do so. By the end of the week, all were done, and most of their designs were hung in the room and in the hall.

❧   ❧   ❧

One morning Mrs. McParlane began the discussion by referring back to the work the children had done with the music, physical education, and art teachers.

MRS. MC PARLANE: This morning, let's talk a little bit about all the work we did in music, gym, and art. I wonder, if you'd listen to some things I'm going to do, and watch me for a minute, whether you'll recognize a pattern or not?

Listen to this. (She claps her hands—first in an erratic rhythm and then in a regular one.) Did you hear a pattern in one of them?

CHILDREN: Yes.

MRS. MC PARLANE: Which one?

CHILDREN: Second.

MRS. MC PARLANE: Why do you think you heard a pattern in that one? Didn't you hear any in the first? What was the difference?

BARBARA: It was arranged.

GARY: The first one wasn't arranged, and the second one was.

KAREN: The first one didn't repeat.

MRS. MC PARLANE: Now watch what I'm going to do. (She walks across the room in a regular three-quarter rhythm, and then she walks back with an irregular sway and erratic rhythm.) Which one had rhythm to it?

CHILDREN: First.

MRS. MC PARLANE: That was quite obvious, wasn't it? Sometimes there is a rhythm or a design, and sometimes there isn't. Then it's jumbled up. That can be true in poetry, or music, or dancing. If we put together a lot of jumbled things, it will just be a jumble. We talked about that the other day.

Let's look at our chalk designs and see how well they are combined and put together. What would you say about this one? (She points to one.)

CAMILLE: The color is repeated.

RANDY: Well, it's organized.

JIM: The lines and shapes are repeated.

MRS. MC PARLANE: I see something else.

DAVID: Well, there are different shapes made out of the lines, and they get smaller and smaller.

MRS. MC PARLANE: Yes. The colors are repeated, but some of the shapes are different.

212

That's what makes it interesting—the combination.

In this way, they continued the discussion for several minutes about many of the designs they had made. This helped to crystallize what they had been experiencing and learning about the integration of rhythm and pattern in a design.

MRS. MC PARLANE: You know we've been doing a great many things, and we've learned a great deal about the jungle people. We've been reading books and writing. We've learned a lot from the music, art, and physical education teachers, and I think you understand a lot about the way jungle people live. I think you have a real good feeling for jungles.

Yesterday when you came back from lunch you felt you wanted to do something, and some of you built an imaginary bonfire and danced around it. And we talked about doing something else together. I don't remember whose idea it was. It was kind of a sharing of everyone's ideas. What did you feel you wanted to do?

RANDY: Paint designs on huts.

MRS. MC PARLANE: Why did you want to do that?

MIKE: The natives do.

MRS. MC PARLANE: Yes. You got that idea from the natives. But there were some of you who didn't want to do that. I think that was Barbara, Wendy, Judy, Mary and Nancy. What would you girls like to do?

NANCY: A mural.

MRS. MC PARLANE: What would you like to show in a mural?

WENDY: We're going to show the green things, huts, people, animals, insects, and trees, and trading post.

MRS. MC PARLANE: Is your mural going to show us what you know about the jungle?

BARBARA: Well, we're going to show how thick it is.

MRS. MC PARLANE: That sounds good. All right now. What is it that we always have a problem with when it comes to drawing and painting? What is your biggest problem?

MARY: We usually paint too small.

MRS. MC PARLANE: I remember Miss Cupelli saying over and over to us: "Fill up the—"

CHILDREN: Page.

213

Classroom Records in the Middle Elementary Grades

MRS. MC PARLANE: Right. I hope we won't see any huts that are one little finger tall and the pygmies just a fingernail tall. We want to see a good-size hut. O.K. I think you have your ideas ready, and as soon as we get back from lunch, we can get started.

When the children returned from lunch, they pushed all the desks together toward the window side of the room to clear as much floor space as possible. They divided themselves into four groups. The five girls were ready to begin their mural. They cut a sheet from the roll of wrapping paper, and took it out to the hall to work. The other three groups were going to paint designs on pygmy huts; they cut their sheets of paper, too. One group mounted theirs over the chalkboard; the second group scotch-taped their sheet over the locker wall; and the third group used the floor. They all began by talking among themselves to decide what things to put in certain places. Then they began to sketch on the paper with chalk.

Here is part of the conversation among the five girls as they began to work on their mural:

BARBARA: We'd better get some trees, and everything in here.

WENDY: I'll make them.

JUDY: But you draw the trees too small.

WENDY: The door on the hut is too small, too.

MARY: It'll have to be a doll house.

NANCY: Hey, you got a good idea.

CHILDREN: (Laughter)

JUDY: Don't you think it'll be too small even for a doll?

WENDY: We'd better make it bigger or it'll spoil the whole mural.

Some such talk went on among the children in all four groups. When they had reached decisions among themselves, they went to work. After about twenty minutes, they had sketched in their basic ideas, and Mrs. McParlane called them together to look at what they had done. Each child had been working on his separate part, and she felt that they should realize the importance of coordinating the parts.

MRS. MC PARLANE: I thought we'd stop to talk about what we've done so far, and to see if there are things we can think of to improve our pictures. Let's look at this one first.

Now I think you should know that these boys decided to paint a

214

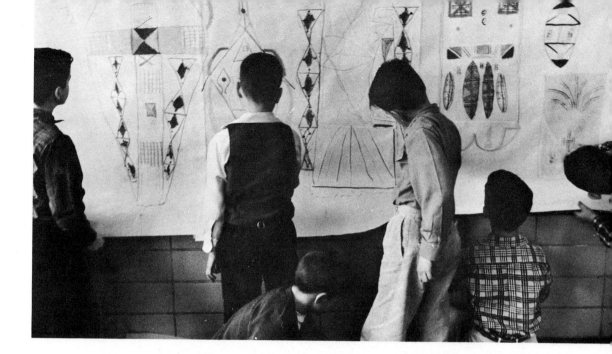

section of the wall only. They just want to make the part with the design. They decided not to include the roof, or door, or windows of the hut.

Now, in the jungle, do you suppose the huts were decorated by one man, or by several men working together?

GARY: Well, in the movie we saw, there were several.

MRS. MC PARLANE: You are right. Several men often worked together. But how did they come out with the design? Let's say there were five men working on it. Were there five separate designs?

RANDY: Well, all together—not the same design but four of one design maybe, and then kind of—if they had lines they'd come like meeting, and they just looked like together.

MRS. MC PARLANE: They'd all be meeting, you say. Then all the five designs you have on your wall should be doing what?

SKIPPY: Joining.

MRS. MC PARLANE: Joining.

JIM: Putting together.

MRS. MC PARLANE: Yes.

JERRY: Join.

MRS. MC PARLANE: Yes. Be joined—be connected together, so that when you are finished, the five parts will look like one connected design. How do you think you can connect them to look as if they belong together and part of one great big thing?

DAVID: Well, you could sort of make other lines that would go onto the other ones.

MRS. MC PARLANE: Have lines connecting? Is that what you mean?

DAVID: They could put other designs in between.

MRS. MC PARLANE: You mean smaller designs in between each of the large designs? Is that what you were thinking about?

DAVID: No. I thought that if you started, you could make triangles, and then kind of put something inside of them.

MRS. MC PARLANE: Are you thinking of a triangle that might be behind part of these designs?

DAVID: Well, just a design—a triangle, and then inside just colored in.

MRS. MC PARLANE: But how would that connect these designs?

DAVID: Well, you can put different shapes in between, and they go together if you arrange them in a certain way.

BONNIE: Colors could connect them together.

MRS. MC PARLANE: Are you boys getting any ideas as we're talking? Before you start working again, I'd like you to talk over this problem among yourselves and decide how you might like to connect your designs.

In this way they talked briefly about all four pictures—how to combine and connect the parts, which parts to make larger or smaller, and what to put into some of the empty spaces. The children were utilizing what they had learned earlier about rhythm and pattern to work with this new problem. After about ten minutes of such discussion in the whole group, they went back to their small groups to decide what they were going to do to their own pictures. This was the conversation among the group of boys whose design was first discussed:

RANDY: Listen. We could do something like this (he points to part of their design) and put it down near here.

JIM: I think we can put triangles and connect them with these (pointing to another part of their design).

SKIPPY: We could make some turn around here, and go over there.

RANDY: We could make some of these over in here.

216

DAVID: Yes, right here—make another one here, and here.

JERRY: Yeah.

DAVID: O.K. Let's begin to do that.

In this manner, they all decided what to do. Then they resumed their work. As soon as they had completed their drawings, they began to paint, and by the end of the work session, a great deal had been accomplished. They spent about two hours on these large pictures during this afternoon. They completed their work at odd times during the following few days.

Here is the design on the wall section by the five boys who started with five separated designs.

Another group painted an entire hut, roof and all.

Here are four stages in the development of the jungle mural by the girls who didn't want to paint a pygmy hut, showing how they worked out the connections among the different parts of their picture.

Four Days in Mrs. Shrosbree's Fourth Grade

Mrs. Shrosbree is a very warm and alert person with a twinkle in her eye. She speaks in a poetic manner, reveals her feelings to her children, and encourages them to express theirs. The sensitivity they thus develop is reflected in their poems and in the work they do in the visual arts. Mrs. Shrosbree has twenty-eight children in her class.

Mrs. Shrosbree teaches in the same school as Mrs. McParlane, and their classrooms are equal in size, equipment, and general convenience. Miss Cupelli works with her children, too, in the same way as she does with all the other classes in the building. The excerpts of the classroom records from Mrs. Shrosbree's class, like the ones from Mrs. McParlane, include Miss Cupelli's work with the children.

The children in Mrs. Shrosbree's class have been studying the north country—Alaska, and the Hudson Bay Region in Canada. They learned how to read a map in order to locate these places. They read about Eskimo life, and discovered that there were sculptors among the Eskimos who carved in whalebone and stone. Miss Cupelli came to their room to talk to them about sculpture. She brought some magazine reproductions of Eskimo sculpture, and mounted these on their bulletin board. She also brought a small Eskimo carving in soapstone of a seal which she borrowed from the local collection. The children fondled the little seal, and they talked about sculpture.

MISS CUPELLI: I knew you'd be interested in seeing the Eskimo sculpture I hung on your bulletin board. Did you get a chance to look through the books and magazines I brought?

CHILDREN: Yes.

MISS CUPELLI: And isn't our little friend the seal just nice to hold in your hands? Did you notice anything about the Eskimo sculptures that you'd like to talk about?

BONNIE: Well, on this one picture—I think it's— and under it, it says made out of soapstone.

MISS CUPELLI: That is soapstone. The Eskimos carve in soapstone. They carve in whalebone, too.

JIM: I say, there was one with an Eskimo and a bear, and the Eskimo

Classroom Records in the Middle Elementary Grades

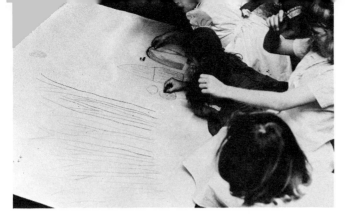

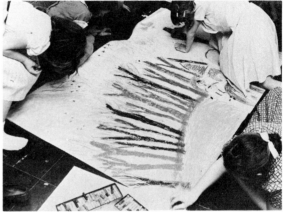

Courtesy of
ction Eskimo Art
Incorporated

had a spear that was right in on the bear.

JANE: Do they use knives in carving them?

MISS CUPELLI: Sometimes. They use knives or files.

DAVID: In that book I saw a man, ah— he sort of was carving out of soapstone with his mouth—sort of like a piece of wood coming across his mouth, then a little long stick, and I think he's filing. He has a little thing across his mouth, then a little stick and he's filing.

MRS. SHROSBREE: Do you remember, we saw that in the Eskimo movie the other day?

DENNIS: Yeah, it was in his mouth. He carves that way.

MARY ANN: He was carving on a face.

MARILYN: I like the fish best, the big fish. What's it made of?

MISS CUPELLI: I think that's stone.

MARILYN: Was it real big?

MISS CUPELLI: I really don't know, but it might be. Some pieces of sculpture are as small as this little seal, and some can be as large as this room. How many of you have seen sculptures that are very big? All sculpture isn't just hand-size like the seal. Have any of you seen any large sculpture?

BILL: Oh, you know the ones about Washington and Lincoln.

MISS CUPELLI: Yes, and they're on the side of a great big mountain.

What is sculpture anyway? We've been using that word. What is it? What makes sculpture different from painting? They're both pieces of art, aren't they? What makes them different?

BONNIE: Well—ah, a painting is, ah— you use a brush and paper—well on a piece of paper. A sculpture is really a rock of some kind.

MISS CUPELLI: All right, that's a very good way of saying it. Now let's see if you can make it a little clearer. Let's have another way of saying the same thing. What is there that's really different about a piece of paper and a piece of sculpture?

DANNY: Well, paint, you can't carve in it or anything.

MISS CUPELLI: Yes, it's a different material. That's true. But there's something else.

220

Classroom Records in the Middle Elementary Grades

ROY: Use a knife?

MISS CUPELLI: You do use a knife, but you use a brush for painting. You use different tools, but what's different about a painting and a sculpture? Bonnie?

BONNIE: With—ah, sculpture you take a knife, you know. You dig in. You know, you carve out. In a painting you just do it on the outside.

MISS CUPELLI: That's a very good thought.

JANE: With paint, you can't get the real shape of it. You can't get it rounded.

MISS CUPELLI: That's it. In a painting, you can't see around it; and one of the most important things about a piece of sculpture is what? What part of your body really helps you see a piece of sculpture?

JEFF: Your hands.

MISS CUPELLI: Yes, your hands, because you have to go around it. And a piece of paper is what?

DANNY: Flat.

MISS CUPELLI: Flat. When you turn a piece of paper over, you can't see the picture because you can't go around it. Sometimes, as in some of our pictures, we feel we could go into it, but we know the picture is flat. Sculpture is round. You move around it, or feel around it, and you want to see all sides of it. To make a good piece of sculpture, you have to do a lot of feeling with your hands.

DAVID: My mother, she gave me a piece of soap. She said it was best soft, so first I washed my hands with it, and then I carved it, and it was real easy.

MISS CUPELLI: Do you think you'd like to do some carving?

CHILDREN: Yes.

MISS CUPELLI: It's very interesting. How many of you have ever carved out of plaster?

JEFF: Oh yeah, yeah. But it didn't look very well after. It dripped a little.

MISS CUPELLI: I don't mean liquid plaster. I mean hunks. You know, like bricks.

JEFF: You mean solid?

MISS CUPELLI: Yes.

ROY: Over at my friend's, his mother, she does a lot of carving and they have balsa wood. My friend and I, we did some, and we bought balsa. We made a real neat totem pole.

MISS CUPELLI: Good. Would you like to carve using some different materials?

CHILDREN: Yes.

MISS CUPELLI: We can mix the plaster and pour it into some milk cartons. Then you can carve it when it gets hard.

Now some of you might have some balsa wood. That would be good to use. Can you think of anything else we could use?

DENNIS: I'm not sure. My mother, she has a creek, and at the side of the creek, it's sort of like a clay, but it's real hard, just about like brick, and she made this great big turkey out of it once, and she broke it up into hunks, and each hunk is about that big (he gestures). I can bring a whole bucket full.

MISS CUPELLI: Well, bring a piece of it, and we'll see whether we can carve in it.

Bill, you told me you know where to get a piece of soapstone. Do you think you can get it?

BILL: Mm, I don't know. I'll try tonight.

MISS CUPELLI: Good, and maybe we can have some soapstone, too. Now, there's something else. We need some tools. How many of you would be able to bring some knives?

CHILDREN: Yes.

MISS CUPELLI: Good. Can some of you bring some files?

BONNIE: I can get some.

MISS CUPELLI: Can you get a chisel?

JEFF: Yes.

MISS CUPELLI: There's another thing. Some of you can bring milk cartons and cottage cheese cartons.

MARY ANN: Glass?

MISS CUPELLI: Just the cartons, not glass. We need something we can tear off, so that we can carve in the block. Now if you can remember to bring all these things by Wednesday, we'll be able to begin to work. What do you think we might be able to carve?

222

Classroom Records in the Middle Elementary Grades

ROY: We could carve a little igloo?

MISS CUPELLI: Would we want to carve an igloo out of soapstone or plaster? What's the purpose of an igloo?

BONNIE: I think we should take a vote on it.

MISS CUPELLI: I don't think that's the kind of thing we'd want to take a vote on, because we need to do some thinking first.

A carving or a piece of sculpture should be something that you want to feel, and touch, and walk around, and look at, and feel real good about. I wonder whether an igloo is that kind of thing? It serves another purpose.

You have some things to think about. You want to think of something that you want to touch and that you want to feel and see around it. So between now and Wednesday try and think of something. It could be a person, or an animal, but it doesn't have to. It can just be something nice to feel.

BONNIE: You mean something that's nothing?

CHILDREN: (Laughter)

MISS CUPELLI: Something that's nothing? Can you explain what you mean, Bonnie?

BONNIE: Well, like you carve, and it's not anything. It's just a—like a, not a picture or anything.

MISS CUPELLI: It isn't anything that has a name?

BONNIE: Yeah, it's nothing.

MISS CUPELLI: Is it nothing?

MRS. SHROSBREE: It would be nice if you would think about the feelings you have, and the things that you love, and the things you want to spend your time with. And then you'll be able to think of something. There's no need to make a sculpture of some things, because if you were going to make them, you'd make the things themselves. And there are other things that you love so much that you can't make, but you get a nice feeling from them. Maybe you could think of something you would enjoy having, and that you would enjoy making. You can also think about the way the Eskimos felt about their carvings. Do you remember the man who bought a beautiful seal carving? What did he say?

223

MARY ANN: He said: "Would you please make me another one." And then the Eskimo said: "Why do you want another one? You see I can do it nicely. Why should I do it over again? I'll make something else."

MRS. SHROSBREE: You think about something that you'd like to make that would really be nice.

❧ ❧ ❧

On Wednesday morning the children were looking at the current issue of the *Weekly Reader* in which they saw a map of the State of Washington. They were interested in maps, because they had learned to read them. They had made maps of the Arctic region in conjunction with their study.

MRS. SHROSBREE: Do you remember when I told you about the trip I took to Seattle, Washington, last summer? When we got to Seattle, we visited some friends. Seattle is a city, and on the map, just a dot shows where it is. Now that city is beside some water. When you look to the east you see a mountain, and when you look toward the west you see another mountain on that peninsula, don't you?

When we were there, we saw those mountains in the distance; and that water was a big beautiful harbor. There were ships in the harbor, and when I see that water on the map, I think about the big harbor and lots of ships in the water.

Now, in the city, from our friends' house, we could look out of the window and see snow-capped mountains. We could see snow-capped mountains if we looked toward the west and if we looked toward the east.

We had already gone through this part of the country, and you remember how I described the Grand Coulee Dam to you? When I look at this map and see where the Grand Coulee Dam is, I remember that great big dam and all that water rushing over it. So, even though this is just a map, it makes me think of a lot of things.

Now, if you use your imagination, you can look at a map and see pictures in it, too. Perhaps you went on a trip to Northern Michigan, for example, and when you look at a map of Michigan, it probably brings back pictures to you, too. You see a dot for a town and you say: "Gee, we went through there and had a good time."

224

And if you were there in the fall, you'd think of the bright colors and the leaves falling. Or maybe if you see the straits of Mackinac you'd say: "I was there."

When I saw this map of Washington in the *Weekly Reader* and I remembered all the things I saw there, I thought that maybe you'd like to make a map. It could be a pretend map. Do you think you'd like to try something like that?

JEFF: What'll it be?

MRS. SHROSBREE: Let's pretend that you are someplace else. Maybe you want to be on an island, and when you get there, you may find many different kinds of things. Think how you could show some of these things on your map to help someone else to use his imagination to think about the same thing. If you feel there are mountains on your island, you can put them on your map; and can you show if they were mountain peaks or if they were rounded?

But, first you'll need to think of a place, wouldn't you? For example, we have a place right here in our room, and you remember we made a map of our room. You remember when we went about making our maps, what did we do?

MARY ANN: Well, we looked at it like we were up in the air.

MRS. SHROSBREE: That's right, we pretended that we were up in the air. Now, to make this map, you're going to have to take yourself from the place where you are, and pretend you are in another place, and take another look, and pretend again. Then it will be easier to make the map, won't it?

DANNY: Does it have to be a place where we've been?

MRS. SHROSBREE: Oh, let's make this our very own place.

BONNIE: A treasure island?

MRS. SHROSBREE: Yes, if you'd like to. You close your eyes and think, and I'll put some paper on your desks. And then, when you're ready to spill it out on the paper—

CHILDREN: (Laughter)

MRS. SHROSBREE: —you can take your crayons and begin to make your map.

Think to yourself because you want this to be all your own. First

225

get a picture in your mind, and then begin to draw it.

BILL: Can I make a fence on the map?

MRS. SHROSBREE: You may make a fence on your map if you want to. Think of all the different things that might happen. It would depend on what your map is about.

While the children thought, Mrs. Shrosbree quietly distributed sheets of 12″ x 18″ manila paper. One by one they took out their crayons and began to work, and within about five minutes all of them were busy.

Several children remembered that symbols were used in making maps, and that a map had a key for the symbols in it. Some of them, therefore, made a key for the pictorial symbols they were putting in their maps.

The children worked at different rates of speed, and in about twenty-five minutes a few of them were almost through.

MRS. SHROSBREE: Some of you are almost through, and some of you still have more work to do. I don't want you to hurry if you need more time.

Those of you who are almost finished have perhaps forgotten something you might want to include. Maybe it's a bay where you're going to land, or maybe it's a peninsula you're going to explore. When you are finished, then stop and take a look. And if you think you're finished, don't put another thing on it. But, if you see something more you want to do, then take care of it before you say you're all done.

Here are two of the imaginary maps they made that morning.

226

Late that afternoon, Miss Cupelli came in to help the children prepare their plaster for carving. She brought with her a cart loaded with sacks of plaster and mixing utensils.

MISS CUPELLI: I brought some materials for carving, and if we take a little time to prepare them now, we can be ready to begin carving tomorrow.

How many people were able to bring wood to carve? (Four children raised their hands.) Good, there are four people who'll be able to carve in wood.

How many people plan to work with plaster? (Eighteen children raised their hands.) O.K. That's eighteen for plaster. Now, did you remember to get milk cartons or cottage cheese cartons?

CHILDREN: Yes.

MISS CUPELLI: Good. We have everything we need. I brought another material called zonolite. It can be mixed with plaster, and it gives the plaster a coarser appearance. It looks very good, and it makes the plaster just a little easier to carve. Some of you who want to work in plaster can mix yours with zonolite, and some of you can mix it just plain.

But first I want to tell you something very important. When you mix plaster, there is one thing you must be very careful about. What happens to plaster when you wet it?

ROY: It gets hard. You can't get it off.

MISS CUPELLI: Yes. It gets like cement. One time we got it in the pipes, and the janitor was real angry. He had to take up I don't know how many feet of pipe, because the plaster hardened in the pipes. So, if you're working with plaster, be careful. No hands with plaster on at the sink. You can shake it off or use a paper towel, and put the towel in the basket. Then wash your hands, and keep the water running so the tiny bit of plaster that's left is washed away. That's all you need to do. Will you remember that?

CHILDREN: Yes.

MISS CUPELLI: O.K. Now, this is how you mix it. You use half of an old volley ball, and it's easy to clean out later. I'm going to show you how to mix one batch, and then you'll do the rest. You put some water in the ball about one-third full, and then you sprinkle the plaster in. Does anyone know how to tell when you've put in enough plaster?

MARILYN: I think when the water begins to cloud up.

MISS CUPELLI: No, it clouds up as soon as you put only a little bit of plaster in.

JANE: When you can't see the water.

MISS CUPELLI: That's almost right. You keep sprinkling the plaster until it makes a whole bunch of little islands on the water that won't disappear. I'll show you how. (She demonstrates, and begins to sprinkle the plaster into the water in the ball.) See the mountain?

CHILDREN: Yes.

MISS CUPELLI: Now you add some of the zonolite and mix it all together with your hands. Then when it's mixed, you pour it into a milk carton to set.

Now, you know how to do it. I'm going to leave you now because I'm sure you can mix your own plaster and fill your boxes.

I want to ask you to do one more thing. I want you to spend some time thinking about an idea for something to carve. If you want to, you can draw right on your piece of wood or block of plaster, and then we'll be ready to carve tomorrow.

Now, those of you who need to mix plaster should choose partners, because it will be easier if two of you work together on this. You can take turns mixing your plaster. By tomorrow I hope you'll be all ready to start your carving.

228

Classroom Records in the Middle Elementary Grades

At the conclusion of this brief discussion and demonstration, Miss Cupelli left. Mrs. Shrosbree then asked the children to choose partners to prepare the plaster. She suggested that they might read or work on their writing while they awaited their turn to mix the plaster.

There were two volley ball halves to use for the mixing, so two pairs of children were able to work at a time. To do the mixing, they held the volley ball halves in basins to avoid spilling the plaster on the table.

Then they poured their plaster into cartons.

Taking turns to prepare the plaster in this manner, it took them about half an hour to complete the mixing job. They planned to tear the cartons off the plaster blocks the next day, and then to begin the carving.

❧　❧　❧

The following day they were anxious to begin the carving. They planned to do so after lunch.

MRS. SHROSBREE: I'm glad you brought plenty of newspapers this morning, because I think we now have about everything we need to begin our carving. You remember when Miss Cupelli was here the other day, we talked about what would be a good thing to carve. You were going to do some more thinking about that. Do you remember we talked about carving something that would feel nice in your hands, and that you'd like to look at? What do you think you'd like to carve?

JANE: A face.

MRS. SHROSBREE: That's a good idea. You could feel the nose, and the eyes, and the ears. Does anyone have another idea?

DENNIS: Just something.

MRS. SHROSBREE: Can you tell us any more about it, Dennis?

DENNIS: Well—ah, just a carving—not a face.

MRS. SHROSBREE: Do you mean something that would just be nice to hold?

DENNIS: Yes.

MRS. SHROSBREE: That would be a fine idea to carve. Did anybody think of carving an animal—maybe a seal, or something else? Nobody?

A face would be very good, and just something nice to hold would be very good, too. Do you think you'd like to start now?

CHILDREN: Yes.

MRS. SHROSBREE: Can anyone tell us how you carve in the plaster?

DAVID: Well, you sort of—it's like you cut, and you dig in.

MRS. SHROSBREE: You can cut, and you can use your knife to scrape. You will want to dig in, too. You remember, a carving is a piece of sculpture, and it's round. It's not flat like a picture, so you can dig into it.

First, let's spread newspapers on our desks. That will make it easy to clean up later. Then you can get your cartons and tear the paper off, and you'll have your blocks to carve in. And you can begin carving as soon as you're ready.

The children cleared their desks and spread several layers of

230

newspaper. They stripped the cartons from the blocks of plaster, and began to work. Some of the children used their pencils first to sketch on the blocks. Many of them began to scratch and cut directly into the material. They worked with intensity and interest. Here is one of the boys carving the plaster with a pocket knife.

One of the boys succeeded in finding a small piece of soapstone; he was carving intently with a knife and a file.

Carving is slow-moving, and they worked for a full hour and a half before any of the children were ready to stop. They then folded the plaster chips into the newspapers, and discarded the waste in the baskets. They needed about seven or eight minutes to clean up and put the room in order for other work. The carvings were stored along the window ledge.

Late that afternoon, Miss Cupelli looked in for just a moment to see what had been accomplished. Some of the children had grasped the feeling of sculptural roundness in their carvings. Quite a few merely scratched lines in their plaster as if they were drawing on paper. Miss Cupelli, therefore, arranged to come in the following day to talk a little more about carving and sculpture.

ⅎ ⅎ ⅎ

231

The next day, when Miss Cupelli arrived, the desks were already covered with newspapers, and the children were just beginning to work. Mrs. Shrosbree had arranged their time so that Miss Cupelli could talk to them as they were beginning to carve again.

MISS CUPELLI: I came into your room yesterday to see what you had done on your carvings. It was late, and you had already gone home. Most of you did a lot of work yesterday. There are quite a few people whose ideas are really good, but some of you seem to be having a little trouble. I thought that before you start today, it would be helpful to talk a little bit more about sculpture.

Let's see how well you remember what we talked about before. What is a sculpture?

JIM: Something you can feel all around.

MISS CUPELLI: Yes, something that feels good all around, and you want to pick up and touch; and something that looks good, too. Do you know, blind people can sometimes do a beautiful job in sculpture. Why do you suppose this is so? What do blind people develop that normal people with eyes sometimes don't?

JANE: Feeling, ah—things.

MISS CUPELLI: Yes. Just by feeling with their hands and fingers they can tell the shape of something. Maybe it would be a good idea to close our eyes as we worked for just a little while. We could feel with our fingers a little bit, and let the shape tell us.

Put your hands on your face for a minute and feel it with your fingers. Your face isn't a shape with holes poked in. Your nose is just like a piece of sculpture, and so are your ears. They come out.

Then, what do you have to do with your plaster?

DAVID: Carve in.

MISS CUPELLI: Can you tell us how?

DAVID: Carve away.

MISS CUPELLI: Good for you. I'm glad you said "carve away." That's very good. And where do you carve away?

DAVID: Around.

MISS CUPELLI: Yes, you carve away all around.

BONNIE: Well, sort of like hafta—I don't know how to explain it. Well, when you've done it, you have to go in deeper. You sort of take your tool or whatever it is, and somehow you cut it.

MISS CUPELLI: I know what you mean, because this is a feeling thing.

BONNIE: I had to do it with mine, because it's sort of like, ah—you can't explain it with your mouth. You have to imagine it, and sort of like—and dig in a little bit deeper to get it.

MISS CUPELLI: Fine, you dig just a little bit deeper. And if you have trouble, you feel with your fingers.

There's one piece of sculpture here that has something very nice about it. Look at Roy's piece. What do you feel like doing when you look at it?

JANE: Laughing.

MISS CUPELLI: Why?

JANE: Because. It's the way the face is made.

MISS CUPELLI: What does it make you feel like?

MARILYN: It makes me feel like I want to touch it.

MISS CUPELLI: Why?

MARILYN: Well, because it has such, mm— it has such roundness.

MISS CUPELLI: What kind of a face do you think this might be?

JEFF: Mm— a happy lazy face.

MISS CUPELLI: Why do you say a happy lazy face?

JEFF: Well, he looks happy, and he looks lazy.

CHILDREN: (Laughter)

MISS CUPELLI: Why do you think he looks lazy?

JEFF: He looks kind of saggy there.

233

Classroom Records in the Middle Elementary Grades

DENNIS: He looks proud.

JANE: He looks kind of jolly.

MISS CUPELLI: This says something to each of us, doesn't it? So Roy's really done something with it. He's made his piece of sculpture talk.

Now I know all of yours will be different, and as you work on them, they'll be fine, too. Somebody said something before that you should remember. She said she wants to touch the sculpture. A good piece of sculpture is something you want to touch, something you want to feel.

Well, you people won't get to work if we keep talking, so let's go.

The children returned to their work with renewed understanding and interest. Roy continued to work on his with sensitivity and feeling.

Bonnie returned to her piece with vigor and determination.

This sculpture activity continued over a period of about two weeks. They worked together only one more time, and then the children worked mostly in their free time carving, filing, and sandpapering their pieces until they felt they were finished. Miss Cupelli dropped in on occasion to look and to comment briefly. Mrs. Shrosbree brought the activity to its conclusion.

Here is Roy's finished piece.

Here is the carving by the boy who found the piece of soapstone.

And this is Dennis's piece of sculpture. He didn't want to carve a face. He's the boy who wanted to make "just a carving."

❧   ❧   ❧

The art activities in the classrooms of these five teachers in the middle elementary grades—Mrs. Brooks, Mrs. Retzlaff, Mrs. Abele, Mrs. McParlane, and Mrs. Shrosbree—were developed as integral components of the total teaching programs. At the same time, there was an accent on the artistic nature of the particular activities. Miss Cupelli, the art teacher, contributed her extensive knowledge of the special field, without once divorcing the arts from the ongoing studies in Mrs. McParlane's and Mrs. Shrosbree's classes. Her teaching of art enriched the learning of the children and the teaching by the two classroom teachers, because she thoughtfully conceived her work within the individual contexts of each of the classes.

The excellent work of these teachers demonstrate some interesting variations and many striking similarities. The things they did and the work of their children are analyzed in the next chapter.

234

ANALYSIS OF

IN THE MIDDLE

The classroom records of the middle elementary grades in the preceding chapter demonstrate how teachers can develop a zest for life and a feeling for adventure. The six teachers whose work was presented taught in their own ways; each of them had developed a style for herself. At the same time, each created the classroom conditions for ideas to come alive for her children.

These teachers did not talk *at* their children; they talked *with* them. They did not just listen to their children; they paid attention to what their children had to say. Although they suggested ideas, the ideas were always broad and open enough for their children to make their own ideas out of them. As the children responded, their reactions were incorporated into the discussions. None of these teachers assigned ideas for the children to accept without encouragement to do something to them.

The general plan these teachers followed was to suggest an idea to the class in order to involve the children in the process of making more

236

CLASSROOM RECORDS ELEMENTARY GRADES

ideas. It was a process of presenting a theme and developing variations. Most often, the teacher proposed the theme; then she and the children created a multitude of variations. Each variation was of particular interest to individual children. It was the point of identification between the child and the idea the teacher had suggested. These variations became the specific focal points from which individual children were able to proceed to develop and express their own ideas.

Yet you surely noticed some important differences in the ways these teachers talked. Mrs. Brooks spoke with high enthusiasm and intensity. She was excited about the circus; her own enthusiasm created excitement in her children. Ideas came to her quickly, and she reacted spontaneously and energetically. Her personality was reflected in her work. Mrs. Retzlaff was no less involved in the work her children were doing, but she was comparatively calm and pensive. Her quiet nature was evident in her discussions. She questioned her children, listened to them, made suggestions, and encouraged them. They knew that it was their own job to make up ideas and to do something with them.

Although the temperaments of these two teachers were different, each helped her children to extend their own thoughts, feelings, and impressions. Each knew that artistic ideas could only come from personal thoughts and feelings. Both encouraged their children to pursue their personal interests, because they knew that personal interests are always prerequisite to personal thoughts and feelings. In their own ways, they created the conditions in their classrooms which encouraged their children to become identified with ideas in order to discover personal purposes for expressing them. Despite differences in their temperaments, Mrs. Brooks and Mrs. Retzlaff taught their children to create their own ideas. Both established a most fertile basis for significant art expression.

When Mrs. Brooks' children sang the song about the circus and composed their dances, they recreated their experiences with a circus. They relived the mood and excitement, and each child achieved a high degree of intimacy with the general theme. Each became able to create his own variation and thus grasp a personal point of interest as impetus for the story writing and art activities to follow. The children thus discovered ideas which they wanted to work on and develop.

When Mrs. Retzlaff's children painted to the rhythm and pattern of the music, they did not just paint to music. They already had listened and danced to the music. They recreated into picture form the gliding, soaring, jerking movements they had personally experienced. They had caught the bird-like feelings of soaring rhythm in their own bodies; they transformed them into their own rhythmic patterns of line and color as they listened over again.

There were other important differences among some of these teachers—Mrs. McParlane and Mrs. Shrosbree worked cooperatively with Miss Cupelli, an art teacher; Mrs. Retzlaff worked closely with her art consultant; Mrs. Brooks taught art independently because assistance from her art consultant was infrequent; and Mrs. Abele worked independently. Each of these teachers had different resources to draw upon. Mrs. Brooks and Mrs. Abele had themselves primarily—their own sensitivity, insight, and knowledge about children and the arts. They had worked in the arts enough to know what was involved in artistic creation. They had learned how to handle art materials, and they had the experience of creating their own ideas. As a result, they were able to help their children to participate in significant art experiences. They knew how to personalize the experiences for their children.

Mrs. Retzlaff, Mrs. McParlane, and Mrs. Shrosbree were no less informed about the arts. They learned a great deal from their consultants,

238

but it was their own knowledge about children and art that enabled them to utilize the assistance of their consultants so effectively.

In reading the classroom records, you were surely impressed by Miss Cupelli's work—her relationship to Mrs. McParlane, Mrs. Shrosbree, and to their two groups of children. She knew what both teachers were talking about with their children; and both teachers knew what she was doing because they participated. That is a major reason why these two teachers were able to continue activities initiated by Miss Cupelli. They were able to carry on their own art activities for the same reason. The three of them taught well because their teaching was truly interdependent.

You noticed also the variations in Miss Cupelli's work in each of the two classes. The ideas were different in each, and so were the art activities. She planned her work in terms of the background and interests in each class. That is why she was able to help the children to create ideas out of their personal experiences, thoughts and feelings. At the same time, her own extended insight into the artistic possibilities of the work in process was continuously evident in the aesthetic accent she provided.

There was one important characteristic in the work of all these teachers. In comparison with the early elementary grade teachers, this group paid more attention to ways in which an art work can be made *qualitatively* better. They helped their children to begin to learn *conscious* ways to improve their work.

These teachers knew how important it is for middle elementary grade children to learn to improve their work. Third- and fourth-grade children have a special desire to learn how to do things better. They want to find out; and they respond to suggestions they can understand.

The growth characteristics of middle elementary grade children provide important clues about their readiness to achieve higher qualitative levels. Their expanding ability for discrimination and control has as great a bearing on their learning in art as it does on other phases of their education. The work of these teachers was based in part on their intimate acquaintance with the developmental characteristics of third- and fourth-grade children. A review of these characteristics will facilitate further analysis of the classroom records.

Major Developmental Achievements of Children in the Middle Elementary Grades

Third- and fourth-grade children are in a period of relatively even and steady growth. The physical development of girls generally forges ahead of that of boys, but they all seem to achieve a plateau of development before their oncoming spurt into pre-adolescence. Their rate of physical growth during these years appears to be slower than it was during the first and second grades; it is also slower than it will be during the fifth and sixth grades.

Their reduced rate of growth is accompanied by important refinements in physical capabilities. Their vision improves, and they achieve almost full ocular maturity. Their eyes become able to focus upon things near and far, large and small. This ability is accompanied by a more refined coordination of large and small muscles; they achieve a greater degree of arm-hand-finger manipulative skill. The combination of visual maturation and extended manipulative skill enables these children to engage in and to enjoy demanding activities.

Children of this age are able to draw and paint with dexterity. Their paintings reveal higher levels of achievement in visual discrimination and manipulative control. They can sew, weave, carve, and cut wood and metal. They love to tinker and to build with a variety of tools and materials. Construction activities which utilize their manipulative skills are a constant challenge and source of interest. This fact was demonstrated in the interest of Mrs. Abele's children in their marionettes, and in the involvement of Mrs. Shrosbree's children in the carving of their sculptures.

Third- and fourth-grade children achieve higher levels of self-awareness; they grow in their capacity for self-evaluation. They want to achieve, and they want to demonstrate their abilities through their own accomplishments. This was evident in the ability of Mrs. Abele's children to solve the problem of cleaning up by recognizing their own deficiency, and by devising their own system of organization.

Most fourth-graders have a tendency toward being perfectionists. Although they want to do things well, they are easily discouraged by undue adult pressure. When their expanding capabilities are sympathetically encouraged, they can develop extended and prolonged interests. The children in all of these classes were able to work on activities for long periods of time, because their teachers helped them establish goals which they could understand and in which they were interested.

The apparent carelessness of third-graders changes toward increasing awareness and responsibility of fourth-graders. The group begins to assume real importance in their lives, and a new level of social consciousness begins to emerge. They develop strong group feelings, but the membership of their groups changes frequently. During this age, most children achieve strong identification with others of the same sex, and they develop close friendships. They take pride in having a "best friend."

Their growing awareness and responsibility to the social group need assistance, guidance, and supervision. As was evident through the help

240

Mrs. McParlane gave to her children, they were able to identify themselves with group activities, interests, and purposes. They were able to evaluate and integrate their individual efforts in order to achieve coordinated designs on their pygmy huts. Mrs. Abele's children demonstrated their identification with the purposes of the group through the suggestions they made in their discussion of how to improve their marionette performance.

In spite of such extended feeling for and understanding of others, children of this age still enjoy teasing others. They still play against others, but they also make increasingly serious efforts to be responsible to others. Fourth-grade children are often outspoken, argumentative, and critical of adults, like the girl in Mrs. Shrosbree's class who proposed that they vote to make an igloo. At the same time, they are responsive to assistance and guidance. They utilize adult assistance, while they seek to assert their own independence. One general manifestation of their desire for recognition and independence is the way these children begin to earn bits of money through odd jobs done for members of their family, neighbors, and friends.

One of the most important achievements during this period is the extended conception of time, place, and people. Whereas the second-grader's awareness of others was largely circumscribed by his immediate environment, children of this age are growing toward an interest in things that happened to people long ago and far away. Events of the past, and life in distant places begin to hold some fascination for third and especially fourth-grade children. The second-grader's "we" world of "me and my mother" changes into an expanding conception of an ongoing world with different kinds of people in various places, both in the past and in the present. This was apparent in the studies of the African jungle in Mrs. McParlane's class, Eskimos in Mrs. Shrosbree's class, and prehistoric animals in Mrs. Abele's class.

The emotional and social achievements of third- and fourth-grade children are integrally interwoven with their intellectual accomplishments. The command of language among most eight-year-olds develops into an active vocabulary of approximately seventy-five hundred words. The stories and poems many of these children wrote, as well as the discussions in all of the classes, show how they made extensive use of adverbs and adjectives. They are growing better able to create a variety of verbal expressions to convey rich meaning.

The insatiable curiosity of second-graders about the "why" and "how" of things changes into a more alert quest for satisfying explanations. Third- and fourth-grade children are eager for information; they seek answers to many and varied questions. Their curiosity is marked by a great desire to find out. This is a period in which children begin to make important strides in developing a variety of skills and understandings. They are able to criticize themselves more meaningfully in order to improve themselves; they show a tendency to utilize sincere and helpful criticism.

Their maturing conception of time, their desire for achievement, and their ability to work on a job over a more extended period of time—all enable them to grow in their capacity to plan the use of their time. They grow in their ability to plan what they hope to accomplish over a period of time. Their plans are sometimes unrealistic, and they often tackle jobs beyond their capabilities; but with assistance, they can project into the future. They can understand some of the problems of time management.

Of utmost significance is their growing ability to perceive relationships. They are becoming more aware of similarities and differences in quantity, size, distance, and speed. They can begin to compare and contrast the present with the past, more important with less important things, big with little things, events that occur in their own environment with things that happened a long time ago or in distant places. When Mrs. Brooks' children were making the large paintings of animals for their menagerie, they understood that the animals needed to occupy the greatest amount of space, because they were most important.

Virtually all of the developmental accomplishments of these children merge into their growing aesthetic sensibilities. They maintain their earlier ability for spontaneous ingenuity and intuitive feeling, but these are now coupled with a growing awareness of their extended environment.

Children of this age extend their grasp of the totality and wholeness of ideas. They pay attention to intriguing details; and they utilize this information to formulate their expressions about people, places, and animals. Mrs. Retzlaff's children talked about the movements of birds and cats, and recreated them through dance and picture. Their awareness of the many things in the world in which they live leads to more discriminating perceptions of the relationships among movements, positions, sizes, and colors of objects and people. They achieve greater capacity to pay simultaneous attention to many parts of an idea with awareness of the interdependency among the parts. Such was the ability of Mrs. McParlane's children when they talked about coordinating the parts of the designs on their pygmy huts.

Their desire to understand more about what is experienced enables these children to direct some conscious attention to improving their aesthetic expressions. They respond to assistance in recognizing some of the qualities of aesthetic relationships. Their eagerness to do things well is reflected in their own work, and in their appreciation of things that others do well in art, music, drama, or playing a game. You saw the children's admiration for Mike, who crawled like a proud mysterious cat in Mrs. Retzlaff's class, and their admiration for Roy, who made the fine carving of the man in plaster in Mrs. Shrosbree's class. The greater aesthetic awareness of these

242

children is coupled with a growing respect for craftsmanship.

Individual differences in interest and ability in all phases of development begin to stand out during these years. The range in reading abilities in any single group becomes greater, and so do differences in capacity to conceive of ideas imaginatively.

As has already been indicated, the classroom records of the middle elementary grade teachers in the preceding chapter reflect these major developmental tendencies and achievements of their children. These achievements are also evident in the art works which the children created.

The Content of the Teachers' Conversations

Insight into the developmental achievements of their children was evident in the things each of the teachers talked about and in the ways they talked about them. Throughout the discussions, these teachers maintained a sensitive balance between the character of the ideas to be expressed, and possible ways of combining parts of a work of art to express the ideas well. They proposed ideas for discussion and work which they knew to be of general interest to children this age. They paid attention to helping their children become aware of specific ways to do their art work well, because they knew this was important for the developmental level and learning of these children.

When Mrs. Abele talked with her children about ideas for their large animated pictures, they not only discussed many variations and possibilities, but they also paid attention to the utilization of the space in their pictures. Many of their ideas were humorous, and Mrs. Abele helped them to see how the placement of the people in their pictures could contribute to the humor. The colors they used were also important, but she was careful to emphasize that color choices are very personal.

When Mrs. Brooks was talking about ideas for the menagerie with her children, she directed their attention to the size of the paper they were going to use. They discussed the importance of using all the space well; she asked them to think about the things they wanted to make large in their pictures in comparison to those that might be small. She emphasized the fact that some ideas are better done on a tall vertical sheet of paper, while others can best be expressed on a horizontal sheet.

This kind of attention to qualities of organization by all of the teachers was done naturally and not formally. Some emphasis was placed on the organization and use of space, size of the forms, and choices of colors. Direct attention was given to the textures and feelings of the paintings and sculptures. These points of emphasis, however, were never imposed through artificial exercises, divorced from the ideas and activities in which the chil-

Analysis of Classroom Records in the Middle Elementary Grades

dren were involved; they were natural corollaries of the activities in process. They were aimed at helping the children to enhance the quality of their art activities—to do the things they wanted to do in better ways.

When Mrs. McParlane talked with her children about how they might connect the parts of their design into one big design, she was helping them to understand how parts of a work of art are joined to make an aesthetic whole. When her children struggled with words to explain how a good design comes together, they were learning to feel, to recognize, and to comprehend the organic relationships within works of art.

When Miss Cupelli talked about sculpture, the children began to realize how sculpture differs from painting. They were able to approach their carving with clearer purpose and greater insight. The explanation of the difference between sculpture and painting was difficult to put into words. As Bonnie said: "You can't explain it with your mouth. You have to imagine it and dig in a little deeper to get it." The feeling created for sculpture through this discussion was reflected in the pieces they carved, because what they discovered in the activity was brought to a level of awareness. They didn't just do things; they were being taught to perceive significance through the things they were doing.

These teachers were able to maintain the essential balance between the character of the idea and the form of expression, because they never lost sight of the quality and spirit of the idea. They maintained the aliveness of the idea because they continuously encouraged their children to become aware of the emotional overtones in their experiences with the idea. They talked about the idea to be sure, but it was more than just talk.

Mrs. Brooks and her children didn't just name and describe information about circus animals; Mrs. Retzlaff's children didn't just enumerate characteristics about birds. In each instance, they directed attention to the feelings involved in the ideas. They talked about important details to capture the spirit of the ideas. The experiences of talking were brought to a feeling level. This is what made the ideas come alive. At the same time, these teachers encouraged their children to consider how to express the ideas artistically. Taken together, these things lead to significant art expressions.

These teachers knew that the arts deal with human feelings; they knew that a work of art is a harmonious and imaginative expression of human feeling. They encouraged their children to feel the ideas, and to pay attention to their feelings in using art materials to express them beautifully.

Although each of these teachers emphasized the feeling quality in the ideas along with ways to make a good work of art, there was a very significant difference among the sources of the ideas which the children used in their art activities. In Mrs. Abele's class, the ideas for art activities had nothing to do with their unit study. Her children were studying prehistoric ani-

Analysis of Classroom Records in the Middle Elementary Grades

mals and the age of the dinosaurs. The ideas for their art activities, however, stemmed from other sources—story books for their marionettes, and the desire to paint for their large animated pictures. In the other four classes, the ideas for art activities came directly from various aspects of their unit studies. This difference, as important as it may be, had no significant effect on the quality of teaching in art, or on the meaningfulness of the art experiences for the children. In each case, the art activities grew out of ideas and desires which were *real and moving interests* for the children.

Good ideas for art activities can stem from many different sources. This fact was as evident in the work of the early elementary grade teachers as it was with this group of teachers. The important question is not the particular source of the idea, but rather the interest and experience children have had with the idea itself. At different times, children are interested in ideas from many different sources. Good teachers capitalize on these interests, and help their children to intensify them by the work they do. To be good, an idea must have at least one essential characteristic: the children must know something about it. *They must have experienced it.* The unit study is a fruitful source for ideas, but it is only one among many which children encounter.

There was another interesting aspect to the work of this group of teachers. You surely noticed that many of the art activities were developed in relation to other forms of expression. In Mrs. Brooks', Mrs. Retzlaff's and Mrs. McParlane's classes, activities in music, dance, and writing were interwoven with art experiences. Ideas and feelings which were brought to life through one form of expression were reflected and developed in another. Each art form was used to achieve sensitive feelings for the content and character of selected ideas. Awareness of such feelings thus enabled these children to raise the expressive quality in the succession of activities they carried through. Mrs. Abele made no direct application of poetry and writing to what her children did in painting. Their attention to the imaginative use of language in poetry, however, had an inevitable effect on their readiness to deal imaginatively with pictorial ideas.

In all these classes, the arts were integral parts of the study program. The art activities were continuous, and they drew as much from the background developed in other studies as they contributed to the conduct of other studies. Art activities were begun as soon as there were ideas to be expressed, and the expression of ideas in art reflected back into the other studies. This was clearly evident in Mrs. McParlane's class with the variety of art activities in relation to their writing, reading, music, dance, and social studies. Art was itself a source of study; it was not merely a culminating activity reserved for the end of a unit study.

Two of these teachers made excellent use of other works of art to help their children deepen their own feeling for and understanding about art. The film, *The Loon's Necklace,* which Mrs. Retzlaff showed to her class, gave the children an opportunity to see the elegant and imaginative masks of animals and people by the Northwest Indians. This was a rich experience at a time when her children were studying things that live. The artistic ingenuity of Mrs. Retzlaff's children was stimulated and deepened through their appreciation of these works of art by others.

The Eskimo soapstone sculpture which Miss Cupelli brought into class, not only created excitement about sculpture, but contributed also toward an understanding and feeling for sculpture. The children fondled the little seal as they passed it from one to another. Their fingers felt the form as their eyes saw it. They experienced sculpture. Their appreciation made their own work in sculpture much more meaningful than it otherwise would have been.

Finally, through the things these teachers did and talked about, it was clear that they knew the difference between significant art activities and other activities which are important, but often mistaken for art. When Mrs. Shrosbree talked with her children about making an imaginative map, she clearly knew the difference between a map which could be an artistic expression, and another which recorded geographical locations. The purposes for each were valuable but different. Understanding the difference herself, she communicated this understanding to her children. They knew that though a dot on a map marked the geographical location of a city, the experience of having been in the city called forth feelings and memories.

If a map is to express feelings, it has to be imaginative. As Mrs. Shrosbree said: "You're going to have to pretend you are in another place." Then you can express your ideas about that place. Such an expression is art.

The Teachers' Use of Classroom Time

These teachers in the middle elementary grades, as did the teachers whose work was recorded and analyzed in the earlier chapters, continued to use time in a regular, yet flexible and functional manner. They subdivided class time to provide effectively for various parts of their programs. In general, time was always planned in terms of a whole week rather than a single day.

Each of these teachers devoted at least three to four hours a week to art activities for their entire class. There was additional time when individual children could work independently after completing other studies. Normally, these classes worked in art about two or three times each week.

Most of the blocks of time for art activities varied from about three-quarters of an hour to an hour and a half in length. The variation was

Analysis of Classroom Records in the Middle Elementary Grades

necessary for two reasons: (1) the nature of the particular activities, and the time required for effective and profitable involvement; and (2) the interest and attention which children in these grades are able to sustain and need in order to achieve what they should through their art experiences.

In addition to these reasons, the physical limitations in Mrs. Brooks' and Mrs. Abele's classrooms caused them to plan blocks of time of about an hour and a half. Because the furniture in Mrs. Brooks' classroom was quite useless for most art activities, all their work was done on the floor. This meant moving the furniture out of the way, and covering the floor with newspapers. It took almost ten minutes to rearrange the room, and another ten minutes to clean up and rearrange things again at the end of the art activity. Thus, a period of an hour and a half gave them an hour and ten minutes for work. They needed this much time for their mask-making and for their large paintings; they needed a whole hour and a half in order to make it worth while to spend twenty minutes of the period for preparation and clean up. While Mrs. Brooks' children were preparing for their circus, they spent three long periods each week on their art activities.

The problem of physical space was somewhat similar in Mrs. Abele's room. To work on their puppet stage, or to paint their large pictures required rearrangement of the furniture, as well as enough time for the activities themselves. Consequently, Mrs. Abele's children spent two long periods a week working in art.

The length of the art periods in Mrs. Retzlaff's, Mrs. McParlane's, and Mrs. Shrosbree's classes was governed by the particular activities in process. When Mrs. Retzlaff's children painted to music, they worked for about three-quarters of an hour. On the days when they were making their undersea mural, they needed a work period of one and one-half hours.

When Miss Cupelli helped Mrs. McParlane's children to make their paper-sculptured pygmies, they worked for an hour. The day they worked on their mural and the designs for the pygmy huts, they needed to move furniture and yet have enough time for the activity; as a result they worked for more than an hour and a half.

The discussion about sculpture in Mrs. Shrosbree's class required half an hour. The imaginary map took almost an hour. On the days when they carved, they spent about an hour and a half in art.

Mrs. Shrosbree even varied the time devoted to art from week to week. When her children became involved in carving, their interest was naturally high, and the activity required several working sessions. That week, they spent over five hours working on their sculptures and talking about them. The following week, they spent less than two hours in art, in order to give more time to their other studies.

Fourth-grade children have the developmental capacity to understand problems of time management. Mrs. Shrosbree's children, therefore, participated in their time planning. They understood that it would be good to take time and stay with their carvings. They also knew that this would mean less art and more time for other studies the following week.

Although these teachers maintained a general balance and proportion between time spent in art in relation to time spent on other studies, there was somewhat less routine than among the teachers in the early elementary grades. Unless their physical facilities dictated otherwise, this group of teachers was able to work within a more flexible time plan because of the developmental achievements of their children. These children were able to participate in the problems of time management because developmentally they were able to understand more about the time required for various accomplishments. As a result, they were able to assume a share of the responsibility for flexible time planning. This enabled the teachers to better use time as an instrument for good teaching.

The Teachers' Use of Classroom Space and Equipment

Workable solutions of the problems of space and materials are crucial to the conduct of significant art activities. Provision is necessary for the kind and variety of activities that children in the middle elementary grades should experience. Each classroom has its physical limitations; and there probably is not a single classroom that does not require some rearrangement in order to be used well for art activities. Desks often need to be rearranged, and even tables sometimes need to be moved.

These teachers created a variety of orderly and efficient ways to solve the important problems of management. Their children were developmentally ready to share the responsibilities for the care of furniture, equipment, and materials; the teachers taught them how to organize their efforts.

On the first day when Mrs. Abele's children worked on their large animated paintings, they had trouble cleaning up, and it took much longer than it should have. The children were as well aware of this as Mrs. Abele, and they were capable of planning a solution to the problem. Mrs. Abele led the discussion, but her children proposed and agreed upon the procedures to solve the problem. They decided to appoint committees to take care of different parts of the clean-up job, and their solution worked.

When Mrs. Brooks' children were ready to work, she asked different groups to take care of moving the furniture, spreading the newspapers, and mixing the paint. When each child had a job to do, the jobs got done swiftly and in orderly fashion. It took them a while to learn how to take care of these things at the beginning of the year, but they were ready to learn how to assume the responsibility.

248

Along with the learning in art, these children also learned how to plan and arrange space, and how to take care of equipment and supplies. They learned to work in an orderly manner, and to share the space and equipment they had at their disposal. When art is taught well, children learn many things *simultaneously*. They learn to create and express ideas through art; and they learn to manage themselves with responsibility. Both go hand in hand. Good teaching produces both.

Even Mrs. McParlane's room needed rearrangement when the children worked on their mural and pygmy huts. Her room was large, and well equipped, but this activity required a great deal of floor and wall space. They moved their desks out of the way to solve the problem.

Mrs. Abele's room was crowded and tiny for the thirty-two children in her class. It was especially small for the particular activities they had in process. When they carried on their regular studies, their desks were arranged in clusters, so that discussion could be relatively easy and comfortable.

Their marionette stage was stored on a table and out of the way in a corner.

When they wanted to use the stage, they pushed some of the desks back and out of the way, pulled the table into the room, spread a curtain across a wire, and arranged a few chairs in theatre style in front of the stage opening. In five minutes, they had rearranged the room and were ready for their marionette rehearsal.

All such changes were possible, because these teachers were thoughtful, flexible, and patient. They knew that space and equipment had to be organized for productive work; and they sought the best possible arrangements. They were aware of the multiple learning values; and they taught their children how to assume responsibility. They were patient with the children as they learned how to follow through.

These teachers knew that thoughtful preparation can make the job easier and more efficient. When Miss Cupelli planned the carving activity for Mrs. Shrosbree's children, she took some precautions. When the children mixed their plaster in the halves of the rubber balls, she was careful to bring large basins in which to hold the balls. She knew that even when children are careful, some plaster might spill over. Spilled plaster was much easier to clean up from the basins than it would have been from the tables or floor. When they carved, they spread newspapers on their desks. It was quick and easy to roll the chips into the paper, and throw the mess out when they were finished.

Rarely was any paint spilled in Mrs. Abele's or Mrs. McParlane's rooms, and the children always had a good choice of colors with which to work. Mrs. Abele prepared her paints in pans, and the pans were kept on small cafeteria trays. They were easy to carry and keep intact.

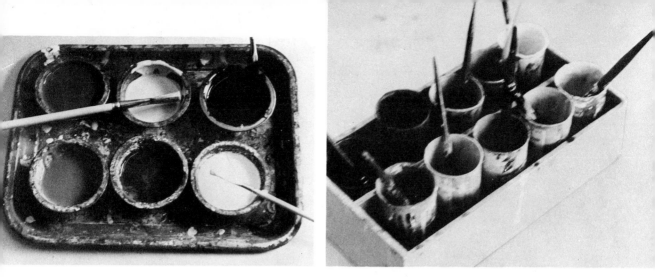

In Mrs. McParlane's school, they collected empty fruit juice tins for paint. The tins were kept in wooden trays, and several children could easily share a group of colors. When they were through, these trays were stacked one on top of another, thereby closing the tops to keep the paint from drying out.

Such simple but ingenious ideas enabled the teachers to provide the children with access to materials and reasonable freedom to work. They were able to choose colors, because colors were available for choice. They were able to mix them, because a group of colors was available at all times. These children learned to paint better, because their teachers provided the combinations of materials when they needed them. Through ingenious yet simple solutions to many practical problems, these teachers contributed an essential element to the effectiveness of their teaching.

The Children's Art Works

Most third- and fourth-grade children have developed beyond the systematic and repetitive symbol-making stage in the way they represent figures of people and animals in their pictures. They have worked through many variations of their basic symbols by enlarging or deleting significant parts. Their general capacity for greater environmental awareness leads them toward more specific attention to the appearance of the things they portray—the way things seem to look.

This increased attention to the way things look takes several forms. The growing awareness of difference in sex is reflected in the pictures these children make; differences in male and female figures are clearly shown. Body parts such as arms and legs are represented with a desire to show their characteristic form. The particular kind of clothing people wear assumes great importance and is indicated with care. And emphasis is placed on selected and significant detail.

In this painting, by a third-grade child, you can see: the clear differentiation between the man and the woman; the attention given to the parts of their bodies—arms, legs and feet; the care to represent the different kinds of clothing—the hat and pants on the man, and the hat and dress on the woman; and the special attention to the design on the fabric of the woman's dress.

In this painting of a fat lady in the circus by one of the children in Mrs. Brooks' class, many of these same characteristics are apparent. Here is the round body of a fat woman with big shapely arms. Her mouth, teeth, and the spotted texture of her dress were details that intrigued this child.

Although it is the general tendency of children of this age to show greater concern for visual appearance, it should be no surprise to find wide differences in developmental achievements among them. The differences in stages of growth which were apparent among the kindergarten and early elementary grade children are just as marked at this age. Not only is this an age in which developmental capacities are refined, but it is also a time when special abilities begin to emerge, and differences in interest and ability among individual children become even greater.

Next for example, are a drawing and a painting by two third-grade children. The child who did the painting of the two figures showed his concern for the sex, body parts, clothing, and detail which is characteristic of this age.

By comparison, the drawing is rather meager, and more reminiscent of the earlier stage of symbolic variation.

In these two animals in the menagerie, made by Mrs. Brooks' children, developmental differences are also apparent, but not to the same extent as in the previous two pictures. The zebra is painted with great attention to the form of the body and legs.

Even though the animal in the other picture is not as maturely painted, notice the attention given to the details of the whiskers, the face, and the decorated blanket.

These differences in ability are natural, and every teacher must recognize them. Good teachers, however, do not merely accept them; they work with children to help them to achieve their maximum potentialities. Although limitations in ability are often the result of limited capacity, just as often they may be caused by limited experience or by inhibitions imposed through past experience. All good teachers, therefore, encourage children to expand their efforts and to surpass their current limitations. This is as true in the study of art as in any other field.

Another important element in the art works of children at this age is their pictorial conception of the environment and the way they depict objects in space, revealed through the relationships they create among objects

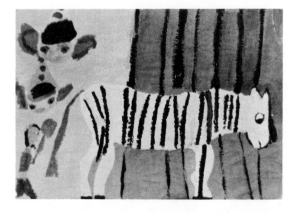

in their pictures. Children in the early elementary grades created base lines upon which to organize the objects that were included. At first, they located people, animals, houses, and trees on the base line; the sky was a line on top, with empty space between. As they began to recognize that objects overlap each other, they began to perceive that space has depth.

Most children in the middle elementary grades have moved beyond dependency on a base line, because they have discovered that objects stand on a surface—a plane—rather than a line. They have discovered that the plane moves back into space. Objects that are far off stand back up on the plane, whereas objects that are near overlap the ones in back and stand on the forward part of the plane. These discoveries are also accompanied by the disappearance of the sky line.

Here is a chalk drawing by one of the children in Mrs. Shrosbree's class made after seeing a film about the mountains of ice in the far north. The overlapping of mountains of ice upon each other and against the sky shows the discovery of the plane and the horizon.

Variations in development which are apparent in the ways children of this age represent people and animals are just as evident in the ways they conceive and depict space in their pictures. Below are two paintings:

The first, by a child in Mrs. McParlane's class of a pygmy village in the jungle, conveys depth in space through the overlapping of huts against trees against sky.

The second shows a tree and a hut standing on a baseline with the sky above and the sun in the corner. The space between sky and ground is not vacant, but there is none of the discovery for representation of depth which is present in the first picture.

Differences among children are not only evident through the ways they convey figures and space, but also in the relative richness or poverty of their ideas. Above are two designs by two other children in Mrs. McParlane's class after they had talked about the rhythm and pattern in African music:

The first is tight, rigid, and meager in thought.

The second, in comparison, conveys a high degree of ease, variation, and interest.

The next pair of crayon drawings show the private treasure islands drawn by two of the children in Mrs. Shrosbree's class. Both are interesting, but the first is more imaginatively conceived in pictorial terms. The child who made it used his crayon richly to achieve interesting variations of texture through differences in pressure.

The second is more limited. Except for the shape of the island in the form of a person, it would be quite devoid of pictorial interest if not for the words the child wrote upon it.

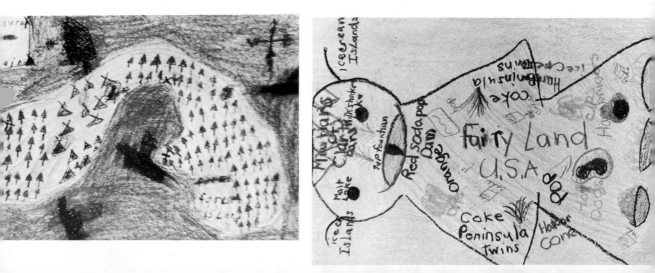

The progress made by children of this age in their ability to perceive relationships is clearly evident in the way they go about making their art works. You will recall from Chapter Five how second-grade children began to work on several parts of their pictures alternatingly and almost simultaneously—that they showed a grasp of their whole idea with many of the parts included when they began a piece of work. This ability to grasp the totality of an idea continues to develop among children in the middle elementary grades. At this age, awareness of the whole idea begins to include greater attention to the size and shape of the paper they use, and the way they use the space. There is the beginning of conscious attention to the way they compose their pictures.

One further element of importance in the art work of these children is the way they use color. The tendency of second-grade children to discriminate differences in color, which you will recall from the discussions in Mrs. Keller's class in Chapter Four, is strengthened and further developed in the middle elementary grades. These children continue to talk in terms of greenish yellow rather than of yellow. They pay attention to the darkness and lightness, and the dullness and brightness of colors; and they use colors which are characteristic of the objects and moods they try to convey. They mix colors to achieve the ones they want.

The general level of development of children in the middle elementary grades and the individual differences among them are reflected in the three-dimensional work they do. The carvings made in Mrs. Shrosbree's class reveal muscular coordination and dexterity. They also show various capacities to discriminate character and detail for the creation and expression of ideas.

Here are pieces of sculpture by four children: The first is something that's nice to hold. This was a "nothing," as some of the children called it in Chapter Six. The boy who made it fondled it as his fingers touched the subtle curves. It felt good to make and to hold.

In the second, this child expressed his grasp of the detailed relationships among the features of the head and face. He used his material with unusual sensitivity to give his idea sculptural roundness.

The third conveys the feeling of sculpture, and is an imaginative expression of the idea the child selected. It is typical of most of the pieces these children produced.

The final one is obviously limited. Except for the form of the nose, the rest of the face was made by scratching the features onto the surface of the plaster, almost as if they were drawn on a piece of paper. Thus this child did not achieve much of the feeling of roundness of sculpture. He was not lacking in physical dexterity, but his ability to conceive his idea in a three-dimensional material was limited.

Summary

During the middle elementary grade period, children refine and extend multiple aspects of their growth and development. They achieve greater awareness of themselves; they begin to comprehend and reach out into an expanding environment; and they are eager to learn. They show discriminating attention to characteristic detail in the figures they draw and paint; their pictures reveal a new level of space perception and interrelationships of objects in space. They arrive at a readiness to pay some conscious attention to the improvement of their work.

Good teachers use these developmental achievements to help children move forward toward new levels of accomplishment. In doing so, however, they remain sensitive to the children's capacity to understand; they do not impose upon them. Although they know that these children want to learn, they are aware that undue pressure can discourage them. Above all, good teachers never lose sight of the fact that the arts deal with moods and feelings. They help their children to attend to some conscious ways of improving their art work, but this attention is never separated from, nor is it ever at the expense of, encouraging personal identification with the ideas the children are trying to create.

Mrs. Brooks, Mrs. Retzlaff, Mrs. Abele, Mrs. McParlane, Mrs. Shrosbree, and Miss Cupelli used their personal abilities, their inner resources, and the facilities of their schools to teach excellently. Each of them encouraged the imagination and sensitivity of their children to create ideas and to express them. These qualities were present in their teaching of art, just as they were part and parcel of everything they taught. Art experiences were continuous for their children, because the spirit of the arts permeated their total programs.

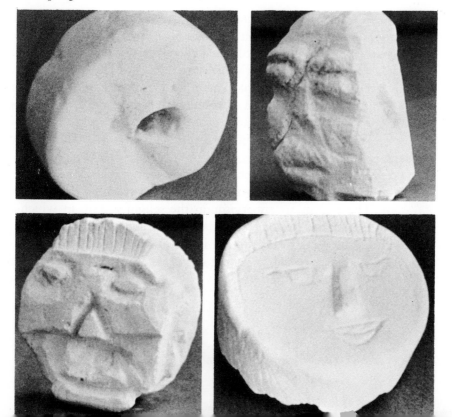

CLASSROOM RECORDS

IN THE UPPER

8

This chapter presents the work of five teachers—one art teacher and four classroom teachers. You already know Miss Cupelli, the art teacher, from Chapters Six and Seven. She is included in this chapter too, because she teaches art to Mrs. Hoyer's fifth-grade class; Mrs. Hoyer and Miss Cupelli teach in the same school. The other three teachers are in different schools. Miss Ellis, like Mrs. Hoyer, teaches the fifth grade. Miss Harrington and Mrs. Williams are sixth-grade teachers.

I'm sure you recall from Chapter Six how Miss Cupelli carried on her work as an art teacher—how she talked with the children, and worked with the teachers in her school. She works with Mrs. Hoyer and her children in a similar manner through frequent teaching and consulting.

There is an art supervisor in the school system in which Miss Ellis teaches, but her responsibilities are many and varied. In addition to the attention she gives to instruction in art in the elementary schools, she also works with the secondary school art teachers. The time she can spend

Classroom Records in the Upper Elementary Grades

ELEMENTARY GRADES

with individual classroom teachers is, therefore, limited, and her visits are infrequent. As a result, she concentrates her efforts on in-service workshops, and on helping those teachers who need it most. Since Miss Ellis teaches art excellently and with confidence, she plans her own teaching of art with complete independence.

There is a travelling art teacher in Miss Harrington's school who visits each of the classes just once a week for a brief period. Miss Harrington considers this inadequate, and because of the background she has been able to develop for herself in art, she has arranged to take full responsibility for the teaching of art to her own class.

Mrs. Williams teaches in the same school system as Mrs. Brooks, whose work you read about in Chapters Six and Seven. You will recall that their art consultant is responsible for assisting the classroom teachers in a very large school district. The time she can spend with individual teachers is consequently very limited, and the contact Mrs. Williams has with her is rather infrequent. As a result, Mrs. Williams is quite independent in her planning and teaching of art.

The abilities and interests of each of these five teachers are reflected in the work they do with their children. Each uses the particular resources she has at hand to develop a program in which the children can create and express ideas. Each teaches to enhance the discriminating judgment of her children, thereby encouraging their development of artistic sensitivity.

Here is some further information about each of these teachers, their schools and communities, together with excerpts from the records of the conduct of activities in their classes.

Five Days in Mrs. Hoyer's Fifth Grade

Mrs. Hoyer is a very sensitive and interesting person who teaches her class in a calm and relaxed manner. She not only believes in the importance of artistic experiences for her children, but she also values them for herself. In visiting her class, it is not unusual to find her involved in an art activity along with her children. She truly enjoys the arts, and sometimes while her children are engrossed in their art work, she makes something of her own. This spirit of working together creates a climate of real adventure in the arts for herself and for all of her children. She has an enrollment of twenty-eight children in her class.

Since Mrs. Hoyer teaches in the same school building with Miss Cupelli, you remember that it is modern, spacious, and well-equipped. It is located in a comfortable section of a small industrial city adjoining a large metropolitan center. Mrs. Hoyer's classroom is very well arranged to facilitate the variety of activities in her program.

The children in Mrs. Hoyer's class have just completed a study of the early New England states. Among other things, they have studied about the arts of that period. Mrs. Hoyer found some magazine reproductions of colonial crafts—silver work, implements, and tools, and the children were fascinated by the beauty and skill with which they were fashioned.

Through conversation around the school, the children had discovered that one of the teachers had a pile of driftwood which they might have in order to do some carving of their own. They could make forms that feel good to hold, and they could sand and polish them with care to bring out the beauty of the wood grain. Mrs. Hoyer joined the children in this activity.

Here are pieces by two of the children in the class.

And then there is the piece Mrs. Hoyer made.

At the conclusion of their study of the New England states, they

260

began a new unit about the southern region of the country. They spent a few days for some general and introductory acquaintance with the South through library work, reading several folk tales, singing some songs of the South with their music teacher, and looking at the documentary film, *The River*. After several days of such general investigation, accompanied by discussion of the material they found, they were ready for more intensive work. They selected a series of topics for study, such as the bayou country of the Mississippi delta, the Southern Highlanders, and the changing South. They organized themselves into committees to carry on their reading, report writing, and art activities in relation to their selected topics.

A group of seven girls selected the bayou country for their work

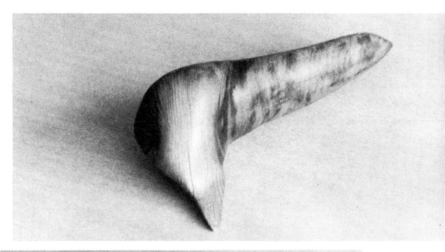

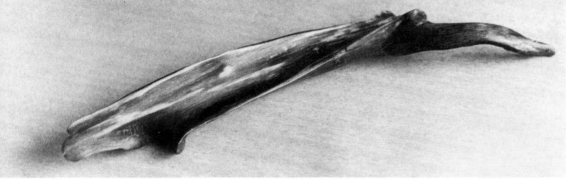

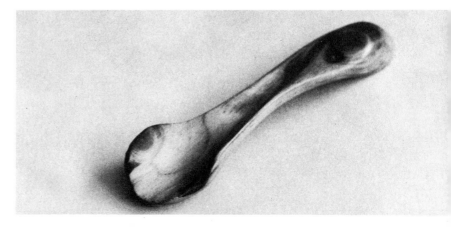

because they were interested in the swamp land—water, insects, and foliage. As they began to carry on their investigation, they decided to use their idea for a large mural painting on a sheet of wrapping paper which was thirty inches wide and about eight feet long.

They worked on their mural in the corridor just outside their classroom. The idea was exciting to them, and they began with enthusiasm. After two days of work, however, they were very displeased. On this particular morning, they had hung their mural on the wall to talk about it, and were engaged in a serious discussion with Mrs. Hoyer.

NANCY: We painted it too much.

SANDY: Well, you see these things (pointing with dissatisfaction to a section of the mural)—

MRS. HOYER: Wait a minute, Sandy. Let's all back up a little, so we can all see it.

JOLINDA: It's too messy.

MRS. HOYER: Well, what don't you like about it?

JOLINDA: The flowers are junky.

KAY: I don't like them.

MRS. HOYER: Well, now, let's slow down and find out what you mean.

JOLINDA: It doesn't look right.

KATHY: We don't think that yellow is good. We don't think that brown— we don't think it looks like really a plant—we don't think there's that many plants at all.

MRS. HOYER: But the plants in the swamp are scrambled all together, aren't they?

SANDY: Did you see those chips of paint (pointing to a spot where some thick paint had chipped off)?

JOLINDA: Look at it!

MRS. HOYER: Look at this part. Doesn't it look like the plants are coming right out of the water?

KAY: That's what we should try to do—more of that.

MRS. HOYER: And don't you like all these different kinds of plants here?

NANCY: No. They're all the same thing. They're too much the same color.

MRS. HOYER: Take a look at this part. Could this be a piece of old wood that had dropped off of a tree?

NANCY: But it isn't.

MRS. HOYER: Could it be?

NANCY: Yeah.

JOLINDA: It's all scratchy.

SANDY: It was all mud. Then we put weeds, flowers. Then we put weeds, mud, weeds, flowers.

MRS. HOYER: Shouldn't some things be on top of other things?

KAY: But we have so much of everything.

MRS. HOYER: What do you think you should do?

KATHY: It's no good. We want to do a new one. Can't we start over again?

NANCY: There's so much paint on it already.

MRS. HOYER: There's one nice thing about this paint. You can paint right on top of it, and change the parts you don't like.

SANDY: But it's cracked too much.

MRS. HOYER: The few cracks don't hurt anything. Take a look at it right now and pick out the parts that look good to you, because there are some parts that are really good.

NANCY: Some of those weeds.

MRS. HOYER: All right, now, is there another part that you like real well?

KATHY: Those weeds over there.

MRS. HOYER: All right. What other part do you like?

JOLINDA: If we're going to make our flowers, we should sketch one first.

KATHY: If everybody will start all over again, that'll make you feel better —get a nice clean sheet of paper and start over again. Now that this is all painted, you can't start over again.

KAY: We know our mistakes, and we know what we want it to be like.

MRS. HOYER: It will be a shame to lose all those nice weeds and swamp.

KATHY: We'll make a new swamp.

MRS. HOYER: What decision are you ready to reach?

SANDY: Well, we're gonna get our—um—and make it what we want it to be.

MRS. HOYER: With a new piece of paper?

CHORUS: Yes.

NANCY: Paint it like you want it, because—

MRS. HOYER: You're going to paint on this some more?

NANCY: No. We're going to start over. We're going to plan a new one. Before, we didn't plan anything. We just painted.

MRS. HOYER: You think you need a little more planning. Well, that's good, but I just hate to think of the time you've spent on this one, and now you're ready to give it up.

JOLINDA: A new one will be better.

MRS. HOYER: If you're ready to settle down, that's O.K. You remember how hastily you went about it yesterday?

SANDY: Don't you worry. It'll be good.

MRS. HOYER: Your idea of making a plan is a good one. Who's going to work on the plan?

CHORUS: All of us.

KAY: Then we'll know what to do in the painting.

KATHY: We can draw with chalk on the old mural.

MRS. HOYER: That's a very good idea.

They quickly went to work with chalk on the old mural making changes and writing notes on it. As soon as they had agreed on the things they wanted to do, they got a new sheet of paper, rolled it out on the floor in the corridor, and went to work again.

In the afternoon on this same day, one of the girls in the group that was studying the Southern Highlands dramatized a story she wrote with the help of one of her friends. Because she had been reading some of the folk tales of the region, she had the idea of making up a tale of her own. With her friend, she painted the scenery, and fixed the costumes.

KAREN: This is a story of my great great grandfather. One day he was coming home late from the fork, and he called to a man: "Henry." Henry said: "O.K. I'll come out to see you." "Henry, you're an old heller." And Henry said: "No, I'm not," and the man went out.

And that night, another man came and said: "Henry, you're an old heller and I'm gonna kill you." Henry said: "No, you're not, because I know your secret." And the man said: "I am," and he ran away.

The next night, another man came, one mile high, half a mile wide. He yelled out: "Henry, you're an old heller, and I've come to kill you." Henry said: "You're not gonna kill me, and I'm not an old heller, and I know your secret, so go away." And the man ran away.

Karen continued her tall tale how more and bigger men came to kill Henry, but he knew their secret. It took her about five minutes to tell the story. Then the class discussed it.

MRS. HOYER: That was very good. Now come sit down while we ask you some questions.

JACK: What do you have in your hair?

KAREN: Powder.

MRS. HOYER: Are there any other questions besides what Karen has in her hair? Are there any questions about the story?

KAY: Where did you find the story?

KAREN: I put it together myself, and Jean helped me.

MRS. HOYER: That was certainly a tall tale you were telling us.

JEFF: How come you kept saying he was an old heller?

KAREN: Because he didn't believe in hell.

MRS. HOYER: Thank you very much, Karen and Jean.

❧   ❧   ❧

Two days later Miss Cupelli came to talk with the children about some other art activities that would be interesting to do. She had already been in the day before to mention a few possibilities, and they were now ready to make some plans.

MISS CUPELLI: Yesterday we talked about a few things you might like to do. Do any of you remember?

JACK: We talked about putting together pictures of the South and make them kind of like a montage.

MISS CUPELLI: Yes, we talked about making a photo montage on the bulletin board with pictures of the South. Some of you were going to bring in some pictures from old magazines. Have you brought them in?

JACK: We have some.

MISS CUPELLI: Good. But we need a few more. There isn't quite enough to work with yet. Will you be able to get more?

JACK: I think so.

MISS CUPELLI:	That will be fine.
MRS. HOYER:	Don't you think it's wise just to start pinning them up to get a look at them, before we try to arrange them?
MISS CUPELLI:	Sure it is. You can pin up the ones you now have, and rearrange them when you collect some more.
MRS. HOYER:	That's what we thought.
MISS CUPELLI:	O.K. Now, what else did we talk about yesterday?
SANDY:	The art of the South.
MISS CUPELLI:	Some of you made some very interesting comments.
JACK:	About patchwork quilts.
MISS CUPELLI:	What about patchwork quilts? Some of you had some very good ideas about them. Why did these people make them? What was their purpose in making them?
NANCY:	For use.
MISS CUPELLI:	Now why did these people have to think about things to use? Why couldn't they just make things because they wanted to make them?
BOBBY:	They don't have a lot of materials like we do.
MISS CUPELLI:	What kind of materials do they have?
BOBBY:	Scraps and left-overs.
MISS CUPELLI:	What other art did they do?
JEFF:	Whittling. They could make a chair and whittle part of it, or a statue.
MISS CUPELLI:	They might, but I don't know that these people made too many statues. Mostly, these people made things to use.
KATHY:	They weave.
MISS CUPELLI:	They did. What kinds of things did they weave? What material did they have a lot of, to weave with?
KATHY:	Cotton.
BOBBY:	Didn't they take dry grass and weave with it?
MISS CUPELLI:	Yes, they wove mats and baskets.
JOLINDA:	They made clay pottery.

MISS CUPELLI: We have some interesting pottery here that was made by the southern mountain people. Look at the way this glaze has been used (spotted running glaze).

KAREN: It makes you feel like you want to touch it.

MRS. HOYER: Did you people get a chance to see this other piece? Look at the way the design is scratched into it.

MISS CUPELLI: I have a movie that you'll enjoy seeing. It's called *The Southern Highlanders*, and it's about the people there. It's very beautiful, and you get a very nice feeling when you watch it. It has some of the crafts in it that you'll want to see. Let's go and look at it now.

In one corner of the school corridor, where there were no windows, there was a permanent screen against the wall, with a projector on a cart. This spot was used by many of the classes in the school to view films. Miss Cupelli, Mrs. Hoyer, and the children went out to see the film. Then they returned to the classroom.

MISS CUPELLI: What impressed you about the film?

KAY: The music. They sang in two parts.

MRS. HOYER: That's right. And do you remember what that man said, that the mountain really wasn't theirs, but it was just there to appreciate? Do you remember his voice when he spoke?

MISS CUPELLI: How many of you noticed the crafts?

NANCY: Chair-making.

KAY: Sewing.

MISS CUPELLI: Was there anything else you might have noticed?

MRS. HOYER: Did you see any kind of craft where they made use of what they had around them? What did they use for some of their weaving?

SANDY: Corn husks.

MRS. HOYER: Yes. They used corn husks in some of their weaving.

MISS CUPELLI: I'm glad you noticed so many things in that film. I knew you'd enjoy it. Now, you need to do some thinking about the things you'd like to make, so that when I come back next time we can begin some work.

During the afternoon, the children continued to work on the

268

Classroom Records in the Upper Elementary Grades

group projects they had in process. The girls who were painting had made considerable progress on their new mural.

KAREN: You couldn't see the lake before, so Sandy made it lighter.

NANCY: It's O.K. now.

KAY: The weeds should curve more. They're too straight.

MRS. HOYER: What else do you want to try to get into it? Is there any movement in the sky, and the clouds?

JOLINDA: Yes. We can make it like it looks.

MRS. HOYER: What are some of the things you can think about, besides what it looks like? You know, our eyes are only part of the story.

KAREN: That gives us a hint.

MRS. HOYER: Could it be anything that you hear? If you look at the picture right now, is there anything you could hear?

KAY: The frogs.

MRS. HOYER: What else?

KATHY: You could smell the flowers.

MRS. HOYER: What would the air smell like in the swamp?

JOLINDA: Moist.

MRS. HOYER: Could you put some of these feelings in the picture? Could you make it feel wet and moist?

Now if you were there, and you looked around, what are some things you would see?

NANCY: Weeds and trees.

KAY: We have only three trees.

SANDY: Vines.

MRS. HOYER: Would you be able to see through them, or would you just see the thickness of the vines in the swamp?

SANDY: All around you, it would be thick.

MRS. HOYER: Now, how are you going to get this to look thicker?

KATHY: We could paint trees back there, and make the weeds taller.

MRS. HOYER: I think I know why you're being so delicate about this. I wonder if maybe you're feeling, that if you paint over something that somebody else has painted, you're taking off her work.

JOLINDA: We're afraid that it will chip off, and we won't like it.

MRS. HOYER: You don't have to worry about that.

SANDY: Yeah, that's what I think.

NANCY: We can make them grow way up there.

MRS. HOYER: Well, now let's see if you can make it really really grow. Ready? Get the colors you want, and find the place you want to work on, and go to work.

In this way, Mrs. Hoyer helped the girls to think deeply and to feel the quality and character of the swamp they wanted to achieve in their mural. While Mrs. Hoyer was talking with the girls, the other groups were busy on their projects. The children who were going to make the photo montage got their work started on the bulletin board.

At the end of this work session, the children in one of the groups took ten minutes to give a puppet play they had been preparing. They had made hand puppets using stockings and odd bits of yarn for the heads. Their play was about a fifth-grade class that was studying the South. Through their puppet characters they talked with the children in the audience, and reviewed some of the things about which they were reading and learning.

❧   ❧   ❧

270

The following day, Miss Cupelli came to help the children begin some new work. She brought a cart loaded with clay ready to use.

MISS CUPELLI: Mrs. Hoyer told me that most of you had decided to work with clay, and a few of you want to make patchwork quilts. I'm going to show you the clay first. There's a very important thing you have to remember about working in clay. The custodian doesn't mind if we use clay, but he minds if we're not careful with it. If you get any clay on the floor, and you walk on it, and it gets dragged into the hall, he knows it. He doesn't even have to ask me who was using clay. So after you get your clay, and you are all set to work, you shouldn't be up on your feet with clay in your hands. Get your material, and sit down at your desks, and work. You'll have to be careful not to go walking around with clay in your hands, because you'll drop pieces on the floor.

Now, how many of you have ever made a pinch pot? (A few children raise their hands.) How many of you have made a coil pot? (A few more raise their hands.) Some of you may have made pots in the third or fourth grades, and I wouldn't want to tell you things you already know.

CAROL: We made some a long time ago.

CHORUS: No.

MISS CUPELLI: Well, since quite a few of you say no, let me show you a few things about clay. When we want to work with it, we have to make sure that there are no air bubbles in the clay before we start, because air holes would make it blow up when we put your pieces in the kiln to be fired. You have to wedge the clay to get all the air bubbles out. You wedge the clay by pounding it carefully, (she demonstrates). You don't smash it like this (she demonstrates).

CHILDREN: (Laughter)

MISS CUPELLI: The idea is to get the air out. You pound it, but you don't make a pancake, because what happens when you fold it over?

BOBBY: You get more air in it.

MISS CUPELLI: Right. You fold the air right into it again. So don't make any pancakes. Just pound it carefully. You'll know when it's ready, because you'll feel the lump getting solid.

Now I'll show you how to do two kinds of pots. Roll a piece of clay into a ball. Be sure its about this consistency. Do you know what that means? This kind of a feeling. (She passes a lump of clay around for the children to feel.) Do you feel how it should be?

CHILDREN: Yes.

MISS CUPELLI: If it's softer and wetter, it's no good, because it's too sticky. If it gets too dry, that's no good either, because it starts to crack. If it doesn't feel like this, then you know that it's not good. Then you roll the clay into a ball.

Now do you remember when we talked about the people in the Southern Highlands, we talked about things they made? What did they have to be able to do with everything they made?

NANCY: Be able to use it.

MISS CUPELLI: Maybe we should think of something we can use.

CAROL: A vase.

MISS CUPELLI: We might. What else?

BOBBY: Ash tray.

KATHY: A candy bowl.

MISS CUPELLI: That's good.

JOLINDA: A statue.

MISS CUPELLI: You could, but what would you use the statue for?

JACK: For a cigarette holder?

MISS CUPELLI:	A statue for a cigarette holder?
KAY:	Weights for papers, or book ends.
MISS CUPELLI:	Can something like that have another kind of purpose? Look at this piece (she holds up a piece of glazed ceramic sculpture). Can this have another kind of purpose?
MRS. HOYER:	I think that's beautiful. What are we using it for right now?
CAROL:	We're all looking at it.
MISS CUPELLI:	Is it important to make something that looks beautiful?
CHILDREN:	Yes.
JEFF:	If you didn't have anything around you, it wouldn't be very nice.
MISS CUPELLI:	You like to look at things like this. It's useful just to look at.
KAREN:	It gives you pleasure.
MRS. HOYER:	Now where else could real pleasure come from in something like this?
KAY:	From making it.
MRS. HOYER:	Making it is such a pleasure, isn't it? If you have a lot of pleasure in doing something, then you feel good about it.
MISS CUPELLI:	And you also get pleasure from looking at it, and feeling it. Then you could make just about anything, and it could be useful. It doesn't have to be a pot.
	Now, if you should decide to make a pinch pot, and you have your ball of clay, put your thumb into it and make a hole, and turn it very delicately. Don't push too hard on it. You have to kind of feel it from both sides—the inside and the outside. If you didn't, what would happen?
CAROL:	It would get bumpy.
MISS CUPELLI:	Yes. It would get uneven, and you would have a weak spot that might break. So, you pinch and squeeze evenly. (She demonstrates.) Pinch and squeeze with one hand, and hold it with your other hand, and keep turning it. You have to feel it all around on the inside and the outside. You can shape it into any kind of form you want.
	Now, I'll show you how to make a coil pot such as the Indians

used to make. Come up a little closer, so you can see what I'm doing. (She demonstrates the rolling of a coil.) You have to move your hands all over from one end to the other to get it even. Then you have to check the ends. Why do you suppose you have to do that?

JACK: For air bubbles.

MISS CUPELLI: Right. Sometimes you can close a whole bubble in there. Then you lay the coil on the bottom of your pot, and work the two pieces together (she demonstrates).

Come up and take a piece of clay now, and you can get started while I talk to the people who are going to make the patchwork quilts.

Through this discussion and demonstration, Miss Cupelli and Mrs. Hoyer did two things alternatingly and simultaneously. They encouraged the children to think of things they would like to make, and to explore their reasons for making them. At the same time, Miss Cupelli demonstrated some of the technical problems in handling the clay. When they were through, the children were ready to go to work.

The children came up and helped themselves to pieces of clay, wedged them at their desks, and went to work on their individual ideas. They worked for about an hour that morning.

Here is one girl who decided to make a piece of sculpture.

The next girl has done a good bit of work on her pinch pot.

This boy wanted to make a patchwork quilt, but he wasn't quite sure how to begin. Mrs. Hoyer sat down to talk with him to help him get started.

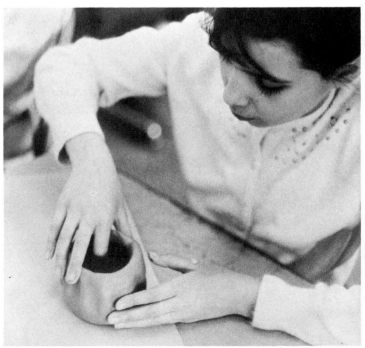

MRS. HOYER: Show me how you are thinking of sewing it together. How would you do it?

JEFF: Well, I'll put the squares together, and sew them onto this (the background).

MRS. HOYER: So all the pieces will be sewn onto this. Is that the idea?

JEFF: Instead of just sewing one, I want to sew a few pieces together first.

MRS. HOYER: That's O.K. But what shapes do you want to cut the pieces into?

JEFF: Triangles.

MRS. HOYER: When you get done, will your quilt be a triangle, or will you put the pieces together into some other shape?

JEFF: I don't know.

MRS. HOYER: How could you get an idea about the shape? Do you start right in with the material and do it?

JEFF: You do it with the material.

MRS. HOYER: You can start whenever you like, and if you'd rather start with the material go right ahead. I just thought that you might like to try the idea with paper triangles first. Then you can see how it will work out before you sew it. But you can do it with the material if you prefer.

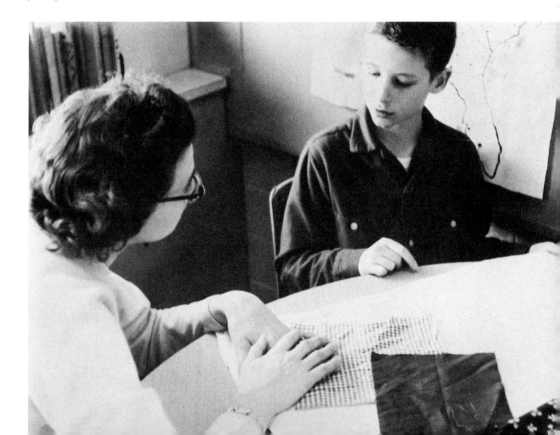

Let's tell the story of "The Changing South" with pictures!

JEFF: I think I'll do it with the material.

At the end of their work period most of the children still needed to finish their pieces. Those who were working with clay covered their pieces with wet paper towels and some pliofilm to keep them soft.

∾ ∾ ∾

The following day, Mrs. Hoyer talked for a few minutes with the children who were making the photo montage. They had collected many more pictures and were continuing to work on their arrangement on the bulletin board.

MRS. HOYER: I thought it would be useful to look at your montage this morning before you did much more to it.

JOHN: We don't like that sign. It's just stuck in the middle.

MRS. HOYER: If you don't like it, then let's take it off.

MARY: I don't think those pictures go together.

MRS. HOYER: Why not?

MARY: They don't fit. We ought to move them around so the same things are together.

MRS. HOYER: Show us what you mean. Move some of them. (Mary moves some of the pictures, and clusters those with similar subjects.) I think you're right, Mary. That's one thing you might do to your montage. Now what else do you see?

BOBBY: I know. We can do like this (and he demonstrates by overlapping some of the pictures).

MRS. HOYER: That helps. You might be able to group them in a more interesting way by overlapping them. What about the colors now, and the dark and light pictures?

276

Classroom Records in the Upper Elementary Grades

JEFF: We need to watch the colors we put together.

MRS. HOYER: Yes. Don't you think some of the pictures might go together better than others because of the colors? And there's another thing. You might watch the textures in the pictures to combine them, too.

Don't be afraid to take pictures off and move them around. Those are a lot of things to keep in mind so your montage won't look scattered.

In this way, Mrs. Hoyer helped these children to become more keenly aware of some of the visual characteristics that could improve the quality of their photo montage. The group went to work, and after half an hour they had made a great deal of progress.

Here is a section of their montage after they had reworked it with greater attention to similarity of subject, color, light and dark, texture, and overlapping of pictures.

The group of girls who had been painting the bayou mural were now finished. They had achieved more of the movement and feeling of the swamp, and they were pleased with their accomplishment.

After several days with short work periods during their free time, the children completed their clay pieces. On the next page are the two pieces you saw earlier, when the children were in the process of making them. The horse's head is spirited; the body of the pinch pot is shaped to give it pleasing form and decoration simultaneously.

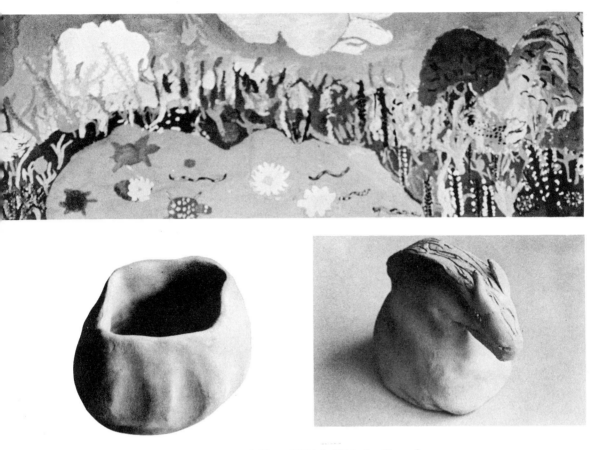

Four Days in Miss Ellis' Fifth Grade

Miss Ellis has uncanny ability to teach very well without talking very much. She is warm toward her children, yet somewhat reserved. She helps them to determine their ideas and to carry on their work; but she expects them to make and to act upon their own decisions. Miss Ellis has wide personal experience in the arts, having done a good deal of work herself with many different art media. She provides a great variety of art experiences for her children.

Miss Ellis' school system is located in a comfortable community bordering on a very large metropolitan center. The children come from professional and business homes.

Although her elementary school building is modern with spacious, well-equipped rooms, the pressure of very heavy enrollment in the district keeps her from enjoying this advantage. Because of insufficient space, her class uses a room in the junior high school building which is located across the street from the elementary school. As a result, she has many difficulties to

278

overcome in conducting a good self-contained classroom program. Her room is small, storage space is limited, and there is no running water. The furniture consists of good portable tilt-top desks with chairs attached. Miss Ellis uses these very effectively to overcome some of the limitations of her room. In addition, there are two long tables which are used for library materials, display, work, and art supplies. Twenty-nine children are enrolled in Miss Ellis' class.

Miss Ellis is talking with her class about the new unit they are beginning to study—"Our Neighbors in Central and South America." They are discussing some of the particular questions they need to investigate, and some of the possibilities they can see for special projects.

MISS ELLIS: Look at the map (Western Hemisphere), and find some of the places you know about; and let's talk a little bit about the way some of these people live. We need to find out some things about the habits of these different peoples. How do you think they dress? What is their climate like? What are their customs? Are the people in these places different from those in the United States?

JAY: Mexico.

MISS ELLIS: The Mexicans would be different. Is there any place else?

BARBARA: South America.

MISS ELLIS: Yes, South America. I wonder why Mexico is different, because it's just right here (pointing to map) and so close to us. Why would it be different?

PEGGY: It's closer to the equator, and I think it's because they had a lot of fighting in Mexico. They used to be pretty powerful, but they got conquered.

MISS ELLIS: Well, maybe you can find out about the history of Mexico. There are things you can read about that.

In this way they commented on some of the brief bits of general information they had about the Latin American countries. By doing so, they were able to identify some of the reading and study they should do. As they continued this discussion their attention shifted to some things they might consider making in art.

MISS ELLIS: Would there be things that we could make? The people in South America and Mexico do a lot of things with handicrafts. Maybe we can make some things, too. Can you think of any things you'd like to do?

VIRGINIA: Weaving.

MISS ELLIS: Yes.

DIANA: We could make serapes.

MISS ELLIS: Yes, you could sew or print on them to decorate them.

PAT: We could make skirts.

MISS ELLIS: What could you put on them?

PAT: We could decorate them with flowers.

MISS ELLIS: That would be good.

JACK: We could make pottery.

MISS ELLIS: That would be a good idea. I have some pictures here of some Mexican pottery. The Mexicans decorate their pottery with interesting designs. When they make a pot, they generally put designs on it going around in stripes. Their pots are of different shapes, and they are made to use for different things. They make water pitchers and bowls.

How many of you would like to make clay pots? (Several children raise their hands.) All right. I'll have to order some clay. I don't believe I have enough clay for everyone who wants to use it, but we can get some more.

They continued their discussion for a few more minutes until they reached some specific decisions for work to do. They decided to spend the next few days getting enough general information to divide into committees to study certain questions and to work on selected projects. They also decided that they wanted to paint some pictures before they started on their special projects.

❧ ❧ ❧

During the next few days, they visited the library and did some intensive reading. They selected their special interests in terms of the countries in Latin America, and divided into committees for more intensive work. In these committees they had begun to plan their study and work projects.

MISS ELLIS: I wonder if some of you people are ready to tell us what you're planning to do for your projects? Jane, can you tell us about some of the people who are studying Mexico?

JANE: Ann and I are going to make some clay pots.

MISS ELLIS: All right. Now, who are the people studying Central America?

280

Jay, what is your group going to do?

JAY: We're reading about the foods in the different countries, and we can make a mural.

MISS ELLIS: That sounds good.

In this way, they talked over a great many of the ideas they had in mind for art activities. They were ready to begin gathering and preparing the art materials they would need.

MISS ELLIS: Now if you are going to need anything from home—some of you people who are going to make serapes—then I think that you had better be planning over the weekend to get your materials to work with. If you have to bring any cloth from home, then be sure to bring it, so you'll have it here next week to start your work.

I don't know how you're planning to design your things, whether you're going to use block printing or whether you're going to sew a design onto it. You need to think about that and decide, so that you can bring your needles and other materials you might need.

DIANA: I've got my cloth. I brought a sheet from home, and it's two yards.

MISS ELLIS: That's fine. Maybe that would be enough for more than one. Would you be willing to share the cloth with someone else?

DIANA: Yes.

LARRY: Well, are you gonna get some clay?

MISS ELLIS: Yes. The clay is already downstairs, and we'll be able to have all we need. But I don't think Friday would be a very good day to work on clay, because if you didn't finish, the clay would get too dry over the weekend. I'm sure that some of you who have worked with clay before remember how the pieces dry out, and then you can't work on them. If we get the clay the first part of next week, then you can work on your pieces more than one day if you want to.

JERRY: Like, if we work on it on one day, we could put a wet cloth over it to keep it soft.

MISS ELLIS: Yes, that way it will keep till the next day. Now for today, you remember you wanted to paint some pictures.

BARBARA: I read about that town in Mexico. There are lots of flowers there. The colors are so beautiful—the different colors, and the rainbow. Well, they wear different colors in their skirts and their blouses.

They've got flowers in their hair. It's so pretty.

JANE: About four hundred years ago they took rafts and planted flowers on the rafts.

MISS ELLIS: And what did the rafts do?

JANE: Well, the branches took root in the water.

MISS ELLIS: Do you know where this is?

JANE: It's in Mexico.

MISS ELLIS: Yes, it is in Mexico, but it's called Xochomilco. Those are the floating gardens. They are very beautiful, and that could be a fine idea to paint.

Do all of you have ideas to paint about? Is there anyone who hasn't any idea?

JERRY: Well, like if I want to make a Mexican with a serape on him, couldn't I just make the serape and have the legs coming out from the bottom? If you're going to draw the whole body, how would you put the serape on him?

MISS ELLIS: Now that's a very good question. Serapes have a split in them to put them over the heads of the people. Maybe you could just make the person's head and feet.

DAN: Can't he make just the serape?

MISS ELLIS: I suppose you could if you'd want to do it that way, but wouldn't it be more interesting with a person wearing the serape?

Now, if you are all ready, would you push your desks back so we can have room to move the paint table out. Let's do this one group at a time.

The children moved their desks, and pulled out the paint table. One boy took a bucket out to the hall and filled it with water. They mixed their paints in small empty milk cartons which they had collected from the school cafeteria, and they went to work. They painted for a little over an hour. Many of the children finished their paintings, but a few completed theirs the following day.

Here is one painting of flowers in the floating gardens at Xochomilco, together with another one of three Mexicans with sombreros and serapes.

෨෧   ෨෧   ෨෧

282

The following week the children began to work on the variety of art activities they had been talking about and planning. Six different activities were in process simultaneously: weaving, ceramics, painting on fabric, sewing, linoleum block printing, and the making of masks. While the children were involved in their individual work, Miss Ellis talked briefly to those who needed help.

MISS ELLIS: (To a boy making a pot) Put your thumb on the inside. Then you can feel if the clay is even or not, and you can work it out.

(To a girl preparing a design for a linoleum block) Work out your idea in black and white. Then you will know which parts to cut out. If you draw just lines, you won't know which parts to cut. When you cut linoleum, the parts you cut won't print and will remain white.

On the next page is one of the girls who is making a serape by painting a design directly onto a piece of fabric.
One of the boys is sewing a design for his serape.
Three of the girls wanted to compose a dance, so they went to the multi-purpose room where they would have more space for their work. When Miss Ellis was able to spare a few minutes, she left the classroom to see how these girls were progressing.

MISS ELLIS: Tell me about the idea you are working on.

JANE: Well, there are Indians and they give the king—mm—what's his name—

PEGGY: Montezuma.

283

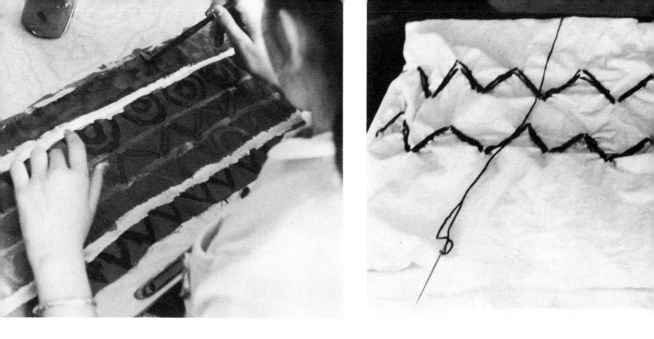

Classroom Records in the Upper Elementary Grades

JANE: He gives Montezuma a gift. So we are the Indians, and we bring Montezuma the gift that Cortez gave us to give him. The Indians were scared, and didn't know what to do, so Cortez gave them presents.

MISS ELLIS: That sounds like a good idea for a dance.

JANE: We'll make a good dance, Miss Ellis.

❧ ❧ ❧

Two days later, they began by talking over their work.

MISS ELLIS: We need to talk a little bit about the work we've been doing, and see if you need any help. If you're having any trouble with your projects, maybe somebody can help you.

KATHLEEN: I can't make a pot.

MISS ELLIS: What kind of pot are you trying to make?

KATHLEEN: Just a dish out of clay. It either gets too big or too small, and the clay cracks.

JACK: I have a suggestion for her. You have to start with a round ball, and then you stick your finger in it, and work it out.

MISS ELLIS: You do have to be careful to see that your clay is moist enough, or it will crack.

JACK: Well, you take a piece of clay, and you make it round. I made it like a ball, and then I put my thumb into it and squeezed it all the way around.

MISS ELLIS: Does that help you any, Kathleen?

KATHLEEN: I'll try that.

MISS ELLIS: Jay, would you like to tell us what you have done?

JAY: Well, I'm making a **serape**, and I have my linoleum blocks all finished, and I'm printing them.

MISS ELLIS: Can you tell us how you're going to do it?

JAY: Well, first thing—first, you have to get two pieces of glass if you want to use two colors. You have to use both pieces, because if you're using red, you can't go over it and mix it with blue.

First of all, you make your block like this (shows his block). You have to make your block and get it cut out, and after that you have to run this (brayer) over it with the ink. You have to put the ink on the glass and then you run it over the block with this roller. Then you print it. I'm not done with it yet, but I've got it started.

MISS ELLIS: It looks very good so far.

In this way, they talked over some of the things the children were doing. Those who needed help asked their questions. Miss Ellis and some of the children made suggestions and tried to help. Then they all went to work again.

Here are three of the things they made:

One girl made this ceramic pot.

Another one of the children made a mask out of construction paper and sequins for their Indian dance.

One of the girls made this block print border on a piece of fabric for a skirt.

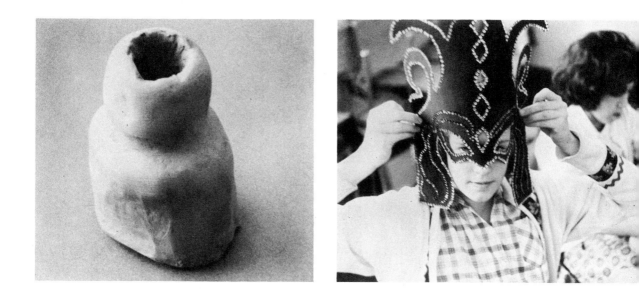

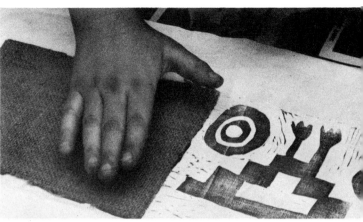

In this series of pictures one of the boys is preparing and printing his linoleum block:

First he developed his design and drew it on the linoleum in preparation for cutting it.

After cutting the block, he spread his fabric on the floor, inked his block, and placed it carefully on the fabric.

To get enough pressure for a good print, he took off his shoes, and stepped on his block.

In this way, he created a repeat design by printing his block a number of times. Here is a section of his fabric.

One of the girls made a huge mask to use in a ceremonial dance.

She started with a very large balloon as the basic form, and covered it carefully with about ten layers of newspaper and paperhanger's wheat paste.

When the paste dried, the layers of paper formed a tough shell, and she was able to cut a hole to pull out the balloon. She trimmed the hole so that it fitted over her head and onto her shoulders.

Then she decorated her mask with colored paper and paint.

Three Days in Miss Harrington's Sixth Grade

Miss Harrington talks to her children in a very friendly and sympathetic manner. She encourages them in their art activities, and brings to them a wealth of background material to enhance their own ability for judging how to improve the quality of their own work. Painting is one of her special interests. She has developed a fine collection of reproductions of works of art which plays an important role in her teaching.

In general, Miss Harrington's classroom program is relatively formal. And yet, her teaching of art has a spirit of adventure and imagination. The activities she provides are varied, and the discussions are stimulating. The children enjoy the frequent and regular opportunities for participation.

Miss Harrington's school is located in a comfortable but modest residential neighborhood of a small city. Most of the children come from business and professional homes. The building is modern; the classrooms are spacious and well equipped.

Miss Harrington's room is bright, large, and comfortable. Adjoining the main part of the classroom, there is a large alcove for special projects with good counter space, adequate storage, and a sink. The furniture consists of individual tilt-top desks with chairs attached. There are thirty-one children enrolled in Miss Harrington's class.

Miss Harrington's children often use their art materials to make charts, diagrams, or illustrations of some of their social studies, but they do not consider these to be art activities. Art to them means painting personal pictures, making pottery and pieces of sculpture, or making an occasional mural.

Here is a section of a mural on which a group of children are working. They are using colored paper and paint, and they call it "The Avenue at Easter Time."

MISS HARRINGTON:	Let's look at our mural and decide on some of the things we still need to do to it.
JAN:	It needs more people.
MISS HARRINGTON:	Some of you already mentioned that to me. It does need more people.
MIKE:	More houses.
MISS HARRINGTON:	Yes, we might put more houses into it.
KATHY:	We could put more cars in it.
MISS HARRINGTON:	The other day, you thought you had all the cars you needed. Do you want to change your mind about that?
JACK:	We don't want more cars than people.
MISS HARRINGTON:	Well, don't you think we can decide about the cars after you put more people into it?
PAT:	We need more trees over near that red building.
MISS HARRINGTON:	We could have more trees if we'd want them.
JACK:	The train siding.
MISS HARRINGTON:	You talked about that before. Where do you think there is a good spot for the train?
JACK:	Right near this building.
MISS HARRINGTON:	I think that's a good idea. It would fill that empty space. Would you like to work on that, Jack? It was your idea.
JACK:	Sure.
KATHY:	A flower stand would be good.
MISS HARRINGTON:	That's a good idea. Where would you put that?
KATHY:	Right there on the street.
MISS HARRINGTON:	Yes, I think you could. Kathy, could you do that alone, or would you want someone to help you?
KATHY:	Jan can help me.

In this way they talked over their mural and decided what needed to be done and who should work on the various parts. When each of the children knew what he wanted to do, they went to work. Each knew where he intended to place the person, car, train, or flower stand he was going to

Classroom Records in the Upper Elementary Grades

make, and he made it of a size to fit. They cut the forms out of colored construction paper, painted them, and tried them on the mural. Sometimes they discovered that they needed to change the position of some of the objects, or repaint others in order for all the pieces to fit together well. Then they pasted them in position.

As they worked, Miss Harrington circulated among them answering questions and offering suggestions.

MISS HARRINGTON: When you get your part painted, try it out, and if it fits then paste it on. That way we can all keep seeing the whole thing as it's coming along.

CHRIS: We need a policeman.

MISS HARRINGTON: Oh, we forgot about a policeman. Of course, we need one. Would you like to make a policeman for us, Chris?

CHRIS: I'll do it.

As their work period came to a close, they had just about finished their mural. They were quite pleased, although they still had a few little things to do to it in their free time.

Before going to lunch, they talked briefly about wanting to do something in sculpture. Miss Harrington suggested a particular material, and they thought they would be interested in using it. She explained how they could use aluminum foil as a base for asbestos powder and paste. They decided that each person should bring a piece of aluminum foil from home.

     🙝   🙝   🙝

Two days later they were ready to begin their sculpture.

MISS HARRINGTON: I'm glad that most of you brought some aluminum foil from home. We have plenty to use. I have a few rolls here for those of you who couldn't bring any. The aluminum foil is easy to use. You can crumple it up (she demonstrates) and squeeze it into the shape you would like. And if you are not satisfied with the piece you are making, you can smooth the foil out (she demonstrates), and try it over again.

Now, what ideas do you have? What do you think you would like to make?

BARBARA: A person.

MISS HARRINGTON: That's a good idea, and I'm glad you suggested it. Don't be afraid to make people because it's so easy. And if you have trouble getting them to stand up, we can anchor them on something. We can make a little platform, and do anything you want with it.

DAN: Is there anything wrong with making just some kind of thing?

MISS HARRINGTON: Do you mean just an interesting shape?

DAN: Yes.

MISS HARRINGTON: You certainly can. I'd like to see some of you people try something like that.

CHRIS: Do you think—can I make a monkey?

MISS HARRINGTON: Sure you can. Now later on, when you finish your pieces, you might want to paint them, or they can be left the way they are. You can do that whichever way you like.

JOE: Can I make some sort of a model of a car—think up a new car with big fins on it?

MISS HARRINGTON: Well, I suppose you could if you want to.

292

Classroom Records in the Upper Elementary Grades

JANE: Can we make any kind of animal?

MISS HARRINGTON: Of course you can. Animals are very interesting to make. Their bodies have such interesting shapes. Does anybody else have a suggestion?

DAN: Can we make like a radio or something?

MISS HARRINGTON: A radio?

DAN: Like a cabinet.

MISS HARRINGTON: Oh, a cabinet. Well you could, but I think there are things that would be much more interesting than that. Wouldn't that just be sort of a square? You could do it if you want to, but wouldn't you rather think of an idea that has more to it, where the shape is more interesting? Animals and people have such interesting shapes, especially when they move and do things.

If you have your idea, then you can go to work. If you don't have enough foil, come up and I'll give you some. Start your idea with the big general shapes first. Then you can add other parts and work out the details. And remember, the aluminum foil can just be the base. You'll be able to add the asbestos paste, and that works almost like clay.

STAN: Can I make it hollow like this?

MISS HARRINGTON: Sure you can. Why not? It ought to work out very well.

The children went to work shaping and forming their pieces. Miss Harrington watched what they were doing, answered questions, and commented on their work.

Barbara got a quick start on her animal.

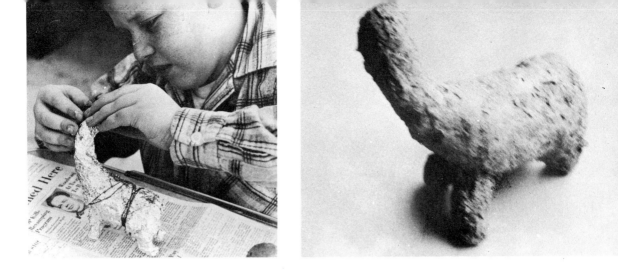

MISS HARRINGTON: Look at Barbara's animal, and see how she has the general shape worked out already. She has a good idea and a real good start.

Some of you are pressing the foil too tightly. If you crumple it too tight, you don't have a good chance to work with it. It gets too hard. If you get to the point where the aluminum doesn't stay together very well, you can tie a piece of string around it. It doesn't matter if the string shows, because you are going to cover most of it with asbestos anyway.

Look at Ted's dinosaur, how nicely he's making it. Look how he's shaping the body and the neck.

BRUCE: This looks like an alligator (pointing to his piece).

MISS HARRINGTON: It does. You can make a real fine alligator crawling on the ground.

Some of you have your shapes about ready to begin working with the asbestos. When you think you're ready, come up and get some. I have the asbestos and paste all mixed and ready in this bowl.

Some of the children worked very rapidly, and by the end of the morning several had finished their pieces. Here is Ted's dinosaur. He was very happy with his accomplishment.

Before cleaning up, they talked for a few minutes about several of their sculpture pieces, and made plans for their next work period. Some of the children needed more time to complete their sculptures; they would be able to work independently in free time, or they could continue in their next work period if they wanted to. Several children asked to do some sculpture in clay, and some wanted to paint. They decided, therefore, that everyone should choose whatever he preferred during the next work period.

294

Classroom Records in the Upper Elementary Grades

Here is a hippopotomus one of the boys made out of clay. Miss Harrington was going to have it fired in the school kiln, and then he would glaze it.

∾ ∾ ∾

During the following week, after they had completed their pieces of sculpture, Miss Harrington brought in a group of reproductions of paintings by well-known artists.

MISS HARRINGTON: I thought you'd enjoy looking at reproductions of paintings today so I brought some to show you. Can you all see as I hold them? John, would you be better off a little farther back rather than sitting so far to the side? Can you see better now?

JOHN: Yes.

MISS HARRINGTON: Now this is a picture by an artist whose name is Utrillo—Maurice Utrillo—and he is a Frenchman. He lives outside of Paris, and most of his pictures are of street scenes.

	Utrillo loves those streets, and he knows them so well that he paints them all the time. He's an old man now; he must be about seventy-five years old and I think he's still painting.
KATHY:	Is that a print that he made himself?
MISS HARRINGTON:	You mean an original?
KATHY:	Yes.
MISS HARRINGTON:	Oh, no. This is a print, but it's a good print.
KATHY:	I thought the man painted the picture and then he did the same thing—he copied it.
MISS HARRINGTON:	No, he didn't do that. Now there are engravings, or woodcuts, and silk screen pictures. With those, the artist himself makes many prints, but this is not like that. Utrillo painted this picture, and then it was photographed. This print was made from the photograph.
JAN:	There are some pictures at our church that are printed from copper.
MISS HARRINGTON:	Do you want to tell us about them, Jan? Jan told me about some pictures she had seen this past weekend. Tell us about them, Jan.
JAN:	They're made by an artist who died, and they're at our church—the whole collection. These have copper plates with them, and the artist printed ten or fifteen of each one. Then he destroyed the plates.
MISS HARRINGTON:	The artist sometimes destroys the plates, so there won't be too many copies. Now who is the artist?
JAN:	Roualt.
MISS HARRINGTON:	During his early years, Roualt painted many religious pictures. Do you know that new picture of a clown which is hanging in the hall? That's a Roualt. I have some more of his, and I'll be glad to bring them and show them to you.
	Jan, which is your church? I'd be interested in seeing those pictures.
JAN:	First Baptist. They've been there about three weeks, and I think they're going to be there about two more weeks.
DAVID:	Our Sunday school class went over there, and our teacher has a

	big folio with a lot of color prints of his.
CHRIS:	The museum has some of his pictures, too.
MISS HARRINGTON:	Well, let's get back to this picture by Utrillo. I'm interested in hearing what you think of it.
BARBARA:	I like the shadows, the way he painted them. And I like the greens in the trees, and the bushes—the way they're painted.
MISS HARRINGTON:	Yes. And do you know, Barbara, when you do your own pictures, you do them something like that. I think that is why you like this painting, and I think that's good.
STAN:	That really does look like the original.
MISS HARRINGTON:	Well, it is a good print, and you can even see the brush strokes very clearly.
STAN:	Yeah.
MISS HARRINGTON:	Utrillo painted many white buildings. Look at his painting very closely, and perhaps you'll get some good ideas for ways to paint your own. He didn't paint his buildings just flat white.
MIKE:	I like the red on the top of those chimneys.
MISS HARRINGTON:	Doesn't it stand out nicely?
JANE:	Some of those dark colors make it stand out, too.
JIM:	I like the way that artist didn't just make the buildings a flat color.
MISS HARRINGTON:	I've read that sometimes Utrillo would go out into the street to paint, and sometimes he'd just sit and paint in his studio because he knew the scenes so well. He had wandered those streets since he was a boy, and he didn't even have to look at them to paint them.
	I'd like to show you some more pictures today. I was looking through this book about Van Gogh and found one here that reminded me a lot of Utrillo. It's not a street scene but it just reminded me about how Utrillo mixed his colors.
BRUCE:	I don't like the hand in that picture.
MISS HARRINGTON:	Well, you know—
JAN:	He painted the way he saw.
MISS HARRINGTON:	He painted the way he had a feeling about the things in his pic-

Courtesy of National Gallery of Art, Chester Dale Collection

298

Classroom Records in the Upper Elementary Grades

tures. Do you remember, we talked about that a few weeks ago when we were looking at a whole group of Van Gogh's paintings.

STAN: Why do all artists have difficult names?

MISS HARRINGTON: They don't all have difficult names, but many of them are from foreign countries, and their names are not familiar to us.

Here's another painting I like very much by Tamayo. He's a famous Mexican artist.

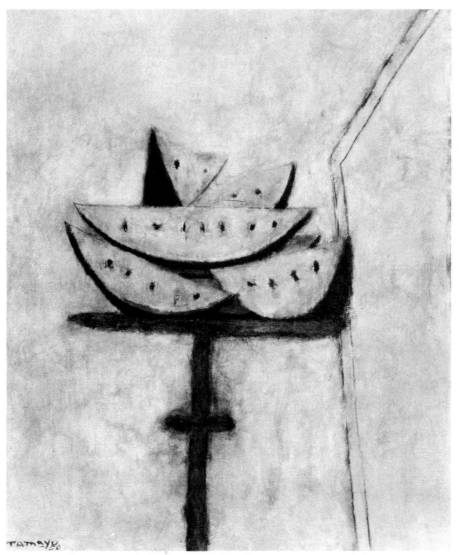

Courtesy of Museum of Modern Art, gift of Mrs. Sam A. Lewisohn

JIM: I like the orange and red colors in that painting.

MISS HARRINGTON: The watermelons are so simple with such interesting colors. And it has such a nice design. I thought you might get some ideas from seeing it.

The last one I'm going to show you is by another French painter. His name is Matisse. Look how he painted the background of this picture. It makes such an interesting design.

KATHY: I like the colors in this painting.

PAT: The background is just like wallpaper—flowers.

MISS HARRINGTON: I thought you'd like the way Matisse made a design out of the flowers.

Now, why don't you come up and look through some of these other prints I have here. You can pick out the pictures you'd like to look at all by yourself.

Courtesy of Collection Loula D. Lasker

Take them to your desk and look at them for a while.

The children came up to Miss Harrington's desk and looked through the prints. This boy picked the reproduction of Utrillo's painting to examine more closely.

Miss Harrington accomplished a number of things through her periodic discussion of the works of great artists. The children became acquainted with many painters and the character of their works. They also became aware of some of the important qualities of artistic form. This experience was enriching for them and was reflected in the way they were able to make and look at their own art works.

Six Days in Mrs. Williams' Sixth Grade

Mrs. Williams is an inquisitive and energetic person. She is very much interested in art, and like Mrs. Hoyer, she too sometimes joins her children to work on something for herself. Her own participation is encouraging and stimulating for the children. She provides continuous and frequent opportunities for them to work in many art activities.

Mrs. Williams' school is located in a suburban area, where housing developments are attracting the population of a large metropolitan center. It is a neighborhood of modest dwellings.

The school building is modern with spacious classrooms; Mrs. Williams' room is large and bright with a great deal of floor space. The equipment, however, is meager. The individual desks are small with a fixed tilt and with chairs attached. Although they are portable, their use is extremely limited for art activities. Mrs. Williams does have two long tables which are used flexibly for a variety of purposes. Storage space in the room is inadequate, and there is no running water. In spite of these limitations, Mrs. Williams provides her children with rich experiences in art. She has thirty-two children enrolled in her class.

Mrs. Williams' class had been studying Latin America—the history of the Indians and the Spanish invasion, the current economy, resources and industries, and the social life of the region. In their art activities, they had already made many individual paintings. Some of the children had made masks by building forms of clay and covering them with layers of paper and paste.

Here is one of the masks painted and decorated with yarn.

They were now preparing for a new group of art activities. As part of their study, they had read and talked about the arts of Latin America. They had been on a visit to the art museum, and Mrs. Williams had brought in reproductions of Aztec and Mayan sculpture of the past, as well as Orozco and Rivera murals of the present. Their examination and discussion of these reproductions created a great deal of interest in ideas for things to do in art. Most of the children wanted to do a mural of Latin American life; a small group wanted to carve.

In preparing for these activities, they were collecting old candles, because they had decided to carve in blocks of wax. They were going to make their blocks by melting the candles and pouring the wax into cartons. They wanted enough wax to make five- or six-inch cubes.

They had already talked about murals and how they differed from paintings. A mural was not only a large painting, but it was made to cover a whole wall. It depicted a composite story with many parts of a big idea. They recognized this from their examination of the Orozco and Rivera murals.

One of the boys had told the class about a large mural he saw in one of the buildings in the city. As a result, they were planning a field trip for the whole class. In the meantime, they were discussing ideas for their own murals. Since over twenty children wanted to work on the murals, they decided that it would be best to make several, so that their work groups wouldn't be too large.

MRS. WILLIAMS: We've made many pictures about ideas we got from the Latin American countries we have studied, but those were individual pictures. Now we need to think in terms of a mural.

You know that a mural isn't just a scene. You found this out when we were talking about the murals that Orozco and Rivera painted in Mexico. A mural isn't just a big picture. When an artist paints a mural, he puts together a lot of important things and makes one big design out of it—something that is pleasing to look at. So, we need to think about ideas that would be good for our murals.

What do you think would make a good general idea for one of our murals, where you could take parts of different ideas and put them together, and weave them into a design?

RICKEY: Well, maybe people bringing the things that they made to a big market.

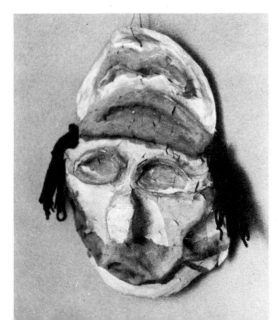

MRS. WILLIAMS: That's a good idea, but do you think that should be the whole mural? Could that be a good part of a mural?

DON: Is a mural something where everything points to the main subject?

MRS. WILLIAMS: Yes. A mural has many ideas about one big subject. That's a good way to say it.

JACKIE: Could you have all different kinds of people put together, and all the different kinds of work that they do?

MRS. WILLIAMS: Certainly, you could. Would you want to talk about the people, and maybe you can make up a good idea about them for a mural?

PAT: The people of South America?

MRS. WILLIAMS: Yes, the people of South America. Let's do that for just a little bit, and see what would be part of that idea.

JACKIE: They were enslaved by the Spaniards.

MRS. WILLIAMS: That's certainly an important part of the idea. For hundreds of years, these people were dominated by the Spanish Conquistadores. Can you think of something else? What kind of people were they? What did they look like?

DAVID: They're poor people.

MRS. WILLIAMS: Most of them were, but were all of them poor?

RICHARD: No. They were ruled by a few wealthy people.

MRS. WILLIAMS: Yes. Most of the land was owned by a few people, and the common people had very little. And this is still true in most of Latin America.

MARGARET: Most of the people have high cheekbones. They are part Spanish and Indian.

JAMIE: They have dark skin.

MRS. WILLIAMS: Yes, the original Indians married with the Spaniards.

Now, if you decided to make a mural about the people of South America, what would you put into it?

LEE: Spanish soldiers and horses.

RICKEY: We could put Indians in it.

MRS. WILLIAMS: How did they dress?

304

Classroom Records in the Upper Elementary Grades

RICKEY:	We could put the Indians dressed in feathers.
DOUGLAS:	Those were the Aztecs.
MRS. WILLIAMS:	Yes, the Aztecs, and the Incas wore feathers, too. What else did they wear?
PAUL:	They wore big masks.
MRS. WILLIAMS:	What did the Spanish soldiers wear?
DONALD:	They wore helmets, and didn't they have suits of armor?
MRS. WILLIAMS:	If you would choose this idea, you'd have to find out some more information about the armor the Spanish soldiers wore.
	What other people would you include in this mural?
BARBARA:	The gauchos.
MRS. WILLIAMS:	Yes, didn't they play a part in what the people are like there to-day?
	What other people would be important to include? What other type of person played an important part in the lives of these people, not only in times gone by, but even today?
JAMIE:	The priests.
MRS. WILLIAMS:	That's right. When the Spaniards came to South America, do you remember the part the church played in the conquest of South America?
JAMIE:	We could put a priest in the mural.
MRS. WILLIAMS:	Now, all this we've been talking about gives us a good basis for the general idea for one mural.

They went on to consider other possible ideas for their murals, enumerating and describing in detail the many aspects that might be included. They developed an idea about the natural resources and industries of South America. Then Mrs. Williams summarized their discussion to this point.

MRS. WILLIAMS:	Now in making a mural with these ideas, you'll want to overlap some of the parts, repeat the colors, and bring the parts together with a rhythm, so our eyes will travel across it when we look at it.
	We need to talk about some more big ideas before you choose

Classroom Records in the Upper Elementary Grades

which one you'd like to work on. Then you will be able to divide up into groups for your work.

In the meantime, you'll need to look up a lot of information. You'll need to do some research on the clothing the different people wore, and you'll need to find out about the armor worn by the Spanish soldiers. See how much you can find out about these things in the books we have. You can take some newsprint paper and make some sketches, so the people who work on these murals can have the information. We can talk this over again tomorrow, and after we decide on all the ideas, you can choose and divide into groups.

🙟 🙟 🙟

They continued their discussion the next day. They still liked the two ideas they had already discussed—the people and the resources of South America. Several of the children, however, mentioned things they had studied earlier in the year—prehistoric animals and Egypt, and they wanted to use these ideas for murals, too. They decided, therefore, to make four murals—people of South America, resources of South America, prehistoric animals and people, and Egypt. They divided themselves into groups according to their individual choices. The largest group had eight children, and the smallest had four. Six children did not want to work on the murals; they preferred to carve in wax.

🙟 🙟 🙟

The following day was the time for their field trip. The school bus took them to see a mural painted by Fred Conway. A shoe manufacturer had commissioned Mr. Conway to paint a mural of the history of shoe-making for the entrance lobby of the company's administration building.

One of the company officials spoke to the children about the mural. He described how Mr. Conway did his work—research into the subject, sketches, and finally the painting. They were impressed by the size of the mural. The official described how Mr. Conway had sketched the idea on the wall with charcoal tied to a long stick, so that he could see the whole wall while he made his drawing. Then he worked with his paints on a scaffold. Before he was finished, however, the scaffold was removed, so that he could look at the whole thing and repaint some of the parts which he thought too bright or too dull. All this was impressive information for the children to hear, and they asked many detailed questions.

306

Mrs. Williams spoke to the group to point out how the various parts of the mural were organized and put together—how they interlocked with each other, and how different sections overlapped others. She compared the work they were planning for their murals with the work the painter had done.

They climbed the stairway of the lobby to get a closer look at the mural, and to examine how some of the details were painted. After spending about three-quarters of an hour in the building, they returned to their bus for the ride back to school. There, they continued their discussion.

KEITH: The man told us how the artist tied charcoal to a long pole to make his sketch on the wall.

MRS. WILLIAMS: He stood on the floor while sketching.

JACKIE: He had to do a lot of research first.

MRS. WILLIAMS: Yes. When the man mentioned that, I was sure it meant something to you. That mural took a lot of research and careful planning before the artist was ready to make his drawing. That's like all the planning you've been doing for your murals. Mr. Conway must have spent a great deal of time studying, reading, and collecting information for each section of his mural.

JIMMY: What do you think he charged for that mural?

MRS. WILLIAMS:	I haven't the faintest idea. What was the main idea in the mural we saw?
DOUGLAS:	How shoes were made. There were a couple of cows in the mural to show where you get leather.
LEE:	When you looked at some parts of the mural, they looked like they were standing out.
MRS. WILLIAMS:	Yes, some parts of the mural did stand out more than others, and some of them were rather indistinct. Now, why do you suppose the artist did it that way? Why did he make parts of it stand out very strongly and other parts sort of fade into the background?
MARGARET:	So it wouldn't look like it was all—it would look like it wasn't just a flat wall.
MRS. WILLIAMS:	It gave depth to it. Do you remember when we talked about your paintings and about the use of color, and light, and dark? You can combine colors so that some things come toward you, and others recede into the background. Do you remember talking about that?
	Now, you will have many different things in your murals, and they will all be important. But some of them may stand out more, and some of them will recede into the background. You'll have to work that out as you go along. You can't predict all those things ahead of time.
	You remember what the man told us about the artist. What did he do?
PAT:	He went back and worked over parts of it.
MRS. WILLIAMS:	Yes. He couldn't tell everything about it, could he, even though he planned it very carefully? He may not even have planned some of the details. It probably developed as he went along. He knew the ideas he wanted, and he probably had the overall plan. Now, we've already spent time building up our plans, but the details will come along as you work on them.
MARY:	Our murals will have lots of parts in them.
MRS. WILLIAMS:	Oh, yes. And Rivera's murals did, too. His murals were also large and complicated. That's why it's so useful for us to look at what artists have done. Some of Rivera's murals are larger and even more complicated than the one we saw on our trip today. I wanted you to see this mural today, because I wanted you to see the size

of it. You know, when you see a real big mural, it's different from just seeing a photograph of it.

I'd like to ask you something else. Why do you think the artist used a piece of charcoal tied to the end of a long stick? Why didn't he have them build a scaffold, so he could get right up close to the wall and just hold the charcoal in his hand? I'm sure if he wanted a scaffold, the people for whom he painted the mural would have gotten one for him. They did put up a scaffold later on when he began to paint, but why did he make his sketch with a long stick?

PAUL: Well maybe it's because if you get back farther you see better.

MRS. WILLIAMS: That's right. With the charcoal tied to a long stick, he was able to get away from the mural and that's important. Because, if you don't get back away from such a big thing, you can't see the whole thing. And if you don't look at the whole thing, you get stuck in little corners, and you can't make it look like it has one main idea that connects all the parts. You can't make a good design out of it. I asked you that question because it will be very important for you to get away and look at your whole mural.

Mr. Conway was just one man, and even though he was planning all his ideas alone, he had to be careful to keep looking at his whole mural. In your murals, several of you will be working together, and each of you will be working on different parts. The most important part of your job will be to put all your separate ideas together to make one big design. That means that you're going to have to invent some ways to move away from your murals to look at them. Do you have any ideas on how to solve that problem?

JIMMY: You can have somebody stand behind you.

MRS. WILLIAMS: Well, suppose I'd stand behind you. Would that tell you what you need to see yourself?

BARBARA: Couldn't we use something that could be erased easily?

MRS. WILLIAMS: That's very important. If you use something that can be erased easily, then it will be easy to change parts to make them fit together better.

DANNY: Couldn't we draw our sketches and then back away from it to see how it looks?

MRS. WILLIAMS: You'll need to do that. You'll discover that all of you who are working on a mural will need to walk back and talk over what you have done. Then you'll be able to make the parts fit together.

JACKIE: In the colors, the artist repeated them a lot.

MRS. WILLIAMS: That was one important way he made the parts look as if they belong together. He also repeated shapes and forms. The repetition of the colors and the forms connected the parts, but you also noticed that all the forms were not the same size. He made a variety of sizes. Sometimes he put in single figures and sometimes there were groups of people. This made the sizes of the sections different. He used his imagination to combine the sections. You'll have to use your information and your imagination just like he did.

Don't you think you're about ready to start your murals? I think you are, and we can plan to begin work on them the first thing next week. In the meantime, you can make some more small sketches to get ready.

The trip to see the mural and the discussion which followed brought the children to the point where they began to understand some of the problems, and they were ready to go to work. They began to realize the importance of using their imagination and judgment to coordinate the many different parts they planned to put into their murals.

❧   ❧   ❧

The following week they began to work on their murals. They used wrapping paper that was thirty-six inches wide, and the four murals varied from ten to twelve feet in length. They scotch-taped their murals over the chalkboards, with two of them at the front of the room and two on the back wall.

They decided to use white chalk to draw their sketches. Then they would be able to erase easily and make changes. They went to work energetically, and at intervals, they stopped to walk away from their murals to decide together what to do. Mrs. Williams talked with the groups individually. As decisions were reached, they placed things in their murals, and rearranged the position of objects accordingly.

By the end of the morning, some of the children had already begun to paint. They were proceeding at a rapid speed.

While the mural painters were busy with their work, Mrs. Williams talked to the children who wanted to carve. Each had taken a box of candles home over the weekend, and each had poured a block of wax.

310

They brought their blocks and paring knives from home, and they got started on their carvings.

To avoid getting the chips of wax on the floor, Mrs. Williams got a few shallow pasteboard cartons. By cutting away one side from each carton, each child had a comfortable and convenient shield to catch the chips while he worked. This avoided a lot of unnecessary clean-up time.

ॐ ॐ ॐ

The following day, during their work period, the children went directly to the painting of their murals. After they were at work for about half an hour, Mrs. Williams asked them all to sit down so that they could talk over what they had done so far.

MRS. WILLIAMS: I think your murals are coming along very well, but we do need to talk about them before you go much further. Let's talk a little bit about each one.

We can start with the natural resources mural first.

Jamie, you're in that group. What do you think about your mural?

JAMIE: It's too dark.

BARBARA: What color can you use? Their skin wasn't very light.

PAUL: The paper is the same color as the face.

MRS. WILLIAMS: Do you just want to leave the paper and not paint it any other color?

CHILDREN: No!

MRS. WILLIAMS: Don't you think it's coming along fine for the beginning? You just need to get more of it painted.

BARBARA: We need to paint the background in.

MRS. WILLIAMS: You're right, Barbara. You've only been painting the figures and you haven't yet painted any part of the background.

Let's take a look at the mural about the people now.

LEE: Those soldiers are good.

MRS. WILLIAMS: I think so, too. They're coming along nicely. Now they need to be painted more completely.

RICHARD: I think the Aztec Indian is very good.

MRS. WILLIAMS: He certainly is. What are you people planning to put in the parts of your mural where there are no figures?

MARGARET: We could put a mountain up there with Christ of the Andes, couldn't we?

MRS. WILLIAMS: That's a good possibility, and you'll think of others, too. You might talk that over in your group and see what you think about it. Then you can decide what to do. What are some other things you like about this mural?

JACKIE: I like the bright colors.

MRS. WILLIAMS: These people wear bright colors, and their music is bright, too. The colors you've used have a good feeling for the people.

MARGARET: I like that priest's robe, the way it's painted.

MRS. WILLIAMS: I do too. Now let's look at this one. This one isn't quite so far along yet, because there are only four people working on it.

DOUGLAS: I like the big flowers.

MRS. WILLIAMS: They are a good shape, aren't they?

PAT: I like the way that man is sitting down. I guess he's making glass.

MRS. WILLIAMS: I think you're right. He does look good, and he is a glass blower. This group needs a little more time to get more of their mural painted. Then we'll talk about it again.

Let's look at the last one now.

KATHY: The colors are too dull.

DONALD: All the people, their skins are the same color.

STEPHAN: You try to get a different color out of that brown.

MRS. WILLIAMS: I think you're right, and if you think all the colors are too much alike, you'll have to do more color mixing to see what different kinds of brown color you can make. You can mix the brown with some yellow, or with green, or with red. You have to try more color combinations.

LEE: I like the mastadon.

DONALD: Well, the woman holding the baby, and the animal, they don't stand out.

MRS. WILLIAMS: You're right, Donald, but don't you think you can improve that by mixing and combining your colors better? You know, sometimes you work too close to the mural, and you only pay attention to your own part. You need to get away from it so you can see all the parts together. Then you can paint them so they look better together. If you think you need to change some of the colors, you can paint over them.

KATHY: The mastadon's legs are kind of short.

JACKIE: I like the way they drew their figures.

MRS. WILLIAMS: Yes. Their figures are well drawn, and they filled their space very well, too. They look primitive, just like the early people.

I think that the main problem you people are having is in the mixing of your colors. The browns do all look alike, and when you go back to work, I'd suggest that you really try to see how many different kinds of brown you can mix. And when you mix your colors, don't just add white or black. Add some yellow, and make a yellow brown. Try some red, and make a reddish brown. Then you'll see that all the colors won't be alike.

In general, I think all of you have a good start. But all of you need to do some talking in your own groups about some of the things that have been mentioned. You need to make some decisions and continue with your work. Let's do that now.

The children returned to their murals, and after talking briefly among themselves, they reached some decisions and continued their painting.

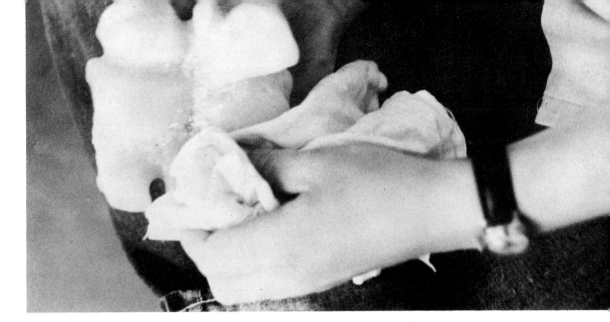

During the next few days the children continued to work on their murals at various times after completing some of their other studies. Most of this painting was done, therefore, on an individual basis. Some of the children talked about their murals among themselves, and Mrs. Williams spoke to them individually and in twos and threes. She kept emphasizing the importance of the background colors in relation to the colors in the figures, and she helped them to see how contrast in colors and overlapping of parts could be useful ways to emphasize different parts and to coordinate them.

At this stage of the work, most of the emphasis was placed on clarifying the relative importance of different parts of the murals. Mrs. Williams helped them to pay attention to the relationships among the colors and forms to convey the ideas and feelings in a well-organized manner. They talked about objects in front in relation to those in back, light in relation to dark, and bright in relation to dull. They were concerned with the design of their murals.

Meanwhile the children who were carving in wax were proceeding with their work; a few of them were almost finished.

This boy is polishing his piece with a cloth.

෨෨ ෨෨ ෨෨

The following week, they were again at work on their murals as an entire class. Before resuming their painting, Mrs. Williams talked with all the children.

MRS. WILLIAMS: All of you have been working individually on your separate parts during the last few days, and you have done a lot to your murals. We need to talk a while before you go back to work, so you can bring the parts together some more. When you go to work, you can paint over parts if necessary to change some of the colors. That's how you can make them even better than they now are.

Let's take a good look at them now to see what you need to do to finish them.

Let's look at the one about the people first.

PAUL: Repeat that red.

MRS. WILLIAMS: Repeat what red?

PAUL: On the soldiers.

MRS. WILLIAMS: Why?

PAUL: That red on the front of that soldier is too light, and we should put some of it somewhere else on the mural.

MRS. WILLIAMS: Do you all see what Paul means?

BARBARA: Well, there's a lot of red—bright red—over here on the soldiers, and there isn't any over here, so you should have some here.

DAVID: All those girls looking toward the priest—well, look like they're moving away from the center.

MRS. WILLIAMS: Do you think that's not good? The body of the priest, though, brings them back into the picture. Don't you think so?

DAVID: I guess so.

Classroom Records in the Upper Elementary Grades

MRS. WILLIAMS: You wouldn't want everything to point in just one direction. That would be monotonous.

JAMIE: That lady back there behind the soldier—you can hardly see her.

MRS. WILLIAMS: She's lost back there. Why do you think so?

JAMIE: She doesn't have enough color in her.

MRS. WILLIAMS: She doesn't have enough contrast against the background. Now maybe you don't want her to stand out as much as your soldiers, but she's almost completely lost.

You mentioned some good suggestions for this mural. Let's go on to the next one.

DANNY: The man with the sugar cane is up in the air.

MRS. WILLIAMS: Danny thinks he's up in the air. Don't you think he's much better now that you have painted the background around him, but maybe you do need to anchor him a little more. You can fix a better place for him to stand.

LEE: I think that cow needs some brightening up. She looks so sad.

MRS. WILLIAMS: Maybe you could make her stronger looking. She is a little lost up there.

STEPHAN: They could put some sides on her.

MRS. WILLIAMS: But they don't want to put a whole cow there. They just wanted to put the head in, and they can do that if they want to.

317

MARGARET: That man on the right—his legs are so thin.

MRS. WILLIAMS: You might work on that a little more if you care to. You have certainly done a lot of work on your mural in the last few days, and you've improved it a lot.

Let's look at the Egypt mural now.

KEITH: That man's hand goes backwards.

MRS. WILLIAMS: Oh, yes. I remember you mentioned that to me yesterday.

KEITH: It's too hard to draw.

PAT: That stick in his hand—make it overlap his hand. That will fix it.

MRS. WILLIAMS: That's a very good suggestion, Pat. That will fix the hand I'm sure.

DOUGLAS: That sphinx looks like it's floating.

MRS. WILLIAMS: Barbara, do you see what Douglas is saying?

BARBARA: I think so. We need to move it behind the figure.

MRS. WILLIAMS: I'm sure that moving it behind that figure will help.

What about the last mural now?

JIMMY: I think it's finished.

MRS. WILLIAMS: How do the rest of you feel about it? Do you see anything else that it needs?

Classroom Records in the Upper Elementary Grades

KATHY: The grass looks too dark, and it's all different colors.

MRS. WILLIAMS: Look out the window, Kathy, and see if you think the grass is all one shade of green. Now if you think that part of the grass is too dark, then lighten it up a little bit.

DONALD: The man that's hitting the boar has hands that are too small.

MRS. WILLIAMS: They are rather small. You can fix that, can't you? You people don't have very much more to do. I think Jimmy was right. Except for a few things, don't you think your mural is almost finished?

Now, let me remind you again. Look at your whole mural often, and talk over what you are doing. At this point, you need to watch the whole thing.

The children then went on with their work, talking over changes they wanted to make. By the end of the morning the children working on the prehistoric mural had completed theirs. During the next few days while the others were finishing their work, those who were through chose to make some collages.

The four completed murals are on the next page.

And there are two of the wax carvings. The Mayan and Aztec sculptures they had looked at not only stimulated their interest in carving,

෨෨   ෨෨   ෨෨

The work of these four upper elementary grade teachers—Mrs. Hoyer, Miss Ellis, Miss Harrington and Mrs. Williams—reveals their consciously balanced attention to the sources of interest out of which children create ideas, and the refinement of the artistic forms through which these ideas are expressed. They helped their children to create beautiful expressions of ideas. Miss Cupelli, the art teacher, used her special knowledge and experience to enhance Mrs. Hoyer's work with her group.

Like all the other teachers whose work was presented in the earlier chapters, this group of excellent teachers demonstrates some essential common qualities through their individual strengths and variations. Their work and the work of their children are analyzed in the next chapter.

ANALYSIS OF

IN THE UPPER

9

For the teachers whose work was presented in the preceding chapter, teaching was as much a form of expression as working in art was a form of expression for their children. Their teaching of art expressed their conception of themselves and the roles they performed in providing their children with education in art. In this respect, these teachers stand out as distinctive individuals, as did all the others whose work was reported in the earlier chapters.

The character of the discussion between Mrs. Hoyer and the girls who were working on the bayou mural revealed her attitude toward the children and their attitude toward her. She respected their feelings, and they knew she did. From past experience, they knew that they could disagree with her, and she would listen to them. At the beginning of the discussion about their mural, Mrs. Hoyer and the girls clearly disagreed. They wanted to scrap their first attempt. Mrs. Hoyer tried to convince them otherwise. She told them what she thought, and listened to what they had to say. Their

Analysis of Classroom Records in the Upper Elementary Grades

CLASSROOM RECORDS
ELEMENTARY GRADES

reasons and feelings were sufficiently strong for her to come to agree with them.

Miss Ellis approached her teaching from a somewhat different perspective. She was brief, direct to the point, and almost crisp at times. And yet through her abbreviated remarks she revealed her own deep trust in her children. They knew she really felt that they could accomplish the things they wanted. They knew she respected their independent interests and desires. They also knew she expected them to develop and to rely upon their independent judgments. She talked to them about their ideas, and commented on the problems they raised; but some of the most useful comments were made by the children themselves. They knew she was confident in their ability to help each other and to stimulate each other's interests.

Miss Harrington talked to her children with warmth and deep personal interest. She enjoyed working with them, and they felt it. Art was rich and meaningful to her, and they felt that, too. When she brought the

Analysis of Classroom Records in the Upper Elementary Grades

reproductions of paintings to show them, they clearly saw how much she admired the artists' sensitive and imaginative creations. In the discussion, there was a revealing exchange between herself and one of the girls. You will recall that while they were looking at Utrillo's painting, Barbara commented: "I like the shadows, the way he painted them. And I like the greens in the trees and the bushes—the way they're painted." Miss Harrington's reply showed how important she felt it was for her children to identify themselves with the painters whose works they were viewing. She answered: "Yes. And do you know, Barbara, when you do your own pictures, you do them something like that. I think that is why you like this painting, and I think that's good." Her children knew that she viewed them as artists. They learned to value their own individuality, because they knew she respected it.

There was an absence of rigidity in the planning for the murals by Mrs. Williams. Although she systematically reviewed much of the content of their unit study as they searched for ideas for their murals, she readily accepted the preference of more than half of the children to work on other ideas. All of them did not need to work on murals about South America, even though that was the subject of their study. She recognized the interests of the children in other ideas, because she knew that interest in an idea is a prerequisite to creating any meaningful expression. Two groups of children chose different ideas for their murals. One group did not want to work on murals at all; they wanted to carve. Mrs. Williams' personal flexibility enabled her to accept the individual preferences of her children. She encouraged them to make their independent decisions and choices.

The distinctiveness of the teaching styles of each of these teachers was more a matter of personal emphasis than of fundamental difference. Each one listened to her children; each respected her children's interests, and preferences. Each encouraged her children to view their own artistic efforts in relation to the work of artists. And each challenged her children to make their own judgments, while at the same time helping them to improve the quality of their judgments. The ideas they worked upon and the approaches to their work were live experiences in the education of these children.

All these qualities were interwoven into their teaching like elements in the design of a tapestry. The distinctiveness of their teaching styles emerged from their particular and personal abilities and temperaments. This led each of them to emphasize one or another element in creating the design of her own teaching.

There was an important difference among this group of teachers —one that was also apparent among the teachers in the middle elementary grades whose work was presented and analyzed in Chapters Six and Seven. Mrs. Hoyer worked cooperatively with Miss Cupelli, the art teacher, whereas the other three teachers worked independently. At times, Mrs.

Hoyer's and Miss Cupelli's individual teaching efforts complemented each other. Just as often, however, both of them worked as a team with Mrs. Hoyer contributing her special knowledge of the children and their immediate concerns, while Miss Cupelli contributed her special knowledge about art.

Miss Cupelli provided important elements of richness and scope to the art program in Mrs. Hoyer's class. At the same time, however, you surely recognized how much Miss Cupelli's work depended upon the background and climate created by Mrs. Hoyer. This was essential groundwork without which Miss Cupelli could not have made her special contribution as effectively as she did.

Mrs. Hoyer's ability to create a climate conducive to artistic experience stemmed from her personal resources—her own knowledge about children and art. She had worked in art enough to know what was involved in creating ideas through art. These personal resources enabled her to work effectively with Miss Cupelli. Miss Ellis, Miss Harrington, and Mrs. Williams drew upon similar personal resources in their teaching.

As you read the classroom records in the preceding chapter, I am sure you detected still another difference among these teachers. The sources of ideas for art activities in Mrs. Hoyer's, Miss Ellis', and Mrs. Williams' classes were their unit studies. In Miss Harrington's class, the art activities had nothing to do with the unit study. The idea for their mural came from the Easter holiday season. The ideas for their sculpture came from their desire to make sculpture.

The difference in sources of ideas for art activities was as apparent among this group of teachers as it was among the teachers in the middle elementary grades. It once again underscores the fact that there are many fruitful sources of ideas for art activities. Through art, an individual can interpret ideas that are significant to him regardless of their source.

Along with the differences in the work of these teachers, there were two striking similarities: (1) the variety of art activities they provided for their children, and (2) the attention they encouraged their children to give to the qualities of artistic form. In varying degrees, these two points of emphasis were evident in the work of each of these teachers. By comparison with the middle elementary grades, the attention this group gave to these two points differed both in character and intensity.

These teachers not only provided a variety of art activities, but different activities often were carried on simultaneously in their classes. The various art activities were not conducted in a sequence, planned by the teacher with each child working in each activity. Every child had an opportunity to choose the activity he wanted to pursue, and the choices were governed by the interests of the individual children and the ideas they

Analysis of Classroom Records in the Upper Elementary Grades

wanted to express.

In Miss Ellis' class, all the children painted when that was a common point of interest. As their ideas developed and became differentiated, however, they were able to choose particular activities to pursue. Simultaneously, they then worked on weaving, sewing, painting on fabric, linoleum block printing, ceramics, and mask-making. In Miss Harrington's class, all the children were interested in finding out how sculpture could be made with aluminum foil and asbestos powder and paste. Some of them wanted to continue this work, but others wanted to paint, or make sculpture with clay. These three activities were then pursued simultaneously.

These teachers provided a variety of activities to expand the scope of each child's work. They encouraged the children to choose among the available activities in order to challenge individual abilities and points of interest. They knew that such challenge was critical to the artistic development of children in the upper elementary grades. They knew that it was more important for these children to choose among a variety of art media in order to become deeply involved with one of them, than it was for all the children to work in the same activities. Hence they encouraged personal selection and deep involvement.

At the same time, these teachers devoted considerable attention to helping their children become aware of ways to make better works of art—helping them to acquire sensitivity to aesthetic qualities in a work of art, and knowledge and skill in handling art materials in order to achieve desired effects. You will recall the beginning tendencies toward such emphasis among teachers in the middle elementary grades. Those teachers were responding to the readiness of their children for some specific attention to the improvement of their work. The beginning readiness for conscious improvement among third- and fourth-grade children expands into a developmental necessity for the fifth- and sixth-grade children. These fifth- and sixth-grade teachers were providing for that need.

Upper elementary grade children are no longer challenged or satisfied by spontaneous efforts in art. Their general development is such that they have achieved extended capacities—physical, social, emotional, intellectual and aesthetic—with corresponding abilities for more demanding activities. Unless they are given the opportunity to exercise these abilities in order to learn how to achieve at higher levels, they tend to lose interest and incentive for work. By paying attention to the quality of their children's work and by encouraging them to pursue activities of special interest, these teachers were helping them to fulfill their developmental tendencies. A brief review of the developmental achievements of children in the upper elementary grades will help you recognize further significance in the work of this group of teachers and in the work their children produced.

326

Major Developmental Achievements of Children in the Upper Elementary Grades

Although most children maintain a slow and steady physical development during these years, there is great unevenness among individuals, as well as between boys and girls in general. Most girls attain a lead of more than a year on the boys. By eleven, many girls but few boys begin to show signs of approaching adolescence.

Gangly long-leggedness produces awkwardness among many children at this age. They are restless and in need of physical activity. At the same time, gradual development of their large muscles, accompanied by a high degree of arm-hand-finger control, produces the ability to perform refined manipulative tasks. Miss Ellis' children, for example, enjoyed cutting and printing their linoleum block designs; Miss Harrington's children created their pieces of sculpture skillfully. Art activities which demand dexterity and control are challenging and of interest to them. They can learn to handle a wide variety of tools with skill and satisfaction.

Fifth- and sixth-grade children continue to grow in their awareness of themselves—their strengths and weaknesses, their abilities and interests. In comparison with children in the middle elementary grades, their behavior is more purposeful and less explosive. They want to achieve a feeling of adequacy; they seek a sense of belonging. They often tend to undertake activities beyond their level of skill in spite of the danger of failure and discouragement. Status gained through achievement is important to children at this age. Their attention span has become greatly increased, and in order to achieve, most of them are able to stay with a job for relatively long periods of time. This was apparent in the extended development of the murals, both in Mrs. Hoyer's and Mrs. Williams' classes.

Although these children need guidance and respond to adult assistance, they seek independence from adult control by asserting themselves, as was evident in the insistence of the group of girls in Mrs. Hoyer's class on starting their mural over again. In general, children of this age want to and are able to assume increasing responsibility for many of the activities in which they become involved.

Most ten- and eleven-year-old children adhere strongly to peer group standards in dress, speech, and interests. Recognition and acceptance are of paramount importance, and one way of achieving these is through the groups they create among themselves. Cliques and clubs are commonly accompanied by passwords and secret rituals. There is strong group feeling, but this is largely restricted to one's own sex. When these children chose others with whom to work, they most often selected from among their

327

own sex. The group of girls working on the mural in Mrs. Hoyer's class is a demonstration of this tendency. Boy-girl relationships are awkward; boys and girls teasing each other is a common occurrence. At times boys and girls are even antagonistic toward each other.

In spite of the alternating uncomfortableness and rivalry between the sexes, there is a strong loyalty among these children to their group. Working with a real team spirit, they exhibit a true commitment to the common good. Their social awareness assumes expanded dimensions. In the discussion about their various art activities in Miss Ellis' class, the children showed a genuine interest in helping each other solve some of the difficulties they encountered. They exhibited a conscious concern for the well-being of others as well as for themselves. Much of the behavior of children of this age is governed by an aware moral judgment and a true sense of justice. Although they are often over-critical of themselves and of others, they are at the same time growing increasingly sensitive to the feelings of others.

In general, the emotional and social development of ten- and eleven-year-old children is marked by the transformation of their concern for self during early childhood to a concern for the wider social group in which they live. This transformation is hardly unexpected, because its characteristic tendencies were already apparent at an earlier age. The development of children in the middle elementary grades toward awareness of group membership becomes crystallized during these years into an orientation toward their social environment—its activities, customs, tastes, and values. The general environmental tastes and values were reflected in the discussion in Mrs. Hoyer's class about making things that were useful through the restricted conception of utility the children at first expressed about pieces of sculpture.

Children in the upper elementary grades develop a conscious aspiration to behave according to the expectations of the group in which they live. This is a period in which basic characteristics of socialization are consolidated; it is also a period in which social conformity establishes its roots. The discussion about the murals in Mrs. Williams' class, with the emphasis upon things looking right, is a demonstration of the attention these children pay to the way things may appear to others as well as to themselves. The way other persons view events and ideas tends to become their own.

These developments are reflected in the virtual disappearance of spontaneous imaginative play and an increased interest in fact and realism. The capacity of these children for fantasy and imagination, however, is not lost. It emerges in new forms, such as their growing interest in adventure, travel, the drama in biographies, and the history of peoples in other lands. This tendency was apparent in the content of the units of study in

Mrs. Hoyer's, Miss Ellis' and Mrs. Williams' classes. It was evident in the tall tale which Karen wrote and dramatized with the help of her classmate in Mrs. Hoyer's group.

The intellectual development of fifth- and sixth-grade children is marked by an increased level of analytical clarity and maturity in ideas and interests. They are able to search for information, generalize from their findings, and organize ideas from what they have learned. Their grasp of time and space relationships indicates an ability to discriminate the meanings of comparative similarities and differences.

The increased ability of these children to deal with ideas and to conceive the nature of time, when coupled with their expanded sense of independence and responsibility, enables them to view the things they do in the perspective of time. They can participate in the planned use of their time. They can recognize value in individual contributions to planning problems, and they can pool their thinking. The character of the discussions in each of these classes attests the ability of these children to explore ideas together, and to develop group goals.

The verbal ability of most children in these grades is expanding into an active vocabulary of approximately twelve thousand words. They read for enjoyment as well as for the purpose of seeking information. The differences in individual abilities which became apparent in the middle elementary grades, however, grow even more emphatic during these years. Among eleven-year-old children there is a range in reading ability of four to six years. Some eleven-year-olds read at an adult level; others have pronounced reading disabilities.

The differences in ability among these children are not limited to reading alone. Variations in physical, social, emotional, and aesthetic development are just as apparent. Such differences are not necessarily linked to each other, although in many cases they are. Most often, however, the particular strengths of individual children become more evident during these years. These are emphasized because of the added attention the children themselves place upon them. Children know that achievement, status, and recognition depend a great deal on the exhibition of their abilities. The recognition of abilities produces satisfaction which in itself encourages further specific development.

The aesthetic sensibilities of children in the upper elementary grades approach a turning point and require support in order to avoid fragmentation and deterioration. Their expanding ability to perceive relationships is accompanied by a more critical awareness and the development of an analytical attitude. Whereas the development of children in the early elementary grades proceeded from a fragmentary conception of parts of ideas toward a more unified grasp of totality in ideas, children in the upper

329

elementary grades develop from a unified grasp toward analytical separation into parts. They notice detail, and tend to pay direct attention to particular parts. This was evident in the discussions about different aspects of the art works in each of the classes. It was also apparent in the efforts of each of the teachers to encourage the children to consider the parts in relation to the whole.

The gradual disappearance of the spontaneous imaginative play of earlier years is accompanied by sharply reduced security in personal intuitive feelings. Children of this age focus a greater part of their attention on the appearance of things outside themselves with the desire to achieve a grasp of external reality. Their expanded social awareness, coupled with their need for social recognition, stimulates their attention to factual accuracy at the expense of imaginative ingenuity. These developmental tendencies are not only natural, but they are also strongly reinforced by the materialistic and conventional pressures from the culture in which these children live.

At the same time, however, this is an age with a renewed sense of drama and adventure. There is excitement in the unknown, and the support of a teacher can create the climate in which it can be explored. A teacher's encouragement and guidance can help these children to achieve some of the analytical understandings they seek, without sacrificing their aesthetic sensibilities. They need to learn sufficient skill to deal with the external realities they value. They also need to achieve a sufficient level of conscious awareness of qualities in a work of art. Above all, they need the assistance of a teacher to maintain confidence in their own efforts and their own personal identities. These were the goals toward which Mrs. Hoyer was working when she encouraged the girls to become aware of their feelings about the swamp. They were Mrs. Williams' goals, when she urged her children to use their information *and* their imagination in the painting of their murals.

Good teaching can help fifth- and sixth-grade children to grow toward the tender feelings for romance and fantasy of oncoming adolescence. It can help them to value and develop the imaginative life—the essence of artistic creation.

The Content of the Teachers' Conversations

This group of teachers, like all the others whose work was presented and analyzed in the preceding chapters, taught their children how to use the visual arts as a living language through which to create and express ideas. They knew the abilities and interests of their children. They also knew the arts well enough to maintain their aesthetic character, while they provided for the developmental tendencies of their children. They recognized the children's analytical attitudes and their concern for objective reality. Simultaneously, they encouraged the children to maintain their individuality and to respect their own feelings about the ideas they chose to represent. They helped their children to solve some of the technical problems they encountered, and they emphasized the importance of achieving a unity of form and feeling in their work—the essence of aesthetic sensibility.

Even though the ideas for the art activities in three out of four of these classes grew out of unit studies, these teachers helped their children to see that art is beyond illustration. Art is the recreation of what you see and feel into an interpretive form. An understanding of the nature of art was clearly evident in Mrs. Williams' discussions with her children. They talked about the many ideas they wanted to represent in their murals. She emphasized the fact that the coordination of these ideas for the purpose of creating a work of art required imagination.

Through their field trip and through their discussions of Orozco's and Rivera's murals, Mrs. Williams helped her children to see how artists design and organize their ideas into a unified interesting whole. She helped them recognize how an artist uses his imagination to make the various parts of his mural interplay with each other. The children tried to make all the parts of their murals look right. At the same time, they became increasingly aware of the relationships among the parts—their sizes, positions, shapes, and colors. Although the ideas for their murals were derived from their social studies, their artistic efforts were not limited to illustration.

If you would refer to Mrs. Williams' classroom record in the preceding chapter, you can recognize how her points of emphasis in the discussions changed as the children proceeded in their work. After reviewing their field trip, they began talking about the murals they intended to make, with primary attention on the various ideas they planned to include. When their work progressed, Mrs. Williams talked less and less about the separate ideas included, and more and more about the way they were included. You will recall that as their work proceeded, their discussions dealt primarily with looking at the parts in relation to the whole, and seeing what needed to be done to make them fit together better.

Thus they talked about figures which did not stand out well, because their colors were almost like the background. They pointed to other parts of their murals which seemed to stand out too much, because they were too emphatic. They were concerned for the parts, with a renewed awareness of the importance of the relationships between the parts and the whole. The things Mrs. Williams talked about encouraged the children to avoid fragmentation and to enhance their ability to create relationships. Even though their efforts were rather methodical and lacked the spontaneity of younger children, Mrs. Williams did help them to strengthen their feelings for aesthetic unity. They were achieving artistic learning.

Similar points of emphasis were apparent in Mrs. Hoyer's discussions with her children. In talking with the girls who were painting the mural of the bayou, she helped them balance their concern for the appearance of the weeds, water, flowers, and trees by encouraging their awareness of the mood, feeling, and "wetness" of the swamp. She encouraged them to discover that a work of art conveys a total mood and feeling. Painting the parts is a problem of combining them to create the mood and feeling one desires.

When Mrs. Hoyer talked with the children who were making the photo montage, she helped them to recognize that a good montage was governed by the same characteristics as any other visual art form. It had to be organized. They grouped the photographs of similar subjects; they were careful to vary the position of the dark ones in relation to the light ones. They discovered that the textures of some of the photographs were different, and that a pleasing distribution could contribute a great deal to the appearance of their montage. They overlapped some of their photographs to create more interesting contrast in arrangement, and in general they became more attentive to some of the specific qualities that affected the unified appearance of their montage.

While the children in these classes worked on their art activities, they encountered various technical problems. Some involved the character of particular materials, and the necessary skill to manipulate them with satisfaction; some involved the ability of the children to draw and represent figures as they would want them to look; and some pertained to their awareness of how color variations can be achieved to create desired effects. The direct attention these teachers gave to such problems encouraged their children to proceed with their work.

When Miss Cupelli talked with Mrs. Hoyer's children about the pottery some of them wanted to make, she demonstrated how clay needs to be prepared, its essential consistency, and possible ways to handle it. The children were then able to maintain reasonable control over the materials and to shape them into the forms they desired. When several children in Miss Ellis' class were preparing to make linoleum block prints, she explained that designing a block print required planning in terms of black and white areas. The white areas need to be cut out, and the remaining surface of the linoleum prints black. The children then understood more about the character of the material, and they were better able to plan their designs in terms of the possibilities of the material.

Mrs. Williams' children were unhappy about the proportions in some of the figures in their murals. Through observation and discussion they discovered which parts were too small or too large. This knowledge

332

enabled them to make the necessary adjustments. When some of the children were displeased with the colors in their murals, she talked to them in detail about ways to mix variations of colors. She pointed to specific possibilities which they then tried and used to develop their murals.

Technical problems were discussed within the context of the activities in which the children were engaged. They were not presented as isolated exercises, but always in relation to the particular activities in process. The demonstrations and explanations helped the children to make the things they wanted in ways which were more satisfying to them. In doing so they expanded their interest and their facility for creating ideas in art.

While talking about the Southern Highlanders with Mrs. Hoyer and her children, Miss Cupelli raised the question of the usefulness of a piece of pottery. Together with Mrs. Hoyer, she helped the children to realize that utilitarian objects can be beautiful, and that something beautiful can have great value even though it has no concrete utility. This discussion reinforced the children's desire to make beautiful things for the pleasure in making and having them.

Miss Harrington talked about artists so that her children would perceive them as real people. Utrillo painted the street scenes he knew and loved. Matisse created beautiful designs in his paintings. Tamayo painted in subtle variations of somber rich tones. These were the achievements of great men, and Miss Harrington helped her children to enjoy them. Of equal importance is the fact that she encouraged her children to create their own expressions. Her discussion of artists and their works contributed toward the interest of her children in creating works of their own.

These teachers talked with their children about qualities in works of art. They brought them into contact with the works of great artists so that they could learn more about the language of art. They helped the children to understand and to deal with some of the technical problems they encountered so that they could achieve some of their desires. Above all, these teachers helped their children to realize that art is a human creation through which people convey their ideas and feelings. A work of art is beautiful because it is unified and orderly. It is achieved through the imagination of the artist.

Because these children were encouraged to approach their work as artists do, they discovered satisfactions in the adventure of the arts. Their analytical tendencies were reflected in their work, and so were their interests in the drama of discovery. The things these teachers talked about were in response to the developmental needs of these children. They devoted specific attention to particular problems in making a work of art, while they maintained the aesthetic sensitivity to the totality of a work of art.

333

The Teachers' Use of Classroom Time

Each of these teachers devoted a substantial amount of classroom time for their children to work in art. In general, each of these classes spent at least three to four hours a week in art activities. You will recall from Chapter Seven, that this was about the same amount of time the teachers in the middle elementary grades devoted to work in art.

The amount of time these teachers provided is a good indication of the time fifth- and sixth-grade children need for profitable learning in art. Furthermore, it is an indication of the importance these teachers placed on effective art experiences in the education of their children. They planned their total classroom programs to provide the amount of time significant art experiences require.

There was another noteworthy aspect of the time these teachers devoted to art. The concerns that upper elementary grade children have for the behavior of others is part of a total complex which includes their tendency toward social conformity. They pay attention to the relative emphasis other people place on different activities. The fact that this group of teachers provided substantial periods of time for art activities contributed to the significance their children perceived in the arts. The amount of time devoted to art was one demonstration of the importance of education in art. It was a factor which influenced the interest and energy of these children in their art work.

Although each of these teachers devoted similar amounts of time to art activities, there was a difference in the way the time was programmed. The art periods in Miss Harrington's class were generally a little over an hour in length, and they were held about every other day. The art periods in the other classes varied both in length and frequency. The reason for this difference was apparent in the classroom records in the preceding chapter, as well as in the discussion of the sources of ideas for the art activities earlier in this chapter.

Because the unit studies served as the sources of ideas for art activities in the classes of Mrs. Hoyer, Miss Ellis, and Mrs. Williams, these teachers tended to modify their time schedule as they progressed with their unit study. At the early stages of the unit, they devoted more time to developing background in the content of the investigation. As the unit study proceeded into its middle and later stages, more time was devoted to art activities to create expressions of the ideas derived from the investigation. The schedule of art periods in Miss Harrington's class, on the other hand, was quite regular, because the art activities she carried on with her children were independent of the social studies program.

As a result, the time devoted to art in Mrs. Hoyer's, Miss Ellis',

334

and Mrs. Williams' classes varied from about two hours during some weeks to almost six hours in other weeks. In Mrs. Williams' class, for example, the children spent less than two hours on art during the week preceding their field trip. When they started to work on their murals, however, they spent more than six hours a week for two consecutive weeks. Mrs. Hoyer, Miss Ellis, and Mrs. Williams balanced the time spent on art activities and the time spent on other studies over a period of several weeks. Miss Harrington maintained the same general balance of time during each week.

In addition to the time these teachers provided for all the children to work in art, individuals were able to continue their art work independently when they had completed their other studies. In all four of these classes, the teachers arranged the time in order to provide for the best education in art within the context of their total teaching program. Like all the teachers whose work was reported in the earlier chapters, this group used time as an instrument for good teaching.

The Teachers' Use of Classroom Space and Equipment

Mrs. Hoyer's and Miss Harrington's classroom were almost ideal. They were well equipped and flexible. There was running water, good storage space, extra counter and table space for work and supplies, and there were good wall spaces on which to hang the children's art work. The desks and chairs were portable and could be rearranged easily to suit the particular activities being carried on.

In Miss Harrington's class, the children would sometimes move their desks together when they were working jointly or sharing some materials. This happened on the day when they were working on their mural of "The Avenue at Easter Time." In Mrs. Hoyer's class, it was hardly necessary to move the furniture. Their classroom was spacious, with plenty of room for the portable puppet stage when they wanted to use it. The corridor outside the classroom was wide, and the girls who were painting the bayou mural worked on the floor just outside of the door.

The space and facilities in Miss Ellis' and Mrs. Williams' classrooms left much to be desired. Storage facilities were extremely meager; there was no running water; and there was hardly any space to hang the children's work. Mrs. Williams' classroom was large, but Miss Ellis' room was tiny and cramped.

When Miss Ellis' children were engaged in their regular classroom work, their desks were pushed together to conserve space and to provide for easy conversational groups. The tables they used to store their work and supplies were pushed against one of the walls.

When they wanted to paint, they had to rearrange all the furni-

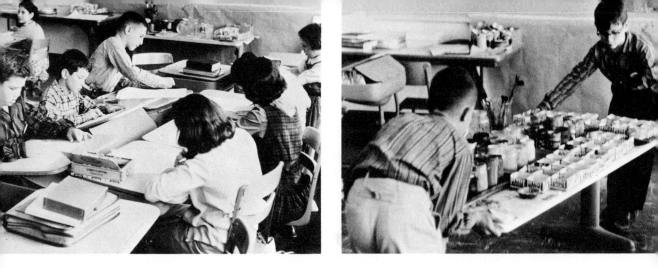

ture by pushing the desks out of the way and pulling the paint table into the center of the room. Then they were all able to reach the materials.

They had a two-bucket system to solve the water problem—clear water in one and dirty water in the other.

When the children were ready to print their linoleum blocks on the fabric, they covered the floor with several layers of paper, spread their fabric, and took off their shoes. They inked the blocks on one of the tables, placed them on the fabric, and stepped on them to get enough pressure for a good imprint.

In Mrs. Williams' class, the children scotch-taped their murals over the chalkboards at the front and back of the room. They arranged the paint on the two tables, placing one at each end of the room for easy access. The water problem was solved in the same manner as in Miss Ellis' room. The children who were carving in wax worked at their desks using the pasteboard shields you saw in Chapter Eight. This system kept the chips from falling onto the floor, and avoided needless time and effort for clean-up.

The physical arrangements in Mrs. Hoyers' and Miss Harrington's rooms were comparatively easy and simple. In Miss Ellis' and Mrs. Williams' classrooms the arrangements were more complex and difficult. In each class, however, the children knew where to find the necessary equipment and supplies, and they had learned how to distribute them quickly and easily. It generally took Mrs. Hoyer's and Miss Harrington's children about five minutes to get their materials to begin their work. Miss Ellis' and Mrs. Williams' children needed about eight to ten minutes to get ready, because they had to move the furniture.

All these teachers created ingenious ways of managing the materials and equipment, and they taught their children to assume most of the responsibility for preparation and clean-up. Although their procedures worked well, difficulties did arise, and on occasion they had to stop and talk over some problem. The children would then suggest solutions just as often as the teachers. They knew that they shared the job of solving the problem with their teacher.

The Children's Art Works

The general development of fifth- and sixth-grade children is reflected in the way they go about making their art works and in the appearance of the works themselves. Their physical dexterity and control are evident in the competence with which they handle materials. Their analytical attitude and their attention to fact are apparent in the way they discriminate comparative characteristics of size, shape, position, and color quality of the things they observe. They want to make things as they look and to resemble physical reality; hence, they tend to concentrate their attention on the appearance of details. Their art works reveal their general transformation in outlook and attitude from concern for self during earlier childhood to conscious attention to the world about them, including the customs and tastes of their social environment. The art works they create are, therefore, a product of a combination of factors—their developmental tendencies, the tastes and values they have absorbed from their social environment, and the leadership and influence of their teachers.

The art works created by the children in these upper elementary grades are a reflection of their natural tendencies coupled with the social and educational influences upon their development. They reflect personal abilities and the effects of prior experience. The variations among individual children are just as apparent in these groups as they were among the classes reported in the earlier chapters. In fact, individual differences in development and ability have become even more crystallized. Through examination of the art works they produced, you can discern their characteristic ways of creating the images of figures, creating the feelings of space in their pictures, modulating colors and tones, and integrating the various parts of their works.

Ten- and eleven-year-old children try to draw and paint the human figure as it looks—its proportion and movement. They attend to details of body parts and clothing; they want to make people "real." At the same time, they are self-conscious about themselves and their efforts, and they pay utmost attention to the construction of separate parts. As a result, the figures they make generally lack spontaneity. Although the parts are carefully included, the figure as a whole is often stilted and even stiff.

In this painting by one of the children in Miss Ellis' class, you can see the careful attention to the proportion of the parts of the figures— the body of the woman in the long dress with her arms growing from her shoulders, the man approaching the woman with his legs in walking position

and holding a vase in his hands.

The figures as a whole, however, are quite stiff. This feeling of stiffness is in part a result of the fragmented and analytical attention to the sections of the figures. Some of this stiffness, however, comes from the analytical manner in which the parts of the painting were put together. Consequently, there is a lack of integration between the figures and the various other objects included in the pictures. Many children of this age tend to paint their figures first and then fill in the background. Their figures often look as if they were stuck on top of the other things. This contributes to and magnifies the feeling of stiffness.

Here are a drawing and a painting by two children in Mrs. Williams' class. By examining them closely you can see that the figures in both are quite well proportioned; and yet they all have the characteristic stiffness that can be seen in the pictures of most children this age.

There is, however, a great difference in the way the figures appear *in each* of these two pictures. The figure of the woman in the drawing is poorly integrated in relation to the rest of the parts of the picture. The two men in the jungle are conceived in closer relationship to the background of trees and foliage. The figures in the jungle painting, all by themselves, are no more flexible than the woman in the drawing, yet they appear less-stilted because they are more successfully integrated into the total context of that picture. They are not just placed as if they were on top of the picture.

One of the most important learning problems in art faced by children of this age, is to discover how to integrate their concern for the accuracy and reality of parts with the totality of their ideas. Learning to integrate is the idea behind many of the things this group of teachers talked about. This is why these teachers helped their children to observe closely, and at the same time to look for and feel relationships. This is why each of

them paid so much attention to the aesthetic unity of the art works their children were making.

Children of this age consciously try to create the illusion of space and depth in their pictures. The merging of sky and ground at the horizon, the surface and plane of the ground as it moves back into space, objects standing on the ground and overlapping each other when something in front obscures what is behind, and the effect of size on distance are all commonplace expressions in their pictures. Their conscious attention to the position of objects in the physical world around them produces a level of understanding which is reflected in their work.

Here are two paintings and a drawing by three children in Miss Harrington's class. The boy who made the first one was intrigued by the boats in the river and the tall buildings in the background. The plane of the water moves back into the distance. The relative clarity of the splash of the water in front compared to the calmer ripples behind contributes to the feeling of distance. This is further reinforced by the small size of the tall buildings, and the intersection and overlapping of the sail against the buildings. All these aspects are integrated with each other through the relative emphasis on detail, line quality, and tone in the foreground and background of the picture. The picture creates the illusion of depth in space through the aesthetic order it embodies.

339

The drawing by one of the girls shows sensitive attention to the variety of textural details in the trees, grass, fences, roof tops, and sky. Through overlapping some of the objects, and through the use of simple perspective to show how the forms of the fields and buildings recede into space, this child created the illusion of depth. The integration of textural pattern and position of objects achieves the aesthetic unity.

The snow scene with the sled on the hill and the boy with the snowman shows awareness of the plane moving back toward the horizon. Each part of the picture, however, is handled quite separately; the figure with the snowball is in fact presented from a different point of view from the one on the sled. In addition, there is relatively little discrimination as to tonal and textural differences. As a result, this picture lacks the patterned integration of the first two, and it appears fragmentary.

The first two children had a richer fund of experience with the ideas they were expressing. They utilized all of what they had observed and knew in order to create the mood they wanted their pictures to have. The third child paid unrelated attention to the individual parts of her picture, and even her awareness of the parts was meager. Her picture, consequently, lacks a unified feeling even though it contains some simple elements of depth in space.

The tendency of many fifth- and sixth-grade children to develop their paintings in a fragmentary manner can be observed through the sequence of stages in which they make their paintings. Here are four stages in the development of a painting of a cock fight by a boy in Miss Ellis' class:

In the first and second stages he was painting the cocks. You can see how he painted each bird in relation to the other, because he kept working on both of them as he went along.

In the third stage, however, he completed the cocks, and went on to paint the fence and the crowd.

He continued to complete the crowd in the fourth stage with hardly any further reference to the cocks. The battle between the cocks is spirited, but the upper and lower parts of his painting are rather unrelated to each other. The upper and lower parts belong together in terms of the idea, but they are not well integrated with each other in terms of the pictorial arrangement. They look as if they were separate from each other.

Since Miss Ellis' class was studying Latin America, several boys were interested in painting pictures of cock fights. In fact, several boys worked together on the same idea. Compare the painting of a cock fight done by another boy to the first one. See how this boy painted his cocks in relation to the ground, the crowd, and the fences. His cocks are not so animated as the ones in the first painting, but the different parts of his picture are more successfully integrated with each other.

340

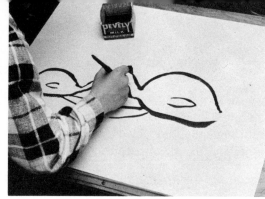

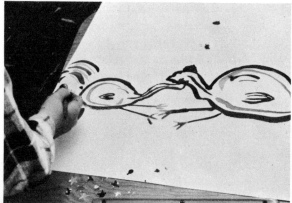

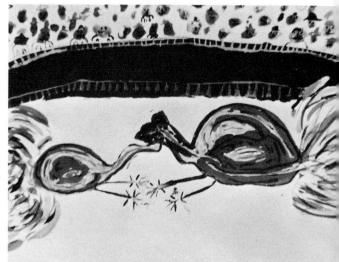

341

Fifth- and sixth-grade children want to use the colors that represent the objects they include in their paintings. They mix and modulate colors, and they can create tonal moods through the ways in which they paint their pictures. They can handle brushes and paints with considerable confidence and control.

In this painting by a sixth-grader in Mrs. Williams' class, you can see the rich tonal variations created by this child with transparent water colors.

The textural excitement in this dramatic landscape was achieved through the use of tempera paint with a wet and dry brush by a boy in Miss Harrington's class.

In spite of their tendency toward conformity, children of this age can react to the encouragement of a good teacher by interpreting

experiences in highly personal ways. Here are three paintings by different children in Mrs. Hoyer's class. In their study of the South, they had seen the film, *The River*, and were moved by the destructive force of the wild rampaging waters. Each of them, however, selected a different aspect from their commonly shared experience. The first child was impressed by the desolate loneliness of tree tops and roof tops sticking out of the debris-laden waters.

The second was intrigued with the pattern of the debris thrown up on the shores and floating down the river.

The third child recreated the dramatic mood and wild excitement in the destructive power of water.

Many of the developmental tendencies and abilities which children in these upper elementary grades reveal in their pictures are also evident in their sculpture. Their three-dimensional work embodies their skill in handling materials, their concern for detail, their analytical approach to their work, their degree of sensitivity to unity and organization, and their relative richness or poverty of individual ideas and conceptions.

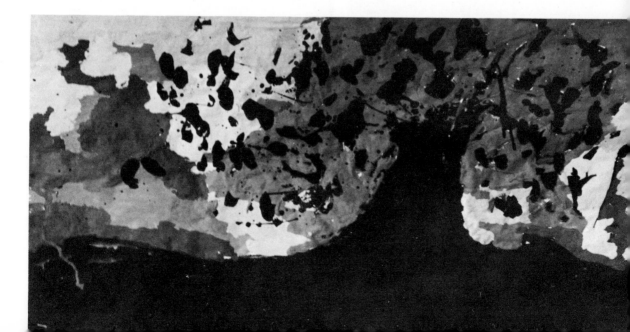

Here are three pieces of sculpture by children in Miss Harrington's class: The first was made by one of the girls with aluminum foil covered with asbestos powder and paste. Through her attention to characteristic detail, she created a whimsical conception of a French poodle dog.

The second was made with clay by another girl whose physical control over the material was limited, and whose ability to discriminate and express characteristic qualities of the figure is reminiscent of the work done by younger children.

The third piece by one of the boys was made of aluminum foil covered with asbestos powder. He handled his materials with good control but his idea suffers from a lack of spontaneity and imagination.

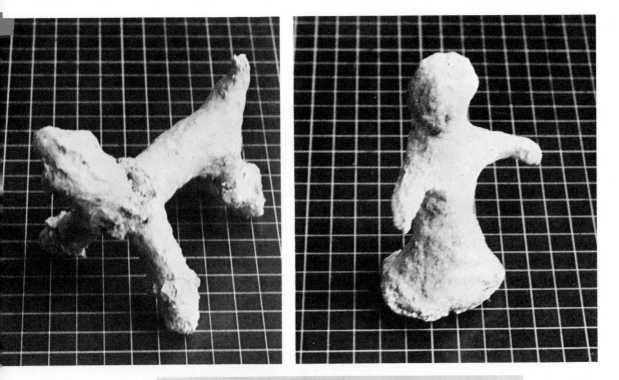

Finally, here are two of the wax carvings made in Mrs. Williams' class: The first is an integrated serpentine form with sensitive attention to the details of the shapes and curves of the individual parts.

The second is composed of fragments with the low part, high part, and hole in the center having little relationship to each other.

Summary

Upper elementary school children are attentive to the world in which they live. They achieve a new awareness of the social environment and the behavior of others—customs, attitudes and values. Their social concern accompanied by their interest in facts and the appearance of things produces a high degree of self-consciousness. The spontaneity of early childhood disappears, but a new interest in drama and adventure emerges. In their art work, they show great concern for the accuracy and reality of detail. They have difficulty in creating integrated artistic expressions, and they need the support and assistance of teachers to maintain their aesthetic sensibilities.

Good teachers respond to the developmental achievements and needs of these children. They help them deal with some of the technical problems that are of concern. At the same time, they challenge them to create ideas in integrated and unified form. They encourage interest, personal selectivity, and individual interpretation, because they know that these are crucial years in the aesthetic development of these children.

Mrs. Hoyer, Miss Ellis, Miss Harrington, Mrs. Williams and Miss Cupelli were individuals in their own teaching with particular abilities and interests. They used all their strengths to help their children build the skills they needed in order to create their own imaginative ideas. They took the artistic efforts of their children seriously, and helped them to see how their own work was an expression of themselves, just like the work of artists.

W HAT IS GOOD

The eighteen teachers whose classroom records have been presented and analyzed in the preceding chapters were selected both for their similarities and their differences. All of them shared certain characteristics, while each revealed a personal style and manner in her work.

These teachers followed many similar procedures. At the same time, their actions in their classrooms reflected as much of their own personal abilities, inclinations, and dispositions, as they demonstrated basic qualities of good teaching of art. Teaching art was for them an art in itself. Through the things they said and did, they created the conditions in their classrooms which encouraged their children to create and express their own ideas with feeling, clarity, imagination, and conviction. They taught their children to create by valuing their creative efforts in the arts and by challenging their extension.

Some of these teachers were energetic and enthusiastic in their general manner of speech and behavior; others were comparatively calm and

10

What is Good Teaching of Art?

TEACHING OF ART?

reserved. None were passive; and none provided merely art materials and some time for their children to use them. All these teachers were actively engaged in teaching art, because they all conveyed their own deep interest in the ideas they talked about with their children and the activities that developed from them. Each one encouraged her children to conceive their ideas through imaginative visual images. Each encouraged them to look at their work in order to discover what was interesting, distinctive, and beautiful; each helped her children to recognize ways to improve their work at their levels of development and conceptual understanding.

Not all these teachers talked in the same way. Some of them suggested particular activities for work, while others provided a greater degree of choice. Most of them, in fact, suggested particular activities at certain times and a greater latitude of choice at other times. None of them, however, imposed any arbitrary restrictions on how ideas were to be developed or how materials were to be used. In their individual ways, each one of these teachers conveyed the realization to her children that every person needs to create and develop his own ideas in order to express them well.

Most of these teachers encouraged their children to use their writing, or their music, or something they were studying in their social studies as sources for ideas for their art activities. Some encouraged their children to use their art materials to create any kind of idea of personal interest. Whatever the source of ideas, each one of these teachers helped their children to pay attention to some particular and specific phase of their own experience in order to discover the stimulus out of which to create ideas.

Although the classroom records in the preceding chapters reveal a great variety of teaching styles, points of emphasis, and procedures, they demonstrate the fact that good teaching of art is purposeful. It is directed toward the accomplishment of particular goals. The goals of good teaching in art are derived on the one hand from insights and knowledge about the nature of art, and on the other from the developmental achievements and needs of children.

Insights about Art Embodied in Good Teaching

All these teachers knew that a work of art is a human creation. It is an imaginative conception of a person's ideas and feelings. An expression of what the person realizes, it is simultaneously an extension and reflection of himself. These are among the reasons why the teachers encouraged their children to pay attention to their own feelings. The same reasons prompted them to encourage their children to admire and enjoy the expressions of the personal feelings and ideas they saw in other works of art. *Their goal was to encourage their children to reveal their own feelings through their art activities, and to become sensitive to the feelings expressed in the art works of other people.* Hence their teaching of art was good because it was true to the nature of art.

These teachers knew that when a person is in the process of embodying his ideas and feelings in art materials, he is sensitive to the possibilities and limitations of both his ideas and his materials. The expression he creates is a harmonious integration of his ideas and materials, because it is a transformation of his idea in terms of his materials. His imagination is as much stimulated by the materials he uses as by the idea he is trying to express. As he works to express his ideas and feelings, he interacts with the art materials he is using. In fact, work with art materials does help to create and crystallize ideas.

These teachers knew, too, that certain kinds of ideas are more appropriately developed in particular art materials. They knew that the material with which a person works has a signal impact on the way he

348

creates and expresses his idea; that the material he uses suggests new dimensions of his idea as he works to express it. These are among the reasons why all these teachers provided a variety of materials for their children to use in order for them to discover how different kinds of materials can help them create different kinds of ideas. They are also among the reasons why these teachers encouraged their children to think of ideas with which to begin to work, while at the same time they provided the freedom for their children's ideas to change and grow as they worked. *Their goal was to help their children to discover how art materials can be used for the creation, development, and refinement of ideas.* Their teaching of art was good because it was true to the nature of the creative process in the arts.

To all these teachers art is an imaginative visual language in which the organization of space, shape, color, and line to communicate ideas and feelings is the essence of aesthetic form. The beauty of a work of art is in the unity and order that has been created. These are among the reasons why all the teachers emphasized the quality of the artistic expressions by encouraging their children to recognize such characteristics as the beautiful colors, the combination of textures, and the relationships among the forms. *Their goal was to encourage their children to improve their judgment through increasing sensitivity to the nature of organic unity in works of art.* This was good teaching of art because it was true to the nature of aesthetic form.

Good teachers know that works of art are infinitely varied, because they are the expressions of individual persons. They present the diversity of human feelings and aesthetic sensibilities. They are the product of human integrity, invention, discipline, and control. Good teachers have achieved these insights about art through their own creative efforts and through their observation of the works of others in our own time and throughout the centuries. These insights are embodied in their teaching; they are reflected in their teaching goals.

Insights about Children Embodied in Good Teaching

The teachers whose work was presented in the previous chapters knew that the growth of children is marked by the development of changing conceptions of themselves and their relationships to the world in which they live. Each stage of growth not only produces developmental achievements, but it also creates its own problems and needs for further growth. In the process of maturation and socialization, growing children are faced with the task of recreating their conceptions of themselves as creative beings, while they expand the horizons of their social-cultural world.

These teachers knew that the creation and expression of ideas through art forms are among the most significant ways in which children recreate their conceptions of themselves. They knew that the art works created by their children were reflections of themselves, their awareness of their environment, and their relationship to it. These were the reasons why they programmed sufficient time for work in art. These were the reasons, too, why none of them imposed ideas or standards of judgment which were beyond the children's developmental level of comprehension. These were the reasons why they admired the art works of their children for their own intrinsic values. *Their teaching goal was to encourage their children to learn how to use the language of art as a potent means through which to formulate their evolving conceptions of their life experiences.* This was good teaching of art, because it was true to the nature and needs of human development.

These teachers knew that all children grow through a series of developmental stages, but that individual children vary in their abilities and developmental achievements. Most children achieve certain characteristic levels at particular stages in their growth. These levels are apparent through their manner of behavior, and the products they produce. The development of individual children, however, does not always fit general chronological expectations. Some fall below, and some exceed them.

Growth toward maturation depends upon an individual child's opportunity to maintain his self-identity and self-assurance. These are among the essential prerequisites for recreating his conception of himself at each stage in his development. They were the reasons why these teachers encouraged and valued the independent efforts of their children, while they challenged their forward movement. None of them rejected what a child said or made. The things that children said or did were accepted as points of departure for the solution of problems and the next advance. *Their goal was to encourage each child to recognize that the development of his own creative powers stemmed from his inner needs to be himself.* This was good teaching of art, because it was true to the developmental needs of the children as individuals.

All these teachers knew that learning to create rests primarily on the desire to create. You cannot teach anyone how to create an idea, but you can stimulate his desire to do so. You cannot urge anyone to create, but you can provide the conditions which foster creation. These teachers knew that children create ideas when experiences are rich and varied enough to enable individuals to identify themselves with aspects of particular personal interest. They knew that children learn to create and express ideas when the ideas are their own. Any idea a teacher may suggest is never more than an initial starting point. To express it, a child must make something out of it. He must make it his own.

These teachers knew that children create ideas when they have access to stimulating materials they are able to manipulate—along with

What is Good Teaching of Art?

assistance to learn how to manipulate them better. They knew that children create ideas when they have the time and encouragement to do so, and when their creations are accepted. To reject a child's creation is to reject him. Creation is personal. *Their teaching goal was to lead their children to want to create by helping them to discover their own purposes for creating.* These teachers taught art well because the conditions they created in their classrooms were true to many of the prerequisites for creative behavior.

The on-going life within the elementary school classroom is the context in which the significance of experiences are realized in order to become stimulating sources for the creation and expression of ideas. The things children study, the events in which they are interested, the books they read, the stories and poems they write, the dances they create, and the songs they sing are among the experiences with which children can identify. These are among the experiences in the life of a child which provide the substance out of which ideas can be created. These are among the reasons why most of these teachers utilized different aspects of life in the classroom to develop the experiences out of which their children could create ideas. *Their goal was to help their children pay attention to and identify themselves with specific aspects of their own experiences as the raw material out of which ideas can be created.* This was good teaching of art because it provided an essential basis for creative involvement.

Good teachers value the individual and independent efforts of their children, while they encourage and challenge their forward movement. They know that the aesthetic sensibilities of growing children are an integral part of their total growth and development. Good teachers have achieved these insights through their study and observation of children—through their knowledge about children who have been taught to maintain their autonomy and self-identity and of those who have not. These insights about children, like the ones about the nature of art, reveal the purposefulness of their teaching, because they are reflected in their teaching goals.

Good Teaching of Art

Good teaching of art is characterized by the integration of insights and knowledge about the nature of art and about the development of children, into the classroom behavior of teachers. These insights and knowledge determine the skills good teachers develop, the devices they employ, the things they talk about to their children, the time they arrange for work in art, the selection of art materials to be provided, and the utilization they make of classroom space, furniture, and equipment. Above all, they lead to the never-ending quest for self-discovery and self-realization, both for teachers and for children. In short, good teachers are guided by their insights and knowledge to create the methods and procedures which best fit their own classroom teaching situations and their own dispositions and personalities. They approach the teaching of art as a creative enterprise.

This group of eighteen teachers did just this; they integrated basic insights and knowledge about art and about children into their own personal classroom behavior. They developed the skills and created the methods most suitable for their local classroom situations to enable them to put their insights to work. The education of their children through significant experiences in art was among the goals they sought as part of their children's general development. The teaching skills and procedures they used were the instruments they created to achieve their goals.

All these teachers played an active and purposeful role; the process of teaching was a live experience for them. They were guided by the goals they aimed to achieve while they interacted with their children in the immediacy of their classroom environments. They proposed ideas to the children for work, but they did not restrict their possibilities for interpreting them. Reactions from the children were incorporated into their procedures and program. They provided different kinds of art materials for work, but they did not impose any arbitrary ways of handling them. Problems encountered in handling materials were treated in relation to the ideas the children were trying to express.

Their children were not left to their own devices, because each individual teacher pursued a conception of teaching which she had created to achieve her goals. Their ways of teaching were varied, because they reflected the needs of specific children within their immediate surroundings; because they revealed the personalities of the individual teachers; and because they embodied basic insights about the nature of art and the development of children. In general, their teaching styles were expressions of their own personalities. They created their teaching styles because they involved themselves in their work. They made the process of teaching a creative experience for themselves.

It is, therefore, quite impossible to define any single way of working or any particular set of methods or sequence of procedures which could produce good teaching of art. Good teachers, to be sure, develop certain teaching skills, and learn many useful methods. These were evident throughout the classroom records, and learning to use them can be tremendously helpful. By themselves, however, they do not produce good teaching.

If good teaching is a purposeful interaction between a teacher and her group of children; if it reflects what the children bring to the situation; if it is conceived in terms of the context of life experiences of the children in the local classroom environment; if it reveals the goals toward which the teacher is striving; if the goals are harmonious with sound insights and knowledge about art and about children; if the teacher is personally involved in the process of exploration and discovery; then teaching methods and procedures *will differ* among good teachers. The quality of the teaching will be recognized as much in the character of the experiences of the children and the teacher as in the teaching procedures themselves.

Good teaching of art is clear in purpose, and yet variable in form. It is guided by sound knowledge; it rests upon the frank utilization of the teacher's own personality—her sensitivity, strengths, and unique background which she brings to the teaching act. Good teaching of art seeks to enhance the imaginative and creative life of children and their teachers.

Who Should Teach Art in the Elementary School?

To teach art well in an elementary school you must know something about art and something about children. But even extensive knowledge, as desirable as this would be, is obviously not enough. The knowledge embodied in good teaching of art rests on close and continuous contact with children, if the children are to achieve the maximum benefits from the experiences you can provide for them. Both requirements—knowledge about art and children, and close contact with children—are essential to good teaching of art. Both are reflected in the work of fine teachers.

Fine teachers have the time and they take the time to build, enliven, and extend the experiences out of which their children can create and express ideas. They take the time to teach their children what to look for in their own experiences as well as what to pay attention to in their art works. They are less concerned with the quantity of things that are done, and infinitely more concerned with the quality of experience, understanding, and achievement. Children need time to create their own ideas and to work with them. Teachers in close contact with children are the only ones who can take the time to help them develop the sensitivity and discrimination for significant creation.

The current assignments of responsibility for the teaching of art in elementary schools vary widely among school systems throughout the country. In a relatively small number of schools, art is taught by art teachers who have close and sufficiently frequent contact with their children. These teachers are responsible for working with a small enough number of classes to permit them to meet with each group of children several times a week. Through the additional contacts many of these art teachers maintain with the classroom teachers, they always know important details about the interests of the children in the small number of groups they teach. These teachers have a rich background in art, and they know their children well enough to teach them well. Many of these people are superb art teachers.

In most of the elementary schools where art is taught by art teachers, however, this special teacher has so very many different groups to teach that her contacts with the children are pathetically short and infrequent. Some art teachers working under such assignments meet with each group of children for less than an hour just once a week. It is by no means unusual to find art teachers on such assignments who can spend as little as twenty minutes as infrequently as every two or three weeks to teach a particular group of children.

Such assignments obviously prevent the art teacher from knowing her children. She cannot know about the other things they are studying, the books they are reading, and the stories and poems they are writing; she cannot be familiar with the many different interests and backgrounds for ideas among all the groups she teaches; she cannot enliven the experiences of her children, because she has little or no contact with the content of their experiences. Consequently, she cannot help her children to draw upon their own experiences to create their own ideas. In spite of her extensive knowledge of art and the work children can do in art, what she is able to teach her children and the values they can derive are highly questionable. At best, her teaching can be only spotty and superficial. Moreover, such teaching is frustrating to any good art teacher, denying her the personal satisfactions she must have from her work to stimulate her own interests for continuous growth in her ability to teach well. She is forced to direct her efforts into unsatisfying, unproductive, and unrewarding channels.

In schools with such practices, those classroom teachers who recognize these serious inadequacies prefer to teach art themselves to their own groups of children. Some of them supplement the infrequent teaching by the art teacher with excellent art teaching of their own. In some schools, the leadership that a good art teacher can provide is used for energetic and effective in-service education programs for the classroom teachers. Through the encouragement, assistance, and good teaching they receive from art teachers, the classroom teachers can learn to develop sufficient insight to extend the very limited work the art teachers themselves can do with the children.

In the vast majority of elementary schools, art is taught by the classroom teachers. Here the quality and extent of instruction in art depend upon: (1) the individual classroom teacher's interest in and knowledge about art; (2) the availability of consultation or supervision of the teaching of art for the classroom teachers by an art teacher with extensive knowledge; and (3) the degree, frequency, and quality of the consultation or supervision.

354

Needless to say, classroom teachers have close and continuous contact with their children. But the quality of their instruction in art varies from the very excellent to the very poor. In those schools where classroom teachers work without the regular assistance of a knowledgeable art teacher, good teaching of art is done by relatively few. Through their own resourcefulness and their firm conviction about the kind of education children require, some individual classroom teachers have developed sufficient personal knowledge about art to teach excellently.

In those schools where special assistance is adequately provided and where the art consultant or supervisor is able to work with classroom teachers directly and frequently, many fine programs of continuous in-service education have stimulated and developed the knowledge of classroom teachers in art. In many instances classroom teachers in such schools, already in close and continuous contact with their children, have developed a sufficient level of knowledge about art to produce excellent teaching of art.

For their education and development, children require and are entitled to good teaching of art. It is the responsibility of every school system and of the group of teachers in each school building to create the ways to provide such teaching. I would also add that the achievement of a general good level of teaching of art is already long overdue in American elementary schools. The fact that art is being taught excellently both by some classroom teachers and by some art teachers should be adequate proof that there is no single formula for an elementary school to achieve a good level of teaching of art. In the last analysis, the question as to who should teach art in the elementary schools must be answered by each school system through utilizing the full potentialities of its own resources, both human and otherwise. If current resources fall short of good instruction in art, they need to be expanded—through the addition of adequate numbers of art teachers and consultants to enrich the program, and through improved teacher competency. Anything short of such efforts merely perpetuates inadequate teaching of art and denies to children an area of development essential to their well-being. The goal to achieve is knowledgeable teaching of art by teachers who can work with children frequently enough to know them and help them.

❦   ❦   ❦

BIBLIOGRAPHY

ON THE NATURE OF ART

Bell, Clive, *Art*, London: Chatto and Windus, 1921.
> A study on the significance of form in art.

Dewey, John, *Art As Experience*, New York: Minton, Balch and Company, 1934.
> A study of the theory of art by one of America's leading philosophers in which he develops the relationships between art experience and common experience.

Edman, Irwin, *Arts and the Man*, New York: W. W. Norton and Company, Incorporated, 1939.
> A brief introduction to aesthetics and the nature of art.

Freedman, Leonard (ed.) *Looking At Modern Painting*, Los Angeles: The Regents of the University of California, 1957.
> An excellently illustrated introduction into the function of the painter and the nature of visual forms and symbols in art.

Ghiselin, Brewster (ed.), *The Creative Process*, Berkeley and Los Angeles: University of California Press, 1952.
> An anthology of writings by artists, writers, psychologists and scientists on their own reflections about the process of creation.

Henri, Robert, *The Art Spirit* (Margaret Ryerson, ed.), New York: J. B. Lippincott, 1951.
> An inspiring collection of notes, comments and articles by one of America's great artists and teachers of art.

Maritain, Jacques, *Creative Intuition in Art and Poetry*, New York: Pantheon Books, 1953.
A study of the nature of art by a leading philosopher.

Read, Herbert, *The Meaning of Art*, New York: Pitman Publishing Corporation, 1951.
A consideration of the interrelationships among various aspects of art by a leading British critic with reference to contemporary and historical works.

Read, Herbert, *A Philosophy of Modern Art*, New York: Horizon Press, 1953.
A collection of essays on aspects of contemporary art.

Santayana, George, *The Sense of Beauty*, New York: Charles Scribner's Sons, 1896.
An American classic on the theory of art.

Seiberling, Frank, *Looking Into Art*, New York: Henry Holt and Company, Incorporated, 1959.
An introduction into the meaning and content of the visual arts. Excellently illustrated with works of art in many media from different periods and styles.

Shahn, Ben, *The Shape of Content*, Cambridge, Massachusetts: Harvard University Press, 1957.
Based upon a series of lectures delivered at Harvard University, one of America's foremost contemporary painters writes on the education and work of an artist.

ON ART EDUCATION

Barkan, Manuel, *A Foundation for Art Education*, New York: Ronald Press Company, 1955.
> A study of the nature of art education in terms of its personal and social significance.

Cane, Florence, *The Artist in Each of Us*, New York: Pantheon Books, Incorporated, 1951.
> An approach to teaching by a sensitive teacher of children and young people.

D'Amico, Victor, *Creative Teaching in Art*, Scranton, Pennsylvania: International Textbook Company, 1953 (Revised edition).
> A statement on the character of creative teaching by one of the leading exponents of contemporary art education.

De Francesco, Italo, *Art Education, Its Means and Ends*, New York: Harper and Brothers, 1958.
> A comprehensive review of directions and tendencies in contemporary art education.

Lowenfeld, Viktor, *Your Child and His Art*, New York: The Macmillan Company, 1954.
> Although written for parents, their statement about the nature of children's art experience is valuable for teachers.

Lowenfeld, Viktor, *Creative and Mental Growth*, New York: Macmillan Company, 1957 (third edition).
> A statement on the nature of teaching of art by one of the leading exponents of contemporary art education.

Mearns, Hughes, *Creative Power: The Education of Youth in the Creative Arts*, Garden City, New York: Doubleday, Doran and Company, Incorporated, 1930.
> Although devoted primarily to the literary arts, the spirit and thought developed is equally significant for teaching the visual arts.

Perrine, Van Dearing, *Let the Child Draw*, New York: Frederick A. Stokes, 1936.
> A sympathetic statement on the experience of children as they work in the arts.

Schaefer-Simmern, Henry, *The Unfolding of Artistic Activity*, Berkeley and Los Angeles, California: University of California Press, 1948, Chapters I and II.
> A conception of creativity and learning through artistic activity.

ON THE GENERAL DEVELOPMENT OF CHILDREN

Cunningham, Ruth, *Understanding Group Behavior of Boys and Girls*, New York: Bureau of Publications, Teachers College, Columbia University, 1951.
> A study of the interaction of individuals in the group behavior of boys and girls.

Jersild, Arthur Thomas, *Child Psychology*, Englewood Cliffs, New Jersey: Prentice-Hall, Incorporated, 1954, (fourth edition).
> A comprehensive treatment of the psychology of children with attention to the internal and external dimensions of a child's world.

Murchison, Carl Allanmore (ed.), *A Handbook of Child Psychology*, Worcester, Massachusetts: Clark University Press, (revised edition) 1933.
> A collection of essays on some of the fundamental aspects of child psychology by a group of foremost investigators in this field.

Piaget, Jean, *The Language and Thought of the Child*, New York: Harcourt, Brace and Company, 1926.
> A penetrating study of how a child thinks, speaks, reasons, and makes judgments.

Strang, Ruth, *An Introduction to Child Study*, New York: The Macmillan Company, (third edition) 1951.
> A presentation of a variety of factors in the growth of children with attention to the overlapping stages of their development.

ON THE DEVELOPMENT OF CHILDREN IN ART

Lindstrom, Miriam, *Children's Art*, Berkeley and Los Angeles, California: University of California Press, 1957.
> A study of developmental characteristics of children's art works.

Lowenfeld, Viktor, *Creative and Mental Growth*, New York: The Macmillan Company, 1957 (third edition).
> A basic text on developmental characteristics of children's art works with particular emphasis on relationships between their artistic and emotional growth.

Mendelowitz, Daniel M., *Children Are Artists*, Stanford, California: Stanford University Press, 1953, Chapters II, III, IV and V.
A readable interpretation of the characteristics of children's art works at the various stages in their development.

ON THE ELEMENTARY SCHOOL

Caswell, Hollis L., and Foshay, Arthur W., *Education in the Elementary School*, New York: American Book Company, 1957 (third edition).
A comprehensive treatment of theory and practice in elementary education. Chapter VIII deals with the development of creative abilities.

Herrick, Virgil E., Goodlad, John I., Estvan, Frank J., and Eberman, Paul W., *The Elementary School*, Englewood Cliffs, New Jersey: Prentice-Hall, Incorporated, 1956.
A general reference on the contemporary elementary school program. Chapter XII is devoted to the arts.

Otto, Henry J., Floyd, Hazel and Rouse, Margaret, *Principles of Elementary Education*, New York: Rinehart and Company, Incorporated, 1955.
An overview of the theories and practices which guide the modern elementary school program.

Shane, Harold G. (ed.), *The American Elementary School*, Thirteenth Yearbook of the John Dewey Society, Harper and Brothers, 1953.
A comprehensive study and appraisal of the American elementary school within the framework of current problems, demands, and limitations.

ON THE TEACHING OF ART IN THE ELEMENTARY SCHOOL

Cole, Natalie Robinson, *The Arts in the Classroom*, New York: The John Day Company, 1940.
A very readable account of a spirited approach to teaching the arts to elementary school children.

Erdt, Margaret H., *Teaching Art in the Elementary School*, New York: Rinehart and Company, Incorporated, 1954.
A readable approach to the teaching of art within the context of the elementary school curriculum.

Gaitskell, Charles D., *Children and Their Art: Methods for the Elementary School*, New York: Harcourt, Brace and Company, 1958.
A comprehensive consideration of contemporary theories and practices in the teaching of art to elementary school children.

ON ART MEDIA, ACTIVITIES AND PROCESSES

Betts, Victoria B., *Exploring Papier-Mache*, Worcester, Massachusetts: The Davis Press, 1955.
A well illustrated presentation of some of the possibilities of paper sculpture.

D'Amico, Victor, Wilson, Frances and Maser, Moreen, *Art for the Family*, New York: Museum of Modern Art, 1954.
A well illustrated presentation of some basic processes and design possibilities in the handling of clay.

Duncan, Julia Hamlin and D'Amico, Victor, *How to Make Pottery and Ceramic Sculpture*, New York: Museum of Modern Art, 1947.
A well illustrated presentation of the processes and possibilities of a wide variety of art activities.

Lord, Lois, *Collage and Construction*, Worcester, Massachusetts: Davis Publishing Company, 1958.
A well illustrated presentation of a wealth of possibilities in collage and construction activities. The quality and range of work done by children is excellent.

Mattill, Edward, L., *Meaning in Crafts*, Englewood Cliffs, New Jersey: Prentice-Hall, Incorporated, 1959.
An well-illustrated introduction to a basic variety of art activities. References to work by professional artists are functionally integrated.

PERIODICALS ON THE TEACHING OF ART

Arts and Activities, Published monthly September to June, The Jones Publishing Company, 8150 North Central Park Avenue, Skokie, Illinois.

School Arts, Published monthly September to June, Davis Press, Incorporated, Printers Building, Worcester, Massachusetts.

INDEX

364

349, 350; -conscious, 337; -contained classroom, 279; -evaluation, 240; -identity, 350; image of, 63; -realization, 351; -sufficiency, 146
Sensibility, aesthetic, 329, 349
Sensuous feeling, 82; satisfaction, 164
Sequence, 59, 325; of activities, 69, 148; of procedures, 353
Serapes, 280
Sewing, 283, 326
Shape, 212, 310, 331, 337, 349
Silk screen, 296
Similarities, 329
Singing, 261
Sink, 85
Size, 63, 331, 337; relationships, 72
Sketches, 306, 309
Skill, 241, 326, 330, 332; of teachers, 351
Skirts, 280
Skyline, 161, 254
Smelling, 86
Soapstone, 222
Social, 62; awareness, 328, 330; behavior, 146; consciousness, 240; development, 5; environment, 337; group, 146, 240; studies, 9, 153, 289, 331, 334, 348
Socialization, 328, 349
Songs, 169
Space, 63, 337, 349; for activities, 70; counter, 86; depth in, 254; -filling, 124; ingenious use, 154; organization, 145; in pictures, 78; relationships, 72; storage, 114, 131
Speed, rates of, 226
Spontaneity, 63
Spontaneous effort, 326
Standards of judgment, 152, 350
Status, 327, 329
Stereotype, 108, 144, 149; representation, 158
Stiffness of figures, 338
Stimulus, 65, 66, 348
Storage space, 114, 131, 169, 180
String, 125
Studio, 297
Style, personal, 346; teaching, 9, 57, 324, 348, 353
Suggestions, 178, 291
Supervision, 354
Supervisor, art, 84, 258
Symbol, 82, 226; dramatic experiences, 158; of people, 75; system, 72, 156; variation, 251

Tamayo, Rufino, 299, 333
Tastes, 328, 337
Teacher: art, 8, 10, 84, 166, 205, 234, 238, 258, 353; authority of, 63; classroom, 8, 167, 353; competency of, 355; differences, 8, 68; individual, 322; music, 182, 210, 261;

personalities, 353; physical education, 182, 210; planning, 60; preparation, 250; role of, 353; skills, 351; special, 354; temperament of, 238
Teaching, 7, 144; a form of expression, 322; goal, 144; interdependent, 239; process of, 353; quality of, 353; role, 322; style, 9, 57, 324, 348, 353
Technical problems, 274, 332
Tempo, 66; changes of, 145; variation, 61
Tension, 59, 66
Texture, 30, 277, 332, 349; materials, 129
Three-dimensional work, 82
Time, 334, 353; art activities, 70; balance, 248, 353; block of, 69, 154, 246; conception of, 63; flexibility, 69; instrument for teaching, 153; of year, 64; management, 242, 248; organization, 145; schedule, 334; spare, 127; teaching, 69; variations, 153; week, day, 246
Touching, 86
Transformation, 348
Trays, cafeteria, 200
Trip, 34, 303, 306, 331

Unit study, 148, 193, 244, 279, 324, 325, 331, 334
Unity, 63, 73, 343; aesthetic, 332, 339
Utilitarian objects, 333
Utilization of space, 243
Utrillo, Maurice, 295, 333

Values, 152, 328, 337; intrinsic, 350; multiple, 250
Van Gogh, Vincent, 297
Variety, 64, 66, 325, 349
Verbal images, 151
Visual: appearance, 252; arts, 150; characteristics, 277; conception, 74; images, 347; language, 349; world, 147
Vision, 240

Wax, 303
Weaving, 283, 326
Wedge clay, 272
Welfare of group, 62
Wheat paste, 288
Window counter, 93
Wire, 192; mesh, 125
Wood, 103, 145, 260; balsa, 222
Woodcuts, 296
Woodwork, 18, 39
Word pictures, 197
Works of art, 245, 289, 333, 348
Workshops, 259
Writing, 9, 88, 348

Yarn, 125

Zonolite, 227

365